Good Enough to Eat
HOW WE SHOP, WHAT WE EAT

GOOD ENOUGH TO EAT

HOW WE SHOP, WHAT WE EAT

Maureen Tatlow

GILL & MACMILLAN

Gill & Macmillan Ltd
Goldenbridge
Dublin 8
with associated companies throughout the world
© Maureen Tatlow 1998
0 7171 2697 8

Design by Identikit Design Consultants
Print origination by O'K Graphic Design, Dublin

Printed by ColourBooks Ltd, Dublin

This book is typeset in 11/14 pt Lapidary 333.

A catalogue record for this book is available from the British Library.

1 3 5 4 2

This publication is intended to provide a summary of
aspects of the matter covered. It does not purport to be
comprehensive or to constitute legal or other professional
advice.

For Conor, Daniel and Clara
with love

Contents

Acknowledgments

Over the years, many, many people have given very generously of their specialist knowledge and a great deal of time. Thanks to: Myrtle Allen, Darina Allen, Jack, Ed and Donal Hick, Randolph Hodgson, Georgina O'Sullivan, Sean Loughnane, Peter Ward, Patrick Wall, Peter Dargan, Mary O'Connell, John and Sally McKenna, Mary Upton, Biddy White Lennon, Rod Alston, Patrick Holden, Feargal Nolan, Phena O'Boyle, Jean Cahill, Stephen and Peter Caviston. Also many members, too numerous to mention singly, of BIM, Teagasc, The National Food Centre, An Bord Bia, the NDC and others. To Joanna Blythman, whose writing first alerted me to many issues. And to those who must remain nameless — thank you as well.

My thanks also to my parents for sanctuary while writing, and for all manner of back-up over the years; Alan for great ideas; Peggy for . . . all sorts! Mairead and Liam, Mary and Conall for the fun; Didi and Clifford, Dermot and Ulrikka for being you; Eveleen Coyle for forbearance; Anne Harris and Deirdre McQuillan for giving me that vital start; and especially to Ros Dee for having faith in me, and all your support!

Above all, I owe it to the indomitable twins, Nita and Putte, who stepped in and saved the day.

Introduction

This book is about how to buy great food. Food which is safe to eat, yes; but safety is only the most basic requirement for our food. What we want is food which goes a step further than just being safe. Food which tastes good. Food which enriches our lives and brings us pleasure. Food which is good enough to eat.

Once upon a time, while we had firm ideas in Ireland about what constituted a good rasher or a tasty potato, we tended to accord more respect to a pint. Now, a real enjoyment of food is blossoming in this country. We have more food in our shops than ever before, and every time you go into the supermarket it seems an entire new section of exotica or convenience something-or-other has sprouted.

Yet a wider selection doesn't always mean a better choice. The variety may have increased, but so have the pitfalls. Where can you find reliably fluffy, tasty potatoes? There are many different types of rashers on every shelf, but where would you find some which sizzle and fry crisply, rather than oozing white goo into the pan? Chicken now comes with garlic butter, with breadcrumbs, with tikka masala sauce, with just about any flavour you can think of — but where do you find chicken with real chicken flavour?

Ultimately, this book was born of my own frustration. Why was supermarket meat so unreliable? How could a fillet steak be tough? Why did potatoes from one producer smell deliciously earthy and taste divine, while another's were watery and bland? Did it have to be that way?

Shopping with Your Eyes Open

The ultimate irony is that despite the rampant foodie consumerism which we're indulging in now, we seem to have forgotten the fundamentals. The supermarket habit has de-skilled us. Many of us are perfectly able to choose between various ready meals, but wouldn't know how to go about finding a great butcher or a wonderful lettuce. 'A generation ago,' says Sallynoggin butcher Jack Hick, 'mothers came in to the shop with their daughters, and explained to them about the meat, and what was good. That just doesn't happen any more.'

This de-skilling has left us less equipped to identify and demand the best. Yet it has never been more important to do so.

Something is Happening to Food

Most of our food is grown and produced quite differently than it was a couple of generations ago. Food production has gone industrial, and on a global scale. The result, whether it's on a pig farm, in a wheat field or a bread factory, is quicker production, bigger yields and cheaper food. Sounds good? Unfortunately there is an invisible price. We may not pay it at the checkout, but we do eventually. That price is the quality and sometimes even the safety of our food.

Fear of Food: Is it Safe?

Time and again, it becomes clear that intensive ways of rearing animals and growing crops leave problems behind. In this book, we'll be looking at antibiotics and pesticides, at food poisoning, at BSE, and more. Above all, we'll consider how you can seek out food which is produced better and more safely.

Does it Taste Good?

Unlike food safety, this subject doesn't necessarily make the headlines. But it affects us all, every day of our lives. Modern production methods have debased the flavour of much of our food. The curious thing is that the more intensively a food is produced, the less flavour it has. You can now, if you want, grow a chicken twice as quickly as it took a generation ago; you can bake a loaf of bread in seventeen minutes, where once it took an hour. You can double the yields of crops. But the result is that we are missing the quality that slower-grown, slower-made foods can offer.

'Grown for flavour'

These kinds of stickers on food say it all. Most food is no longer grown for flavour. Shelf-life, handling, and appearance are all paramount now, and when food technologists talk about 'quality', it's most likely they're referring to microbiological counts, not flavour and aroma. 'Eating quality' is not the top consideration of large-scale food producers.

Better Value?

It's what we all want, and usually we are drawn to the lowest price. But if your food comes with less flavour, more added water, or more air, you're not getting better value.

Time: The Secret Ingredient

These days, no-time food is often considered the best food of all. Yet time is the secret ingredient in many of the best foods — they need time in the growing, time in the making and baking. If we want great food, we need to be prepared to pay for the little bit of extra time it takes to grow or produce it. The people who produce our food are doing an important job for us, and if they are doing it well they deserve our respect, and a fair price for their work.

Take Charge of your Shopping

This book is intended to be a shopper's friend. Don't forget that as shoppers we have a great deal of power. If we know more, we can demand better. Ultimately, that is the recipe for getting tastier, and safer, food onto our plates.

1

Beef

Once, the quality of the meat you ate was a matter between you and your butcher. If your dinner wasn't good enough, you could let him know in the morning. But things have changed in the last few decades. Many of us only have access to supermarkets now, and the quality of beef — in both butchers and supermarkets — has sometimes been variable. And then of course our faith in beef has taken a battering in the last ten years, with the long trickle of tales of growth promoters, and finally the cataclysmic episode of BSE.

Where can you buy? How can you know? And is it safe?

How to Choose

Standing at the display counter, looking at the steaks, or at the mince, how can you know whether this meat will be good? Most of us, apparently, choose our beef based on how it looks. If it seems fresh and bright, we go for it. This is hopeless. The way meat looks tells very little about how it will taste; two identical-looking pieces could be vastly different in flavour and tenderness. Yet choosing well probably matters more with beef than with any other meat, since good handling makes all the difference to the way the meat will taste.

The fact of the matter is that you just can't tell by looking at the steak. However, you can tell quite a bit by looking at the shop, and by talking to the butcher. Don't be shy!

Look at the Shop

Just because a butcher does a smart line in jagged grapefruit halves and black display trays doesn't actually mean his meat is going to be good. A well-tended shop can be a good clue, with creative displays and many different preparations of meat. But don't be seduced by these extraneous factors. Producing magnificent beef is a slow, painstaking process which starts way back on the farm, and the best meat comes from a butcher who cares about all the details. Indeed, a simple shop with hardly any display may be an indication of a butcher who concentrates on the things that matter most.

Look for evidence that the butcher knows where the meat comes from. Ideally there should be information about which farmer(s) sells it to him. Some proud butchers are now posting up evidence and even photographs of their suppliers. However, it often won't be evident, so you'll need to get talking.

Talk to the Butcher

A good butcher will be delighted to tell you about the details of how his meat arrived at the counter. About the farm and abattoir it came from, about how long it was hung for, about the breed of animal. This means you need to know a little about these things, so we'll have a look at them below. But you don't have to be a world expert in beef rearing to be able to seek out a good steak. What you are looking for, the most important thing, is a sense of intent in the man or woman who's selling it to you. Is this a person who just wants to palm you off with a bit of superficial patter about 'it's all quality assured', or is it someone who is genuinely painstaking about the small details which can bring you the best beef?

Finding this out means taking a little bit of time to have a chat, but it's a small investment if the reward is a source of great meat. Try to get to talk to the owner of the shop; younger staff may be inexperienced. A good tip is to make a first visit at a quiet time. Friday afternoon may be ideal for banter at the counter, but it's not the best time to investigate!

Aberdeen Angus and All the Rest . . .

'Aberdeen Angus' is often used as a selling tag these days. Does breed make a difference? Experts differ on this one. Ultimately, the flavour of the meat is probably determined most by what the animal ate.

Broadly, there are two kinds of beef cattle in Ireland. There are the new arrivals, the 'Continentals', European breeds like Charolais and Limousin. These are larger, leaner beasts. And then there are the smaller Hereford Crosses and Aberdeen Angus, classic beef breeds from these islands. Herefords and Aberdeens are more inclined to have a delicate tracery of fat within their meat. Cookbooks call it marbling. It melts away during the cooking and contributes to succulence and flavour. 'The Continentals are colossal-looking cattle,' says fine third-generation butcher Andy Nolan of Kilcullen, Co. Kildare. 'But they haven't the eating quality.'

All other things being equal, you certainly couldn't detect a difference between Continentals and Herefords/Angus in some mince or stewing steak. And the situation is pretty confusing in Ireland anyway, since there are 'an awful lot of mongrel-type animals out there', as one commentator fondly put it. However, Herefords and Aberdeen Angus are *crucial* for the best prime cuts: a nice thick sirloin or a rib roast is just much too big from a large Continental animal.

How Old Was It?

Again, opinions differ on the optimum for flavour. Whatever your own butcher favours, the important thing is that he should know and care. Some say a young eighteen-month-old is perfect. Robin Tormey insists twenty-four months is essential. (He finishes cattle in Kinnegad to supply his three sons' shops in Mullingar, Tullamore and Galway. The beef is some of the best I've ever tasted.) At that age, he says, there is enough fat for flavour, though not enough to spoil the meat.

Ireland is unusual: we have traditionally had a very clear preference for heifer meat. (Heifers are young female cattle who have not given birth.) We feel it has the most delicate flavour, though experts say it can be clearly shown there's no detectable difference between heifer and steer meat. (Steers are castrated males.)

Cow beef, though liked in France, isn't approved of in Ireland. It comes from a dairy cow, five to seven years old, which is slaughtered once her milk yields reduce. The meat is much tougher. (Dairy cow beef is the kind which in the UK has been primarily implicated in BSE, because the animals are more likely to have been fed concentrated diets.) Some unscrupulous operators pass cow beef off as heifer. Any butcher knows the difference.

However, you may encounter cow steak as very cheap beef in certain bargain shops, or at large functions such as tours or weddings . . .

'Sweet Eating'

We may often curse our weather, but our mild wet climate gives us grass, and plenty of it. As a result, Irish beef cattle live a natural, outdoor, free-range existence for most of the year. Extra winter feed, for the best, is not anonymous concentrates, but silage (stored, fermented grass) as well as beet, hay and grains — 'sweet eating', as one butcher described it. This contrasts greatly with the situation in countries with harsher climates, where the cattle are most likely housed indoors and eat much more concentrate-based diets. These natural advantages give us the potential to have the best, most natural of all possible beef.

Truly delicious beef comes from animals which have fed on excellent pasture with a wide variety of grasses. You can't know what the steak you are looking at was fed on, but if your butcher cares, he will.

How Carefully Was It Handled?

This is the crucial question, and this is where supermarkets got their reputation for unpredictable meat. You can take a perfect animal, yet treat it carelessly immediately pre- and post-slaughter, and the meat is ruined.

The animal must be comfortable and not stressed. It must meet its end quietly, carefully and with respect. And afterwards, a very slow chill down to storage temperature is vital. Try to rush this and the meat's fibres will seize up in shocked reaction — this is called 'cold shortening', and results in tough meat.

As you can imagine, these are not strictures which marry naturally with the hectic demands of a meat factory which measures turnover in the thousands. If you have memories in the past of tough and unreliable supermarket beef, this was the most likely cause. Over-hasty chilling in particular was very common. The lesson of chilling has been learned, and factories pay more attention to 'eating quality' factors now. But they still can't match the care of an excellent, small-scale butcher.

Hanging meat

The meat then needs to hang in order to mature. As the days go by, water evaporates from the meat to make it less wet, and then enzyme action softens the fibres and develops the flavour. Beef needs fourteen to twenty-one days to achieve this. To get the best meat, you should be prepared to pay the butcher for that time and also for the weight loss on the meat. It's worth it. It will cook and taste so much better.

Some butchers feel seven to twelve days' hanging is enough. It may be adequate, but it won't result in a superlative steak or roasts.

A new practice is the ageing of beef. It is matured — but not traditionally. After just two days' hanging, the meat is cut up and vac-packed. It then 'ages' on in plastic. This is the way beef is matured for almost all the major supermarkets. Theoretically, there's nothing wrong with it; the enzymes still work to create tender meat. However, I'm not at all sure I like the idea of my meat maturing in a plastic bag. It's done primarily to minimise 'drip loss', not in the interests of creating the best beef. The expert technologists tell me there's no detectable difference, but I feel this is one of the differences between the best butchers and the best supermarkets.

Butcher or Supermarket?
Butchers

There's still no doubt about it: the best of all possible meat comes from a butcher. But not from any butcher. It comes from one who controls every step of the process. He 'finishes' the cattle himself, growing the animals on his own land until he judges them perfectly ready, or he buys direct from farmers he knows. He has his own abattoir, or, having bought the animals himself, sends them to a local abattoir which he trusts implicitly. He hangs the meat carefully and for long enough for beef's wonderful minerally flavours to develop.

Next best is a butcher who buys the meat from a local abattoir with which he has a close relationship. Butchers tell me it's preferable if this is an abattoir which works on a small scale for the Irish market, rather than an export factory. That way, a butcher has a chance of having control over the quality of the meat he's putting on the scales for you. If he buys from a large factory, he may just have to settle for what he's given.

Poor-quality butchers

Just because the shop is small and the aprons are striped red, doesn't mean the meat will be good. There are sadly plenty of poor-quality butchers around, who are more akin to semi-skilled retailers than well-trained crafts-people. They are buying from wholesalers who are selling them an anonymous commodity. If *they* don't have stringent specifications for the meat they're buying, they can't give *you* any quality guarantees. They may buy their meat ready-cut in vac packs. All they have to do is open a plastic bag, seam out a few joints, and slice a few steaks.

Supermarkets

Beef in supermarkets has improved beyond recognition since a decade ago, with Superquinn leading the way. Most supermarket meat is now better and more consistent than meat from a poor butcher. With very stringent specifi-cations for the factories from which they buy, supermarkets now generally sell well-matured, well-handled meat. And all the major multiples are now members of An Bord Bia's Quality Assurance scheme.

Best of all are the supermarkets who can tell you which farmers they buy from.

Which one?

Is there anything to choose between supermarkets? I conducted a blind sirloin steak taste test in 1996, expecting to find huge differences. In fact, tenderness and flavour were good all round, and almost identical between the major stores. However, butchery standards of the pre-pack sirloin steaks were very poor indeed — all had great variations in thickness.

In a later comparison of rib steaks, Ballybrado organic beef (bought in Quinnsworth) came out with flying colours, noticeably better-flavoured than the rest.

One well-informed source in the meat business commented: 'Superquinn fly the flag when it comes to quality. Super Valu is also very interested in meat quality. Dunnes is not too bad. And I'd expect meat in Quinnsworth to improve since the Tesco take-over.'

The Butcher Himself: Have a Relationship with Him!

There's more to a butcher's than just the meat. A great butcher will transform shopping from a mindless chore to an enjoyable exchange. He will listen to your queries. He will save you a great deal of time in the kitchen, boning and trimming meat to your needs. He will help you out with an unusual cut of meat. If you like to cook, you will know how important this is, since most cookbooks come from countries whose meat cutting and naming habits are different from ours (see below for more about this). And if you can't cook, a good butcher will tell you how to roast that rib.

There are some well-informed, experienced butchers in some supermarkets. But they are extremely rare. (Again, Superquinn is way ahead of the others on this score.) All too often, supermarket butchery counters are window-dressing. Supermarkets discovered that we didn't trust pre-pack meat, so they put butchery counters back in. But usually the meat comes in from central depots, and the staff are vague and under-trained.

Ultimately, the difference between supermarkets and butchers is this: a supermarket may, if it's exceptional, train its staff well. But a supermarket does not set out to train you. Yet learning from an experienced retailer is a vital experience — and half the fun — for every shopper and cook. As the following tale will tell.

Fat Is Where the Flavour Is

- For many years now, we have been given health advice to reduce fat intake. Some of this advice has been fair enough. But some has had unfortunate consequences. In the case of meat, the holy grail of 'lean meat' has meant that animals are being relentlessly bred and reared for ever leaner meat production.

- Mary O'Connell of Bosco's in Carlow and a leading light of the IQ Butchers' Guild explains what happened in her shop. 'About six years ago, we responded to the demand for totally lean beef. We went over to the Continental breeds. Our sales dropped. Another member of the Guild visited our shop. "For God's sake, what are you selling there?" he asked, horrified. "Your customer might say she's looking for it — but she won't eat it!"

- 'He was right. We went back to the Hereford Cross, and have had a steady increase in demand ever since. We now look for marbling in the meat, and a little fat. Not great lumps of it, just a neat covering. This meant retraining our customers, though! We had to explain to them: cook with the fat, then trim it afterwards.'

- If you're thinking this is just a butcher talking who wants you to pay for the bits you won't eat — ask the chefs. In 1996, Myrtle Allen of Ballymaloe conducted a Europe-wide survey of Eurotoques chefs. These men and women may be at the pinnacle, but tight restaurant margins mean they certainly can't afford wastage. Unanimously, though, they called for meat *with* fat. This, even though they cut the fat off before serving, because we don't much like it. They wouldn't cook without it.

- **What is marbling?** A fine filigree of delicate fat within the meat. It provides the meat with an internal 'basting' as it cooks. Look out for it. Ask for it!

The Butcher: An Endangered Species

Now that I've sung the praises of the perfect butcher, here's the bad news: they are thin on the ground.

The demise of the butcher has primarily been fuelled by changes in the way we eat. Once, Irish families ate twelve to fourteen meat meals a week; now, this is down to six or fewer. Butchers have been squeezed by our increasingly cosmopolitan diets. In this context, it has been frustrating to watch 'health' regulations deal further blows to an already weakened sector. European Union (EU) requirements for the upgrading of abattoir facilities, enthusiastically endorsed by the Department of Agriculture, have made it impossible for some excellent, small traditional butchers to continue.

Some closed their abattoirs and bought meat from wholesalers. 'That was when my heart went out of it', says Vincent Morrissey, who presided over the busiest butchers' shop in Dungarvan, Co. Waterford. 'The meat used to vary enormously. We had people getting quite angry with us. It's very hard to stand over a product someone else has given you. It's like selling meals in a restaurant which you haven't cooked yourself.'

Myrtle Allen has long been a staunch defender of the value of locally-produced food. Where outstanding meat is concerned, she despairs for the future. 'Send a good animal into a large abattoir and you don't know what will come out. Meat from my local butcher is of a quality and a consistency which I cannot replace.'

The Department of Agriculture asserts vigorously that no-one has been put out of business who didn't deserve to be. Butchers and chefs don't agree. They say that many of the costly 'improvements' are entirely unnecessary for the small butcher who deals in just three or four cattle a week. In 1997, the Irish branch of Eurotoques passed a resolution calling on EU-required alterations to small abattoirs to be EU-funded. This, unfortunately, is highly unlikely to happen.

Yet the basic inequity remains: abattoirs geared for export are eligible for large grant-aiding.

The general assumption seems to be that the big meat plants, being more 'modern', will result in better, more hygienically-produced meat. Not necessarily. Animals travelling greater distances to abattoirs means more stress, which can often lead to worse meat and also to increased likelihood of dirty carcasses. In addition, large meat plants provide much greater opportunity for cross-contamination. Bugs like E coli O157 may become more common in our meat as a result.

E Coli O157

This nasty little bug has been in the news a lot in the last few years. It has crept into our lives since the 1980s and can cause kidney failure and death.

E coli bacteria typically live in the intestines of animals and man and cause no problems. Some may cause mild diarrhoea. But at some point in the last decades, O157, as part of the natural process of evolution, acquired dysentery genes which cause it to produce a powerful toxin. This can result in haemorrhaging in people whose immune systems are vulnerable, such as children and the elderly.

The outbreak in Scotland which killed twenty-one elderly people showed that no-one could afford to be complacent about this bug. And in the US, in August 1997, twenty-five million pounds of mince were destroyed after it was found to be contaminated at a meat plant in Nebraska.

E coli O157 has particularly been associated with cattle, and with beefburgers. Cattle which are dirty at slaughter are a particular danger. It has also been found in other meats. E coli O157 may be on the surface of raw meats. This means that it can be found all the way through mince or a burger, since the meat is all chopped up. However, it is easily killed by cooking, once it reaches a temperature of about 70°C. So any meat, once properly cooked, is perfectly all right.

Remember:
1. You can eat a cut of meat as rare as you like, once the outside is seared. But burgers and sausages should be cooked through, until the juices run clear and no pink bits remain. Be particularly vigilant with children's food, and if you are in a restaurant with them, check that their burger or sausage is cooked.
2. Don't buy cooked meat from a butcher who has handled raw meat and not washed his hands before going to the cooked meat counter. And tell him why! See also milk, page 81; cheese, page 95; and food poisoning, page 231.

BSE, Growth Promoters and All That

Beef was the first big food scare in Ireland. For many years, there were only rumours, and the very occasional conviction for the use of illegal growth-promoting drugs in beef cattle. The sordid revelations of the Beef Tribunal, with its tales of large-scale, well-organised corruption in the largest processing plants in the country, did nothing to help. Finally, in 1996, came the announcement from the UK that BSE-infected beef was most likely responsible for a new variant of the human brain disease CJD.

Can you trust the beef you buy?
BSE

In truth, neither BSE nor its relationship to new variant (nv) CJD are fully understood yet. Scientists are still debating the finer details. It is believed that prion protein, when 'folded' the wrong way, causes other proteins to change shape too; the result is a degenerative brain disease. The most likely cause of BSE is the feeding of infective meat and bonemeal (rendered cattle remains, a concentrated source of protein) back to cattle. The most likely cause of nvCJD in humans is eating infective material — beef offal, most likely in cheap processed products such as pies and burgers — from animals which had BSE. Both meat and bonemeal itself is thought to have become infected as a result of cost-cutting in the rendering business; the temperatures at which cattle remains were turned into cattle feed were lowered. Exactly how infected material got into the food chain in the first place is not yet clearly understood.

We were relatively lucky here in Ireland. Our grass-based system of rearing cattle as described above has meant that we escaped with low levels of BSE in the national herd — about two cases per million cattle a year since BSE was first diagnosed in the Republic in 1989. Cases have been found predominantly in dairy herds, those ones most likely to be fed concentrated feeds, though some suckler herds have been affected too.

There are scientists who dispute the BSE/nvCJD connection. There are those who believe the process is the result of a virus, as yet unidentified. There are scientists who predict Britain will see a thousand or so cases of nvCJD in the future — and those who are predicting millions. There are those who are researching the possible infectivity of bone marrow, of tongue, of milk. 'You have got to be careful though,' cautioned one scientist, who did not wish to be named. 'There is money in BSE research now.' He warned that some dubious research and many scare headlines are emerging as a result.

The slow drip of bans and warnings causes anxiety for consumers. First, we were told that only brains and spinal cord were infective, and that removing them at slaughter would make everything safe. In 1997 it was concluded that dorsal root ganglia (found embedded in backbone) had infectivity. In the UK, beef on the bone was consequently banned, although the ban is reportedly widely flouted. In Ireland, a recommendation was issued not to eat rib of beef on the bone, or T-bone steaks. Some consumers began to get an uneasy feeling. If bones weren't safe, what next?

So what *do* we know? The most important thing to remember is that *if the animal does not have BSE, then every part is safe.* This simple fact is often forgotten in the hubbub of headlines and bans. The consensus is that Irish beef is extremely safe now. Some people may still be uneasy, and understandably so. The feeding of meat and bonemeal was banned in 1990, yet the trickle of BSE cases in Irish cattle continues. Clearly the ban was not enforced sufficiently rigorously. However, sources agree that since 1996 it has been enforced strictly. 'I don't know how they've done it, but they really have,' said another source who did not wish to be named. 'You'd want to be making a huge effort to feed meat and bonemeal to cattle now, it's all so tightly controlled and closely audited. We should start to see a drop in the number of cases around early 1999. You could even eat brains now,' he added.

If you still don't quite trust the system, but you'd like to eat beef, you could try a few options. Organic beef has always been produced without meat and bonemeal or other such 'concentrates'. Beef from a Quality Assured system should be particularly well audited (though see Quality Assurance, page 15). Or you could buy beef from Super Valu. All their meat is Enfer-tested before being released for sale — the only supermarket to do so. This test for BSE, carried out after slaughter, was developed in the Republic. It has been evaluated by the Department of Agriculture and is considered reliable, especially since it detects BSE infectivity at that most dangerous stage: when it is high but before clinical symptoms have emerged in the animal. Sources say that a BSE test for live animals, however, is still a few years down the road. Finally, you could avoid cheap meat products, those where you are most likely to find 'leftovers'.

The BSE disaster was a consequence of intensive food production systems which tried to increase output and reduce cost — at any price. (The price, as it turned out, was high: human lives plus many billions of pounds in the UK to deal with the aftermath.) The scale of the disaster in the UK was a result of the government shutting its eyes, hoping that an absence of evidence meant there would be no problem.

There are two lessons which we should learn:

1. We should be suspicious of intensive food production systems. Some of their potentially dangerous consequences are still being ignored. See, for example, the sections on Antibiotics in Pork, page 30 and Chickens, page 44.

2. We should approach any new and untested method of food production with a great deal of caution. The risks are just too great. Sadly, most of the world's governments are failing to observe this precautionary principle, at present particularly where genetically modified food crops are concerned. See Genetic Engineering, page 215.

One final concern: although cattle may no longer be fed meat and bonemeal, this is not outlawed for pigs. There are experts in the field who are most concerned about this. One requested anonymity and said baldly, 'We just don't know if it is safe. It is really not a good idea.'

Growth Promoting Hormones

Growth promoting hormones are used in beef production primarily to make cattle gain weight faster and to encourage the development of more lean meat on the animal. They promise greater profit for the farmer: it has been estimated at up to an extra £100 per animal. Some growth promoting drugs were previously legal in the EU but all have been banned since 1988. Some are permitted in the US, Canada, Australia and New Zealand.

These drugs divide into several groups. There are '*natural*' hormones, synthetic copies of naturally-occurring hormones such as testosterone. There are *synthetic* hormones, which do not occur naturally but which enhance the effect of natural hormones. *Thyrostatic* hormones inhibit thyroid function to speed weight gain. *Corticosteroids* help muscles retain water. And *beta-agonists* are used against asthma, but have the effect of converting fat to muscle (clenbuterol, or 'angel dust', is the most famous of these).

There are heated debates taking place worldwide about whether some of these should be permitted for beef production, and whether any are safe. Reports from Italy in the 1970s described babies developing breasts and enlarged genitals after eating French veal which contained traces of DES, a synthetic hormone. European public opinion has since been strongly against the use of hormones of any kind in beef production.

However the EU's 1988 ban was not imposed for health reasons in all cases. In 1984 the Commission had recommended limited use of 'natural' hormones, but the Parliament and Council of Ministers insisted on a total ban. In 1995 the Commission's scientific conference on growth promoters agreed with earlier studies which had suggested that there is as yet no evidence for health risks where 'natural' hormones are used to produce beef. (Other experts say that any increase in our intake of hormones, however tiny, is potentially risky.)

Other drugs such as beta-agonists and corticosteroids are considered to be potentially dangerous for humans (and animals).

The United States, which permits some 'natural' and synthetic hormones, considers Europe's ban on beef grown with growth hormones to be a trade barrier with no viable foundation in science. The matter is currently in dispute at the World Trade Organisation. It may yet be that the EU will be forced by this body to lift its ban — although whether European consumers would accept beef grown with hormones is another question.

Meanwhile, in Ireland, there is no doubt that illegal growth promoting drugs were very widely available some years ago. Many farmers did not consider the use of 'natural', previously permitted, hormones to be a serious offence. The IFA did not eject members found guilty of such offences. The black market was well controlled, in some cases by terrorist organisations.

Have hormones and other growth promoters been present in the beef we ate? To some degree yes, although this is hard to quantify precisely. Europe-wide tests of steak and liver in 1994, conducted by consumers' associations and supported by the European Commission, showed residues in meat from every European country except Denmark. The Consumers' Association of Ireland, when it published the results in *Consumer Choice* in March 1995, suggested that due to the sophistication of users' techniques, results obtained probably represented 'the tip of the iceberg'.

In that survey, three per cent of Irish samples were positive for illegal synthetic hormones. The figure for Belgium was highest at seven per cent.

Two per cent of Irish samples were positive for clenbuterol ('angel dust', a beta-agonist). Other figures were: Luxembourg and Netherlands ten per cent; France thirteen per cent; Belgium twenty-three per cent; Spain thirty-six per cent.

Many growth promoters (but not all) produce meat which is extremely tough and easily recognised by an experienced butcher. Most use of illegal growth promoters in Ireland is thought to have taken place in steers, which are primarily sold into intervention rather than for the retail market in Ireland. However, the Irish samples which tested positive in the above survey were all bought in butchers' shops.

You may have noticed many reports during 1997 of farmers and dealers being convicted of handling and using illegal growth promoting drugs. Most belonged to a legislative backlog and related to offences in earlier years. It was gratifying to see the courts handing down high fines and stiff custodial sentences. There may always be a few cowboys. However the consensus on the ground now is that the situation has changed radically — aggressive action on the part of the Department of Agriculture has dried up supply.

Which beef can you trust? Once more, it's a question of sourcing it either from butchers whose relationship with their suppliers you trust, or buying beef from an accredited Quality Assurance Scheme.

And once again, it's worth considering the problems which can be caused by intensive, large-scale food production. Where food was being sold anonymously into intervention, and not for eating by neighbours, it was all too easy for some farmers to close their minds to the possible consequences.

Quality Schemes

Once quality was something assured by the butcher's knowledge of his sources, and your trust in him. Now that this is no longer possible in the case of most beef, audited schemes are necessary to step into that gap.

Quality Assurance (QA)

This Bord Bia scheme aims to offer two-fold assurance: traceability and eating quality. It features traceability of the animal back to the farm (though not to birth). It also stresses basic animal welfare and specifies slow carcass chilling to ensure tenderness. It began in 1990, designed for the export factories; with the BSE scare, it was decided in 1996 to extend it to the home market (and about time too). Superquinn was the first to operate it; interestingly, while beef sales suffered in Ireland, Superquinn actually sold more. In 1997, Quinnsworth, Dunnes and Super Valu joined the scheme.

The guarantees offered by QA have been questioned by some commentators, such as vet and farmer Peter Dargan, Chair of the Consumers' Association of Ireland, who are concerned that the tags used to identify cattle may easily be knocked off or removed.

Eating quality is addressed by watching animal welfare and stipulating a minimum seven days' hanging; but these factors will depend on the individual tailoring of the scheme as each retailer requests.

Taste of Kerry

This scheme offers traceability to the farm of beef and lamb in Kerry. It has two laudable variations: it extends to hotels and restaurants, so you can sit down and be served a traceable steak! And no animal travels more than twenty miles to an abattoir. The scheme stipulates seven days' hanging. Two-thirds of beef sold in Kerry is now derived from this scheme, including Dunnes in Tralee, and most Super Valus.

IQ Butchers

This is not an assurance scheme, but an all-Ireland group of independent butchers. They aim to combat the demise of butchers by being exceptionally skilled. They meet to exchange skills, with each other and with national and international specialists. They are closely audited twice a year, and are expected to show constant improvement. One disadvantage of the scheme, from a shopper's point of view, is that they only allow one member per town; there are six in Dublin. (Contact: c/o Boscos, 132 Tullow Street, Carlow. Tel.: 0503 31093.)

Meat: Buying the Best and Tips for Cooking It

Which Cut For Which Dish?

One of the biggest mistakes we make these days is thinking that a more expensive cut of meat will make for a better dinner. So we might use, for example, round steak for mince, burgers and stews. Yet other cuts, cheaper (and no fattier if well trimmed) would taste so much better. The problem? That perceived notion that the leaner-looking a cut of meat is, the 'better' it will be. As a result, butchers now seem to be recommending an awful lot of round steak; for many dishes the result can only be tough and dry.

The vital thing to remember about meat is that, if good tasty food is what you're after, the butcher you buy from matters much more than the cut of meat you buy. Now that our society is becoming more affluent, we are forgetting about the delectable dishes which can be cooked with cheaper cuts of meat. Cuts like beef shin and flank, pork belly or lamb shoulder don't taste worse, they just need different cooking. And in fact they have more robust and rounded flavours than an ultra-expensive fillet steak.

Unfortunately, although we do have butchers who sell superb meat in Ireland, those who are equally well-versed in the best way to cook each cut of meat are few and far between. They tend to be OK on the basics of roasting, but after that I suspect most are suffering from a marked lack of experience in the kitchen! As a result, there's a fair bit of misinformation being distributed out there.

Roasting

Butchers are unanimous, and they're right: try some of the less expensive cuts of meat. They recommend rib of beef above the more expensive striploin or fillet, and neck and shoulder of lamb and pork in preference to loins and legs.

I used to find this unconvincing: yuk, all that fat! Then one day I finally roasted a shoulder of lamb. Yes, there is more fat — but the sweet, sweet succulence of the lean will seduce you. The constant internal basting provided by the fat and connective tissue makes for incomparably rich flavour. It makes the leg and loin seem forever insipid by comparison. Of course, there are times when a leg of lamb or fillet of beef is perfect. But since you're getting more flavour, for less money, the other cuts are a great addition to a roasting repertoire.

Worried about the fat? Just cut any remaining fat away after roasting, and remember to strain the pan juices well before making gravy.

Butchers also recommend joints and cuts on the bone. They all chorus this advice. 'Every time you cut meat,' pork butcher Ed Hick explains, 'you lose moisture, and that makes for less succulent meat when it's cooked.'

Stewing meat

Whether beef, pork or lamb, stewing meat is usually sold ready-cut. The problem is that: a) it's rarely trimmed carefully enough of its fat; b) it's usually cut too small, making for an itty-bitty stew; and c) it probably comes from several different cuts, all of which will cook at a different pace.

Here's what to do. Buy a piece of stewing meat (see each section below for suggestions). Explain to the butcher you would like it carefully trimmed, and watch as it is done. And then have it cut into pieces larger than the norm, about one and a half inch cubes. They won't cook much slower, and the resulting stew will seem much more satisfying for having chunky pieces of meat in it. (If you're stuck with meat that's fattier than you'd like, let the finished stew settle off the heat before serving. The fat will rise to the surface and can be skimmed off. Easier again is if you cool the stew and chill it. The fat will solidify on the top.)

Spice Mixes

Spice mixes are used far too often by butchers and account for the fact that so many marinated meats taste the same, and taste of awful dried herbs and additives. And while we're on the subject, I can't recommend stir-fry mixes from butchers. I have yet to see one where the meat is cut finely enough. They tend to be finger-thick and good only for semi-stewing.

Beef Tips

1. For prime beef cuts, butchers insist on Hereford Crosses and Aberdeen Angus. Galway butcher Sean Loughnane explains: 'The Continentals are too big. A nice thick sirloin steak from a Continental is about one and a quarter pounds; that's just too much. From a Hereford, it's a nice three-quarters of a pound. And a roast? The Continental cuts are the wrong shape. Three pounds of rib from a Continental is so wide, it's only a thick steak really.'

2. The best *roast beef*? The butcher's choice is the rib, not the 'finer' sirloin or fillet. And the best rib roast? From the sirloin end of a properly-finished, long-enough-hung Hereford Cross. (See page 2 for more on this.)

3. *Stewing*, casseroling or braising beef? Watch out. All too often, Irish butchers now recommend round steak. Don't take it! It will be much too dry. Well-trimmed rib, shin, flank or brisket will be infinitely better, as these cuts have connective tissue which melts and gives the sauce savour.

4. *'Round' mince*? Many people are now paying a lot for round mince. As one expert butcher put it: 'Ridiculous!' Again, the stewing cuts like rib and shin provide moisture and flavour. Brisket, shoulder and neck are good too. The vital thing is that they are well-enough trimmed first, so that when the meat is minced, it's not fatty. If your butcher minces too much fat in, it may (as with stewing meat) be necessary to buy a piece of one of those cuts; then get your butcher to trim it in front of you to your satisfaction, and mince it fresh for you. (Be sure you don't get a

lump of what was last in the mincer.) If a butcher gives you the feeling that this is too much trouble, find another butcher!

5. What goes for *mince* goes for burgers too. Only it's even more important to have some connective tissue to hold the burgers together. With the right mince, your burgers will be more moist.

6. For *pot roasting*, the best cut is brisket, though it must be well-trimmed. Silverside, top rump, chuck and blade are good too.

7. For *braising*, look for *shoulder pieces*, *brisket* or *housekeeper's cut*.

8. For stir-frying, use *topside* (part of the round; every other part of the round is too tough) or sirloin. You can get away with using rib, but only if your butcher hangs his meat very well. It is important to slice meat extremely thinly for stir-frying. And it will be much more tender if you slice it across the grain. This means that you shouldn't see the meat fibres running along the length of the slivers you have cut. See which way they run in the piece of meat, and then cut at right angles to them.

9. Insist on thick, evenly cut *steak*. If it's thin one end and thick the other, it won't cook evenly. This slapdash butchery is all too common. Don't settle for it. Pre-pack steaks add insult to injury by being a measly half-inch thick, sometimes even less. Much too thin. A thin steak does look bigger on the plate. But if you want it to taste right, crusty outside yet still juicy within, it must be at least three quarters of an inch thick.

10. *Spiced beef* is not just an annual event for lucky Corkonians who can buy it year-round. Unfortunately, all too many butchers dump a vast quantity of cloves into the spice, the result so unsubtle it numbs your gums (cloves are a natural anaesthetic.) Approach with caution. My favourite butchers' spiced beef are Downeys and F. X. Buckleys, frequent winners of Master Butchers Federation spiced beef competitions.

Some Confusing Beef Terms Explained

Most cookbooks available here are written for the English market. When it comes to meat, we don't always speak the same language.

English rump steak is called sirloin in Ireland. Meanwhile, what's called sirloin in England, a favoured roasting cut, is not the same as Irish sirloin: it's called striploin here. And, just to add to the confusion, if you see rump for sale in Ireland it's probably not sirloin, but rather the round. English cookbooks often refer to chuck steak, for casseroling, etc. The cuts to use here are neck, shoulder or rib.

The T-bone steak has of course been temporarily suspended from duty. The small side of it is the fillet, the larger side is the striploin.

Lamb Tips

1. Buying a whole *leg*? Ask the butcher to remove the 'H' bone. It makes for much easier carving at the fillet end. And if the leg came with a part of the lap rolled around it and tied on, take it off. Roast it in the tin with the lamb, where it will crisp up beautifully; left on the leg, it just tends to stay fatty.

2. *Rack of lamb* — ask the butcher to remove the chine bone. Again, this makes for easier carving. (Many loosen it but leave it on, which can be a little tricky to handle when carving.) But watch out! When he reaches for the saw, don't let him destroy the rack, as many Irish butchers do, by cutting into the meat at each chop.

3. *Shoulder of lamb* is fabulous roasted, but it is undeniably fiddly to carve when on the bone. If you ask for it boned and rolled, beware. Many Irish butchers are in the habit of rolling the shank end into the centre of the boned joint. This makes for a neat parcel. But the shank is the toughest end of the cut, and needs most cooking, not least. Make sure that if the shank comes with the shoulder, it has been rolled onto the outside.

4. Shoulder of lamb is also excellent cut into steaks for braising, minced for lamb burgers, and is excellent boned and grilled flat on the barbeque.

5. *Stewing lamb*? Neck, shoulder, or gigot/shoulder chops.

6. A *butterflied leg of lamb* is making more and more appearances in recipes. This is a boned leg of lamb laid flat. Since it's very uneven when laid out (it lies in three hillocks), a couple of cuts are made into the thicker parts of the meat to help it lie flatter. Alternatively, the boned leg can be turned into lamb steaks: the three sections of meat are separated. Cut each crossways into slices about half an inch thick. Then lay them on a chopping board, cover with cling film and beat flat with a heavy frying

pan or pot; this tenderises the meat. Marinated, then barbecued or grilled, they are quite delicious.

Confusing Lamb Terms Explained

Shanks of lamb — confusion has been known to reign about these now trendy cuts making several appearances in cookbooks. An English shank is the very lowest, thinnest end of a shoulder (the front leg) or sometimes the back leg of lamb. You need one per person. An Irish shank of course is the lower half of the (back) leg, and will serve several!

Rack of lamb may also be called fairend; English cookbooks may call it best end. Two racks tied together make a guard of honour, or a crown roast.

If the bones are removed from a rack of lamb, you then have an eye fillet. This slender, tender piece of meat is great for barbecuing, quick roasting, or for slicing into medallions and pan-frying.

The loin may also be called *centreloin* or, if both loins are joined, the saddle. And if a loin is boned, rolled and sliced, the pieces are called noisettes.

Pork and Bacon Tips

1. Like all butchers, Ed Hick prefers the flavour of less expensive cuts of meat, which have plenty of internal basting. His preference is for neck, 'a divine roasting cut, but you've got to cook it slow'. Since it is the cut used for collar of bacon you will probably have to order it in advance.

2. *Belly pork* makes a wonderful roast too. Indeed, Galway chef Gerry Galvin, one of the country's finest, won the hotly-contested Bord Bia New Irish Cuisine competition in 1996 with a superb stuffed and rolled belly pork roast. It was most refreshing to see such an underrated cut given a bit of respect.

3. For great crackling, roast a *shoulder joint*. You won't get crackling if you cover the joint with foil. Not if there's no skin on the joint, either . . . Most butchers are very slapdash about scoring the skin, reckoning that a few slashes will do. For good crackling, the skin must be scored with a sharp knife at small, regular intervals.

4. A *loin of pork* for roasting is, just like a rack of lamb, best if left on the bone, although not often seen that way in Ireland. But like a rack of lamb, the chine bone must be loosened or removed to allow for easy carving. This cut may also be called rack of pork when on the bone.

5. *Stewing or braising pork*: neck, shank, hand, knuckle, shoulder. Leg can also work.

6. Take care if boiling ham or bacon. You can dry meat out if you actually boil it. Never let the water come to the boil — cook it at a bare shiver.

Confusing Pork Terms Explained

There are two *pork fillets*. One is the fillet end of the leg, and looks just like the same cut of lamb. The other is the long thin boneless fillet (it's the same cut as fillet steak); this may also be called pork steak or pork tenderloin.

A *hand of pork* is not, as you might think, its little front trotter, but rather part of the shoulder joint, good for stewing and braising.

Green bacon is not ready for the bin, but rather plain salted and cured bacon; it is more often referred to as pale. Smoked bacon is dried and smoked after curing. Back bacon is from the loin of pork and streaky is from the belly.

Gammon is the hind leg from a side of bacon, whereas ham is also a hind leg but is cured separately, so it usually has a different flavour.

Storing Meat

The basic rule is: the smaller the bits, the quicker it must be used. Meat can be kept for:

- Mince — preferably use fresh on the same day; store one day only, or freeze.
- Stewing meat — one to two days.
- Joints boned and rolled — two to three days.
- Joints on the bone — three to four days.

Meat should be taken out of packaging when you get home, unless it's in a vac-pac. Moisture speeds up spoilage, so dry the meat with kitchen paper if it's a bit soggy. Cover with greaseproof paper or clingfilm. Always store meat at the bottom of the fridge, where it can't drip onto or touch ready-to-eat food.

2

Lamb

There are three things about lamb which make it rather special:

1. The meat varies with the time of year; it's one of the last of our foods to remain truly seasonal.
2. Sheep don't take to intensive rearing, so it remains a basically 'free-range' meat. If you're unsure of your source of meat, lamb will likely be the purest.
3. Our regional mountain lamb. It's the best of all. It comes from the rugged, inhospitable areas of the country, where the breed of sheep is different and the herbage it nibbles at is quite distinct. We ought to be clamouring for its sweet eating, yet we hardly notice it!

The Season of Lamb

Lambs get larger through the year, so you need to vary cooking with the seasons.

Spring

At Easter, the spring lamb arrives, the first of the new season's lamb, from young animals which were born in late December or January. At three months, it's just beginning to lose its most baby-like flavour. It's extremely tender, and very popular, but still rather bland for my taste.

Remember that a spring lamb is much smaller than the wintry ones it is just replacing, so although a leg costs about the same, there's only half as much meat on it, three to three and a half lb, as opposed to six and a half to seven lb.

Spring cooking

The briefest roasting and most delicate sauces are usually recommended, so as not to overwhelm the delicate flavour. (Try to find fresh mint if you're making a mint sauce, rather than those vinegary ones in jars.) Italians also balance the blandness of baby spring lamb most successfully with the strong salty punch of anchovies.

Summer

From May, lamb is in its full glory. Not only is the animal a little more mature, but it has also had a chance to feed on plenty of grass. It has more flavour now than the namby-pamby stuff of spring, yet it's still tender enough for quick roasts and grills, yielding a perfect layer of sweet, crisp fat and juicy, tender pink flesh within.

Summer cooking

Roasting, quick grilling and barbecuing are all ideal for summer's prime cuts, as well as for lamb breast and ribs. Stews are good with summer lamb too.

Winter

When is a lamb not a lamb? When it's a hogget. And hogget is what you're getting for about three months of the year, though you may never have heard of it. 'Years ago, we used call it hogget at home,' says Galway butcher Sean Loughnane. 'But lamb is a, shall we say, more user-friendly word.'

That depends on the user. 'Lamb' certainly sounds more genteel than the rather inelegant 'hogget'. But using the same term year-round means we are no longer reminded to cook the meat differently. The closest I've encountered as an exception to this is Oughterard butcher Eamonn McGeough. 'I call it teenage lamb,' he grins. 'That explains it's more mature, without confusing people.'

From September, lamb starts to become a more robust meat. It is larger, and slightly more chewy, but you can't beat it for depth of flavour. We all seem to yearn for the cachet of younger animals these days. But why not value post-Christmas hogget for what it is? The colder winter months are the time to be grateful for its hearty flavour.

Winter cooking

Hogget is magnificent braised and slow-roasted. It's also perfect for Indian and Middle-Eastern dishes; their marinades and spice would annihilate tender spring lamb. Just don't cook a rack quick and pink and expect it to be meltingly tender like it is in early summer.

'Spring' lamb all year round

Just when I was rejoicing in the seasonality of lamb, along comes Superquinn to knock that one on the head. In 1997, they trialled 'Spring lamb all year round'. From October through the winter, young lambs were supplied. Of course, these would be primarily indoor animals, much less likely to get out on grass. It was popular, apparently. I found the flavour disappointing. Selling small lambs through the year also means the legs and shoulders are smaller.

Mutton Dressed as Lamb?

Reputable butchers tell me time and again that some of the cheaper outlets indulge in this. Beware suspiciously cheap offers of lamb. You may be being off-loaded with some very mature meat indeed. Of course, there would be nothing wrong with selling mutton, as long as you called it that. Indeed I wish someone would — it's a rich-tasting meat, which we've sadly abandoned. Many traditional Irish recipes taste bland made with hogget, let alone with lamb.

Mountain Lamb

Anyone else would be serving it as a prime delicacy and protecting it with Denominations of Origin. By and large, we ignore it. And yet mountainy lamb from Kerry, or Connemara, or Donegal, or the Nye Valley is something very special. These hilly regions have none of the lush grass which lowlands can boast. Life is harder, and the sheep more hardy. They feed on the heathers and the rough mixed grasses, the natural herbage of the area. The black-faced mountain lambs are originally Scottish, but over the last century they have evolved into distinctive strains.

They lead a very different life than their pampered lowland cousins. As a result, the meat is different, often a little more dense; rather similar, Sean Loughnane reckons, to a 'well-finished wild deer'. The flavour, though, is unmistakably lamb. Only sweeter, a little more intense. Just delicious.

Where Can You Get It?

It's only available from summer on; the lambs must be born when the weather is kind enough for them to survive, so mountain lamb starts in July or August. For obvious reasons, lamb from the more forgiving hills of Kerry comes in earlier than from the harsher climes of Connemara. By a lucky coincidence, this means the timing's just right for you to encounter it on your summer holidays. Very few butchers make a feature of mountain lamb, though many sell it; in western areas, it's likely to be their standard stock later in the year.

There is one exception — Sean Loughnane in Galway. Nearly half of his sales of lamb from August on are Connemara lamb, he's proud to say, though he warns that, because the animals never become as heavy, the meat is about ten per cent dearer than that of lowland sheep. A small premium for such deliciousness. But in general, the only way to get mountain lamb is to go to a local butcher and quiz him about where his lamb has come from.

Organic Lamb

Mountain lamb is often described as 'practically organic', which indeed it may be, since its grazing is rarely sprayed or fertilised. However, depending on your reasons for choosing organic, 'practically' may not be good enough.

Organic lowland lamb is becoming more widely available, and can be found in some branches of Quinnsworth, as Ballybrado lamb, as well as from the few organic butchers which do exist.

Tips for Cooking Lamb

See Meat: Buying the Best and Tips for Cooking It, page 16.

3

Pork and Pork Products

Finding really good porky things in Ireland is not so easy. This is surprising when you consider that we love pork and its products, and eat more of it than any other meat. And yet — fry a pork chop from almost anywhere in the country and it will be dry, a little tough and sadly lacking in flavour. It's not your cooking, it's the meat.

Most of our bacon and ham are sorry things as well. They're pumped to the gills with added water, usually needing a shot of polyphosphates to hold the water in place. If there's one question I'm asked most often (apart from 'What has happened to the potatoes?'), it must be: 'Why do my rashers ooze all that white goo in the pan?'

Added to all that, there are the antibiotics. In October 1996, the Consumers' Association announced the results of EU-wide tests for antibiotic residues in pork. Ireland showed a shocking seventeen per cent of pork products with excess antibiotic residues. This was twice as high as the next worst offender, Greece. It only emerged later that Department of Agriculture testing, not publicly released, had earlier shown the problem to be even worse.

And finally, there is salmonella. Over fifty per cent of pig herds in Ireland are positive for salmonella. Among the strains present is the multi-drug-resistant salmonella typhimurium DT 104.

What has happened?

Pork
In Pursuit of the Perfect Chop

Pork has suffered terribly in the last few decades. Apart from chicken, it is the most intensively-reared meat we have, and much of its quality and flavour have been lost. It *is* possible to find a pork roast which will be succulent and full-flavoured, or a juicy, tasty chop which will be worthy of the simple partnership of some crunchy fried onions. But you will have to search hard.

Even industry sources, usually so defensive about what they're producing, agree that the way pork tastes needs attention. 'There should be more emphasis at factory level on the eating quality of the pork,' one conceded. You'd have thought that, since this is food they're producing, 'eating quality' would be top priority. You'd be wrong.

The Lean, Lean Pig

Thirty years ago, there was a lot more fat on a pig. This has progressively been bred out of the animals, especially along the loin. Back fat is down to a fraction of what was once to be found.

All well and good, you might say. And indeed none of us wants to be faced with great clumps of fatty meat. Unfortunately, though, it has gone a bit too far. As we saw (see page 7): no fat, no flavour. The intramuscular fat has largely been bred out of pigs too, that delicate lacing of fat within the meat. It's a tiny amount, not something you could see, but it's one of the things which makes meat juicy and tasty.

Intensive Production

No longer is the pig a farmyard companion, eating scraps and swill. Pigs in Ireland — as in most of the world — are now reared in very intensive conditions. Where cattle and sheep mostly graze outdoors or are fed a grass-based diet, pigs are kept entirely inside, usually in barren concrete housing with slatted floors, and are fed concentrated rations in pellet form. Margins are very tight, and the profit is in volume. The temptation can be to pack in a few extra pigs. In intensive systems, everything is geared towards getting the most meat from the least amount of feed, and doing so as quickly as possible.

These are not conditions which are conducive to producing the best meat. They also carry with them other problems, such as excessive use of antibiotics. Another concern is the poor welfare of pigs housed in these systems.

Feed

'The quality of the feed is a very, very big thing,' bacon producer David Rudd points out. But since it comes in pellet form, it can be difficult for farmers to have control over this. It still isn't even required for feed compounders to list feed ingredients on the bags; they may be listed according to groups of ingredients instead.

Meat and Bonemeal in Pig Feed?

Concern was raised by SEAC, the UK government's BSE Committee, about the possibility of BSE-type disease in pigs and poultry, since they carry the PrP gene just as cattle do, and since they may also be fed meat and bonemeal from their own species, as cattle were. The chances are thought to be small, but are being investigated. Scientists think that the issue may be different for pigs since they, unlike cattle, are naturally omnivorous. If you don't want to take your chances while they're figuring out the science, An Bord Bia's Quality Assured pigmeat has banned the feeding of meat and bonemeal to pigs.

How was the Pig Handled?

The health and welfare of pigs is a very pressing issue, so see below for more about that. But as far as the quality of the meat is concerned, the bit that makes the most difference is probably the way the pigs are handled, and how the meat is treated before it is sold to you.

Pigs are Very Sensitive

'The pig,' says Ed Hick, 'is peculiar.' Ed is the youngest member of the Hicks of Sallynoggin and Dalkey in Co. Dublin, where you will find two of the best pork butchers in the country. 'Cattle and sheep are more docile. But small things can distress a pig, and that affects the meat.' His father Jack adds that pigs are 'more jumpy than they were thirty years ago', and so need even more care.

The Hicks operate the last slaughterhouse in the Dun Laoghaire/ Rathdown area of Dublin. Although they buy standard intensively-reared pigs, their pork is quite exceptionally good. They put this down to care before slaughtering and afterwards. Their pigs have a short final journey and then rest overnight in lairage. This differs considerably from many other producers. For example, An Bord Bia's Quality Assured strictures (see page 32) are for a limit of an eight-hour journey and then minimum two-hour lairage before slaughter.

Avoiding stress for the pig can be difficult, even in well-run large-scale operations.

Has the Meat Been Hung?

Another problem is that it is not at all common for pork to be hung in the factories, which supply most of the pork eaten in this country. It is rapidly chilled — the very thing which once caused so much tough beef from large processors. And then it is sent out immediately.

A careful chill, and hanging for a number of days (up to seven) would make the world of difference. Any butcher could tell you as much. And in 1996, research at the National Food Centre confirmed this. Unfortunately, An Bord Bia's Quality Assured scheme does not recommend hanging pork.

Antibiotics

The routine use of antibiotics in intensive animal systems is common the world over. They may be needed because large numbers of animals, housed in close proximity, are prone to catching and passing around disease. Antibiotics are commonly used as a preventative in the feed of young pigs in Ireland.

Antibiotics as growth promoters

Antibiotics are also used to speed up animal growth. The particular drugs given are not used in human medicine and are used in very small quantities. It's not quite known how they work, but they increase the absorption of feed.

The term 'growth promoters' is a bit sensitive because of the publicity given to illegal growth promoters used in cattle, so they may be called 'digestion enhancers' instead. These drugs are perfectly legal; nine are authorised for use in pig feeds by the EU. Most pig feeds in Ireland will contain a growth promoter, except for the feeds they receive for about the last seven weeks of their lives.

Problems with antibiotics

There are two problems with the use of antibiotics. Firstly, antibiotic residues in meat are unacceptable, and there finally seems to be general acceptance of this. Levels in pork have now, with new vigilance, dropped to negligible amounts. However, the reaction of the pig meat industry has unfortunately generally been to call for better adherence to withdrawal periods and more frequent testing, not to question a system which sees the need to use antibiotics on such a wide scale.

Secondly, intensive animal rearing systems which frequently use antibiotics are a problem per se, for they are causing the development of strains of bacteria which are resistant to many major antibiotics. *This has possible health implications for us all.* This is something which the World Health Organisation is highlighting. And the Scientific Veterinary Committee (SVC) of the EU, in its September 1997 report to the Commission, has recommended that preventative and growth-promoting antibiotics should not be used in pig feeds.

Ireland should cease to use growth-promoting antibiotics in all animal feed and should work at EU and world levels to bring an end to this practice. It is causing a threat to human health.

Growth-promoting antibiotics are also often used in intensive systems to rear chickens (see page 42).

Salmonella

Department of Agriculture tests show twelve per cent of pork samples positive for salmonella. Food safety sources tell me that over fifty per cent of pig herds are positive. A Control Programme for salmonella in pigs came into effect in mid 1997 and it is hoped that levels will now reduce. 'They'll have to deal with it,' the source said. 'They're in competition with the Danes. Food safety is now a big trade issue.'

The Welfare of Pigs

The welfare of pigs in intensive systems is highly questionable. Pigs have been bred for lots of lean meat and fast growth, to the detriment of their own health. The SVC put it this way: 'Selection for large muscle blocks and fast growth has led to leg problems and cardiovascular inadequacy', which results in 'increased risk of mortality and poor welfare during handling and transport'.

Particular attention is now focusing on how sows are housed.

Sow stalls and tethers

Breeding sows — the ones which provide piglets for pig production — are typically kept in narrow pens, in which they cannot turn around. They can only stand or lie. They are in addition tethered by a collar and chain to a bar in the stall for the duration of their pregnancies, so typically they spend nine to ten months of the year chained up. About eighty-five per cent of Irish sows are kept tethered. This system is due to be outlawed in the EU at the end of 2005. Consumer pressure has resulted in an earlier ban being enacted for Britain: the end of 1998.

Sows confined this way show sign of considerable stress, have increased levels of disease and injury and perform repetitive, abnormal behaviour. The SVC has recommended that sows should be kept in groups (loose housing, or group housing), and that no individual pen should be used which does not allow the sow to turn around easily. Yet there doesn't seem to be any rush to move to other housing systems here. Indeed, many producers are just switching to stalls, which still confine the sow and don't allow her to turn around.

How are the pigs housed?

The basic system keeps pigs which are raised for eating in barren concrete housing on slatted floors. Better systems use more open barns and supply plenty of material such as straw for pigs to snuffle and root around in, something they love to do. And a happier pig seems to make for a healthier pig. Research on breeding pigs, published in Sweden in 1994, found that, 'Herds using deep straw bedding systems used three or four times less medicated feed than those with other weaning systems.'

An Bord Bia's Quality Assured Pork, Bacon and Ham

This was revamped at the end of 1997. The scheme provides some basic assurances. It now includes an entire new section, a Code of Practice for the farmer. Including the farm in quality control is a step in the right direction.

Antibiotics In the case of pigs, farm quality control is to be welcomed if it means antibiotic-residue-free pork and pork products. However, QA still allows the use of all permitted growth-promoting antibiotics, and thus does not address the more urgent, wider problem of antibiotic-resistant bacteria developing in our animals.

Meat and bonemeal in feed No meat and bonemeal may be fed to pigs in this scheme.

The conditions in which the pigs are kept QA addresses the issue of sow housing only by saying a research review is under way. There is no time-frame for the conclusion of this research, which is expected to be several years away. This is particularly ironic, since the Code of Practice itself refers to the fact that 'good pig welfare' means pigs should be free to 'express normal patterns of behaviour', something which sows are most certainly not able to do in over eighty-five per cent of current systems.

What's the QA guarantee worth? QA will not guarantee you pork or bacon with really excellent eating quality, since it does not address the extremely intensive conditions in which most pigs in Ireland are reared. There is no provision for hanging pork for better flavour. Up to ten per cent water may be added to bacon and ham.

The QA scheme has gone for the lowest common denominator. It is not a guarantee of the best possible pork quality.

How To Find Good Pork

At the moment, your best chance for reasonable eating quality is probably to steer clear of the supermarkets and find a good butcher. One who does his own slaughtering preferably, or one who buys a small amount from a local abattoir whom he trusts; and one who will hang the meat for a few days.

Pork reared by better methods

This is currently very hard to come by in Ireland, though I suspect that this is set to change. I certainly hope so. You can make an enormous difference by asking for it from your butcher or supermarket.

Some producers are somewhat more enlightened than others. For example, all the 'Tender and Lean' brand pork in Quinnsworth/Tesco comes via Avonmore from farmers who rear the pigs in straw in large open barns; the sows are housed in groups, not in stalls or tethers.

Free-range

These pigs are very rare in Ireland. It's hard, because we have such a wet climate: oceans of mud often result. More welfare-friendly indoor group housing may prove to be the best option.

Organic Pork

This is hard to come by, but can be a great treat when you do. At least you can be sure that strict organic standards mean the pigs have led a better existence. However, the final quality of the meat is just as dependent on careful slaughtering and hanging as any other; just because it's organic doesn't mean it'll taste exceptional. Growth-promoting antibiotics are not permitted in organic production.

Tips for Cooking Pork and Bacon

See Meat: Buying the Best and Tips for Cooking It, page 16.

Bacon

The problem with rashers is that they won't fry any more. Put them in the pan, and they sweat a white liquid. The rashers boil in this until it evaporates off. It leaves a hard, dark brown deposit stuck to the rashers. The culprit? Added water. Bacon is now one of the most debased foods in Ireland, an example of the mess industrial-scale food processing can make of a simple food.

How bacon is made

Bacon is made by 'curing' fresh pork, with salt and preservatives. Once upon a time, this would have been done by scattering dry salt over the side of pork and allowing it to draw moisture out of the meat. Alternatively, the pork could be cured in a tub full of brine — a salt solution. Later, it was discovered that by injecting brine direct into the meat, it could cure more evenly. As technology progressed, this injecting became more refined. Nowadays it's done with precise multi-injection needles.

Done carefully and with restraint, brine injection can be fine. Unfortunately, it allows for something which would once have been impossible: for water to be *added* to the meat during the process of curing, rather than taken out of it. Using polyphosphates (sometimes listed as Emulsifier on the label) enables the joint to swell with even more water.

This is a brilliant wheeze. Take water for free, add it to meat, then charge £4 per lb for it. You can even give the customer the illusion that they're getting great 'value' by knocking a few pence off the price. Of course, the value is an illusion, since the water evaporates in the pan.

Perhaps this wouldn't matter so much if the end result tasted good. It doesn't. Excessive brine injection makes bacon wet, soft and pasty. It makes for rashers which ooze slimy goo. Don't worry about that, butchers and food technologists say nonchalantly, it's only protein and water. But they don't like to say what it's doing there, making your rashers sloppy instead of crisp.

Irish food laws are no help. Anyone can pump as much water into their bacon as it will hold. They don't even have to tell you how much added water is in it. Fractional reassurance is available from bacon which carries An Bord Bia's Q mark (see above). But don't get too excited. The Quality Assurance provided by this scheme just means that the processors can add no more than ten per cent water to their product. Every single rasher I have tried which bears that symbol oozes white goo, as do the own-label rashers from all the major supermarkets.

Rashers
Too thin

Most rashers nowadays are cut very thin. Indeed it means that your rasher costs less. But the great texture of an old-fashioned rasher is lost.

Better rashers

Are there any alternatives? Yes. Even with brine-injected bacon, you can seek out a butcher who cures it conscientiously. Above all, this means hanging the cured meat so some of the injected salt solution can drain out again, 'or else,' as one butcher graphically put it, 'it's sloppy, gooey, slimy yuck!'.

Properly-cured brined bacon will only release a few droplets of liquid when cooking.

Another factor in rasher flavour may be time. The interactions of flavour chemicals are difficult to pin down, but the ultra-speedy factory processes in current use don't seem to allow the best flavour to develop.

Dry-cured rashers

There are a few precious souls who dry-cure bacon. Prue and David Rudd do it in Co. Offaly. They pierce the pork with a pair of curved carving forks. It is scattered with salt and cured in the brine that forms. 'We start off with 100 lbs meat and end up with 94 lbs,' they explain. Clearly, this is not as attractive a business proposition as starting off with 100 lbs and ending up with 110 lbs. But the result is that you and I get more meat for our money. The Rudds have tested their rashers against others, and have concluded that a typical leading national brand of rashers, which sells for a few pence a pound less, costs 48p per lb *more*, once the weight loss in cooking has been allowed for.

Better again, it also means that we get to eat lovely rashers and firm bacon, truly tasty with a genuine firm, meaty bite to them. It is available in selected supermarkets around the country.

O'Flynns butchers in Cork city have recently begun making a masterful dry-cured bacon. Sold in the piece and in rashers, it would convert you to dry-cure for ever more.

Bacon Tips

1. Most recipes suggest soaking bacon. But most modern low-salt cures don't require this. Check with your butcher if in doubt.

2. How to fry an oozing rasher: put the rashers in a pan, without any added fat or oil. Heat until they ooze goo. Blot this off with kitchen paper. Wipe the pan clean. Add oil to the pan and fry them. And contemplate the madness of paying less for more water.

Ham

Ham fares no better than bacon. Ham is made by curing a leg of pork (whereas bacon and rashers come from the back, belly or neck of pork). The added water problem is just the same as it is for bacon. A good butcher will find that the hams he makes weigh less than the leg of pork he started off with. Most processors add water to ham, however. And often about another eleven ingredients. Water doesn't have a lot of flavour, so high water use inevitably brings with it plenty of additives such as flavourings, flavour enhancers and sugar. In fact, ham may be even worse than bacon, for nowadays it is often made not with a pork leg but with leftover bits of meat. These are 'tumbled' together with the emulsifiers necessary to make them stick to each other during the cooking. The worst culprits here are the hams which have an irridescent sheen like the slick on the ground at a petrol station, and a rather plastic texture. Unfortunately, these are often the products which are considered most suitable for children.

A 1997 survey by the Consumers' Association discovered that most Irish hams contain phosphates which help water absorption; over twenty-five per cent had flavour enhancers; thirty-three per cent had high sugar levels. In the Europe-wide survey, Ireland had the samples with the highest nitrite levels — these are suspected of being carcinogenic, and are limited in levels since March 1997.

There is no legal limit to how much water may be added to ham. Manufacturers are not required to say how much added water is in the product and not all of them do. The EU Directive on Additives, introduced in 1996, permits many more water-binding additives in ham.

Real Cooked Ham

This is easily spotted. Whole, it looks like a leg, not like a smooth shaped round. Sliced, you can see the fibres running along it.

Cooked hams have a lot of creative names. Some may indicate a genuine process, like 'baked', 'roast' and so on. Others may be using the terms rather more impressionistically. It is curious, for example, that there are at least two 'honey roast hams' on the market which don't actually include honey in the list of ingredients. Read the label carefully . . .

Smoked hams and bacon are under no obligation to have ever been near smoke. A liquid flavouring may be used instead.

Picnic Ham is often the worst; they may have only seventy per cent meat.

Kasseler

This cured and smoked loin of pork, a finely-flavoured roasting joint, is actually a German speciality, hence its name. But it seems to have taken off with a few speciality butchers spread across the country, with the result that it's beginning to feature on great Irish restaurant menus, and was even one of the featured foods for Ireland's showcase catering for the Tour de France in 1998.

The beauty of Kasseler is that it requires no more work than switching on the oven: the butcher has already done all the flavouring for you. The result is a succulent joint, lightly smoky, with a unique and subtle flavouring from its cure and a light and crispy skin.

Kasseler is available from: Hicks of Sallynoggin, Co. Dublin; O'Flynn's of Cork; McGeoughs of Oughterard, Co. Galway; and Continental Sausages of Fossa, Co. Kerry.

Ham Tips

1. Look for a percentage meat declaration on the label, and a short list of ingredients. Real ham has no need for polyphosphates, flavour enhancers, MSG, emulsifiers, glucose syrup, carrageen, flavourings and so on.

2. Better is a guarantee like 'made from prime pork legs, cured and cooked with no added water'.

3. Best of all is a good ham which your deli has cooked on the bone, and which is sliced to order from the bone.

See Chapter 1 Beef, page 21 for further tips.

Sausages

A sausage is a most personal thing, and everyone has their own idea of what a great sausage tastes like. Unfortunately, all too many sausages nowadays taste the same. This is because so many butchers are no longer mixing their own spices for sausages, but rather taking the easy option of ready-made spice mixes. They are liberally available at trade fairs.

What's In Them?

The sausage is a most honourable place to put porky leftovers, the bits of the meat which don't really sell as cuts. That's if you're a trustworthy butcher or company. There are no regulations in Ireland, however, governing what may or may not go into a sausage (or indeed any meat product); nor is there any requirement that the type of meat used be declared on the label; nor is there any definition of how much meat a sausage or other meat product must contain. So what's in them is anyone's guess.

Your sausage, which you assume to be pork, might contain beef as well, or even chicken. Trade guidelines were developed in 1988 for the contents of the Irish Standard Pork Sausage, known as IS 414. You might be surprised to learn that even this Standard required a *total* meat content of only fifty-five per cent, and a total pork content of only forty-four per cent. In a 'pork' sausage! So forty-five per cent of the sausage could be made up of things other than pork, and eleven per cent or significantly more could be meats other than pork.

You might think that this standard is very low, but trade sources agree that even it has fallen by the wayside.

Some *rusk* is essential in the mix to make a traditional Irish sausage — unlike other countries, we like our sausages very soft. The temptation is to overdo it, since rusk can absorb a lot of water. *Soy protein* is a cheap way of bulking out a sausage, especially likely to be found in the catering variety. *Cheap chicken meat* is another possibility. This may be mechanically recovered meat (MRM) — chicken carcasses are put under pressure, the scraps on them become softer and flow off.

Labels provide scant information. 'Meat', it may say, at the top of the ingredients list. How much meat that is, and how much pork, or beef, or chicken meat that might make up is anyone's guess. In practice, most producers and butchers are honourable. Good ones use pork, and limit additives. But there's no way of regulating the cheap end of the market in this country and that's a most unsatisfactory state of affairs.

Sausages Which Fry in Stripes

If you have wondered why some sausages don't brown properly, here's an answer. The sausages which brown in thin stripes, rather than all over, are made with collagen casings, not natural ones. You can spot collagen casings: they look rather plastic-like and dry; the uncooked sausages are not linked, and are perfectly uniform, without that homely squishy look that a naturally-cased sausage has.

Irish Sausages

Despite the fact that we clearly love them, Irish sausages are nothing much to write home about. This is bound to bring howls of outrage, I know. But there is the soft, mild Irish Breakfast Sausage . . . and nothing else. There is nothing to hold a candle to the output and variation of another pork-loving nation, Germany. So there is definitely room for innovation here, especially since a well-flavoured main-course sausage is such a great convenience food.

Dubliners can find out about the pleasures of a variety of sausages at the Temple Bar Market, where Hicks of Sallynoggin and Dalkey sell a selection of their imaginative range: Orange and Fennel, Garlic and White Wine, Chorizo, and many more.

Black and White Puddings

These have really started to come to life again. The rise and rise of black pudding as a star ingredient in restaurants has been one of the more unexpected features of the way Irish food and cooking has been transformed in recent years. The Irish Master Butchers Federation holds annual national competitions for puddings (as well as sausages, burgers and spiced beef). These have had a significant impact in bringing a tasty Irish food back out of the doldrums, as well as giving butchers pride in the value of their regional traditional foods. And unlike sausages, black and white puddings continue to be much more individual, with great regional variations.

Black Puddings

Soufflé of black pudding? Why not? Warm salad of black pudding? Certainly. Pizza with black pudding? I'm not joking . . . The humble blood sausage, once scorned, is back with a vengeance. And of course it is just great for a morning fry as well.

You might be forgiven at times for thinking that the only black pudding in the country was Clonakilty black pudding. Now available country-wide, this was the one which started the black pud gourmet revolution. It is good and crunchy, with a high proportion of pinhead oatmeal. But I find it rather bland; there is an exciting variation of black puddings out there — different kinds of spicing, texture, cereals, fat size and so on. It's well worth trying various ones to look for a favourite. Aficionados recommend McGeoughs of Oughterard. Hicks of Sallynoggin even do a smoked one, which is surprising and rather good.

White Puddings

These are, when they're good, hugely underrated compared to their black cousins. Or so I think. Ed Twomey of Clonakilty Puddings tells me it's because I'm a city person. Apparently we prefer the white, whereas in the country the black sells much better.

Most white puddings are a bit sticky and lacking in texture nowadays, more like liver sausages or pates, which smear on the knife when you cut them. Clonakilty is my favourite: very peppery and crunchy. But, no more than with sausages, this is an immensely personal thing.

Tip

For excellent puddings, sausages, burgers and spiced beef, look for winners of the annual Irish Master Butchers Federation Awards, or contact the Federation for information at 01 830 6380.

4

Chicken and Other Poultry

Chicken ■ Turkey ■ Duck ■ Guinea Fowl ■ Goose

Chicken

Olive Pierce is a sprightly sixty. She rears free-range chickens for the Kilternan Country Market in County Dublin, and also sells some to a few other outlets, among them Dublin free-range butcher Danny O'Toole. 'When I make my deliveries, there are people waiting at the shop, just to talk to me, they just want to see the woman who raises the chickens!' She shakes her head in disbelief.

She shouldn't be surprised. Her chickens are superb, with a rich depth of flavour that is hard to fathom when a diet of supermarket birds is your only alternative. What once was an ordinary skill has become as rare as hen's teeth.

Intensively-Reared Chicken

It fits every bill for our modern times: it suits all kinds of cooking from around the world; it's low in fat; it's ideal for processing into any shape or taste; and it's cheap. Pity it doesn't taste of anything anymore.

Where chicken is concerned, we have decided to pay a price for cheap food, and that price is the flavour. The standard chicken nowadays represents the apotheosis of intensive farming. It is a pappy, watery-fleshed, largely tasteless bird, but it provides cheap, plentiful protein, so we ought to be grateful for it.

Or so the logic goes. The low-fat brigade have seen to it that chicken is now viewed as the 'healthy' meat par excellence, but healthy food doesn't begin and end with its fat content. What are the *chickens* eating? How are they reared? And how likely are they to deliver a little bout of food poisoning?

Growing at breakneck speed

Modern chicken rearing is done at astonishing speed. Where once it took a chicken eighty-four days to reach slaughter weight, now it's done in about half that time. The little chicks are placed in vast sheds, typically housing thousands or tens of thousands of birds. About forty days later, the chickens are tightly packed in, with very little room to move.

Ultra-speedy growth has been achieved by intense genetic selection of chickens which put on meat — especially on the desirable breast — as quickly as possible. In addition, the birds' environment — diet, lighting and temperature — and the feed are closely controlled to get maximum efficiency in 'feed conversion'.

What Chickens Eat

Margins are very tight indeed in the poultry growing business, and the feed chickens receive is the 'least cost formulation', for optimum growth. This doesn't add up to optimum quality or flavour, however. Well-flavoured chickens are produced by allowing them to feed on a wide variety of grains, grasses and other foods.

It is standard to include poultry offal meal — processed chicken leftovers — in feed. If adequately heat-treated, this should not recycle disease. However, SEAC (the UK's BSE advisory committee) has raised a concern that feeding poultry and pigs remains of their own species may make them vulnerable to a BSE-type disease, since they contain a PrP gene like cattle. Set against this is the fact that poultry are natural omnivores, unlike cattle; but the matter is under investigation. The FSAI (Food Safety Authority of Ireland) is awaiting the European Commission's Scientific Committee's advice on the matter.

Some companies are now eliminating poultry offal meal from their broiler feeds.

Antibiotics

In order to speed growth still further, low doses of growth-promoting antibiotics are given. Most chicken feeds in this country contain these; five compounds are permitted by the EU. They can improve feed conversion; exactly how they work is not understood. The term growth promoter isn't much liked by the industry, so these antibiotics are often called 'digestion improving additives'.

The widespread worldwide use of antibiotics in feeds for intensively-reared animals is a matter of great concern. It is encouraging the growth of bacteria which are resistant to these antibiotics.

The World Health Organisation estimates that over half of the world's production of antibiotics is currently being used in farm animals, and that a large proportion of these is not even being administered to fight disease but rather to make animals grow faster. 'As a result,' it concludes in a 1996 report, 'E coli and salmonella . . . are highly resistant to antibiotics in both industrialised and developing countries.' It warns that this can affect us anywhere in the world, since we travel, and buy food from all over the world.

The FSAI now believes that the 'medical and public health consequences' of antibiotic use in animal feed 'should be considered', and the EU is currently examining ways of reducing the use of antibiotics in feedstuffs.

In 1997, the EU banned all use of avoparcin in animal feed. It had been approved for use as a growth promoter in chickens in 1976, and was later used for other farm animals as well. Avoparcin is closely linked to vancomycin, a 'last-resort' antibiotic used in human medicine. Studies have found vancomycin-resistant bacteria in pig and poultry farms where avoparcin was used, but none where avoparcin was not used. The link between the two is not yet considered proven, but the precautionary ban is to be welcomed. However, many other growth-promoting antibiotics continue to be used.

It is time the authorities stopped dithering. Routine inclusion of antibiotics in all animal feeds should be discontinued at once. The use of growth-promoting antibiotics in animal feeds is unnecessary. It is symptomatic of an approach to animal rearing which has an eye only to the balance sheet, and pushes animals beyond their natural limits — and it poses a threat to human health.

Pigs are also reared using growth-promoting antibiotics (see page 30).

Chicken — A Dose of Food Poisoning Bacteria?

In 1994, a Consumers' Association Europe-wide sampling of chickens found that nearly one in two Irish chickens sampled carried food poisoning bacteria. Thirteen per cent had salmonella and twenty-nine per cent had campylobacter; since there was no overlap, forty-two per cent of birds were affected. This was about mid-way in the European league.

In 1996, two separate Teagasc samples found very high levels of contamination of poultry: thirty-five per cent poultry meat samples contained salmonella. (In comparison, just 6.6 per cent of pork sausages were contaminated, and none of the minced beef tested positive.)

The poultry industry points to Department of Agriculture figures which show salmonella contamination in home-produced poultry at twenty per cent, and likes to say that with Scandinavia we lead Europe. Our levels are certainly not as high as some European countries, but we are a long way behind Sweden, which has no salmonella in its poultry.

The Teagasc study provided further cause for concern. Nearly a third of the salmonella strains found were resistant to three or more antibiotics. As we have seen, this development of 'multi-resistant' bacteria is one of the most worrying side-effects of the overuse of antibiotics in intensive animal farming.

A second survey conducted by Teagasc in 1996 found a massive fifty-six per cent chicken samples contained campylobacter. This sort of level is a matter of great concern. Many in the industry appear to be complacent about campylobacter, which causes no illness or economic loss in birds, but can deliver a dose of diarrhoea to us. Campylobacter has become the leading cause of food poisoning in the UK. Eradicating it completely would appear to be unrealistic, but the high levels found in chickens on sale in Ireland are completely unacceptable.

Chicken: handle with care

Fortunately, salmonella and campylobacter are both easily killed by cooking, but in view of such figures, extreme care must be exercised when handling the raw meat while shopping and in your home. Wash hands, boards and knives used in preparing poultry immediately. Make sure raw poultry meat doesn't come into contact with food which will not be cooked. And cook poultry meat until the juices run clear.

Levels of salmonella and campylobacter in Irish-produced chickens leave much to be desired, but levels in many other countries are even higher. Yet we import a great deal of poultry for processing from other countries. The label may say 'Made in Ireland', but it doesn't tell you where the raw ingredients came from.

The Unhealthy Chicken

Broilers suffer so that we can eat extra-cheap chicken. (Broiler chickens, the ones reared for eating, are not to be confused with battery hens, the ones which lay eggs and which are kept in cages.) The intense selection for speedy meat growth and a high meat to bone ratio means that they suffer bone and joint disorders — they grow too fast for their legs to support them properly. They have also been found to outgrow their heart and lung capacity. In addition, the fact that they have weak legs, and that the litter is typically not changed in the sheds during their lifetime, means many are reported to suffer breast blisters and ulcerated feet.

A Slower-Reared Chicken: The Eighty-Day Bird

Professor John Webster is Professor of Animal Husbandry and Head of the Veterinary School at the University of Bristol. He believes that farmers have a right to a decent living, and that the public has a right to buy cheap, wholesome food. Yet he also describes the fate of broiler chickens as 'the single most extreme example of man's inhumanity to another sentient creature'.

Professor Webster recommends that action to improve the lot of the broiler chicken 'need not be drastic. The problem of chronic pain could be solved if supermarket shoppers only bought birds reared more slowly . . . i.e. those that state that no bird was killed before eighty days of age.'

The search for flavour

An eighty-day bird would also have a much better chance of bringing us some of chicken's natural, delicious flavour, which is so absent in the forced, speed-reared birds on supermarket shelves today.

Slower = safer?

It is possible to raise chickens speedily and intensively without a high disease level by closely controlling every step of the way, as the Swedish poultry industry has shown. Still, the fact remains that the closer animals are confined, and the younger they are slaughtered, the greater the possibility of disease. Research at the Food Microbiology Research Division of the Department of Agriculture for Northern Ireland concluded in 1994 that: 'The manner in which the animals are housed will directly affect the microflora of their exterior, whilst the age at slaughter will have a major effect on the microflora of the (gastro-intestinal) tract . . . Those animals which are intensively reared and slaughtered young will have the greatest potential for carrying pathogens.'

Free-Range Chickens

Are free-range birds the answer? Not necessarily. We all have an image of a free-range bird, pecking contentedly about a yard and delivering wonderfully-flavoured chicken. What many people don't know is that there are, according to EU rules, several levels of 'free-range'.

If you have tried a supermarket free-range bird and were disappointed, having paid the extra, to discover that the flavour isn't noticeably different, that's because they are reared on an industrial scale, to the lowest of the EU's three free-range standards.

Three different types of 'free-range'

EU basic 'Free-range' standards are much too low. Birds have just a square metre space allowance outside, for half of their lives. There's no restriction on flock size. Flocks may be huge, typically up to around 7000 in size. While feed in the fattening stage must be at least seventy per cent cereal, there are no restrictions on the type of proteins used, so they may contain soy for fast growth and also poultry offal meal. Antibiotics are permitted.

The birds can be of the same fast-growing broiler breeds, and there's no guide to the age at slaughter. Because the birds are outdoors, they don't grow quite so fast as indoor birds in controlled conditions. Still, they are ready at a young fifty to sixty days — not enough to develop flavour.

There are two other EU free-range grades: 'Traditional free-range' and 'Free-range total freedom'. These correspond a little more to the idea of free-range birds which we have. Flock sizes are limited (albeit to a massive 4800 birds per house). Above all, the birds must be of a slow-growing strain and must reach a minimum age of eighty-one days. These are more likely to deliver 'free-range' flavour, but are very rare indeed.

The supermarket free-range bird

There is only one free-range chicken producer registered with the Department of Agriculture in Ireland; less than one per cent of the country's annual production of nearly 60 million birds.

Most commonly, free-range birds in the supermarkets are from Manor Farm and Moy Park (produced in the North). Moy Park's birds come with an impressive-sounding 'Free Range Charter' on the pack. It refers to 'traditional husbandry', 'small farms', 'farming methods much the same as thirty years ago', and a 'traditional diet'.

If this conjures an image in your mind of a small number of birds pecking at the back of someone's farmyard, the reality is rather different. The birds are kept in huge flocks of 20,000 birds, in groups of about 7000. Flocks of this size would not have been standard here thirty years ago, when free-range chickens were typically reared in dozens. Chickens are thought to find large flocks very stressful if they cannot establish a natural pecking order.

Moy Park explained that 'traditional husbandry' refers to the fact that account must be taken of the weather when rearing free-range birds; this compares to standard broiler production, which takes place entirely indoors. The 'traditional diet' advertised is free of animal by-products and growth-promoters (though they may use growth-promoting antibiotics in their standard birds, depending on customer specifications). The birds reach slaughter size at fifty to sixty days, depending on the weather.

I then asked *Manor Farm* about rearing conditions and diet of their free-range birds. They stated that they were reared to 'EU standards . . . including stocking density, age of kill and type of feed etc.' (They stated that no growth-promoting antibiotics are used in their chicken production, either standard or free-range.)

Birds reared to basic EU free-range standards have, at least, been able to get outdoors and move around a bit. But they are a 'half-way house', especially since they are most likely to be of the standard fast-growing breeds, and thus subject to similar problems as described for broilers above, and are most likely to be ready at a young fifty to sixty days.

'Real' free-range

This is a rare item in Ireland. By 'real' free-range, I mean birds which are raised in small flocks and reach slaughter weight slowly, birds which have plenty of flavour. Olive Pierce rears birds like these. They are gently cared for, no more than 400 at a time. The result is astonishing. The meat tastes of — well, chicken. Suddenly, you realise what you've been missing. Suddenly, you know why a roast chicken was once a tremendous treat. It's the kind of food which has everyone at the table humming with pleasure: the kind of food which really is good enough to eat.

Flavour is a factor of age above all

And yet Mrs Pierce doesn't use a different breed of bird. She supplements their free-range peckings with carefully-chosen but standard broiler feed. So what does she put the huge difference down to? 'The fact that they're not forced. They're let live until they're ready to be killed,' at an average of eighty-four days. At this stage, they are bigger than the chickens we're used to seeing in the supermarkets — they weigh over 4 lb on average, and would feed eight. And they cost more, around £6-£8. But once you've tried one, you'll long for the flavour for ever.

Where to find 'real' free-range chickens

I only wish I could tell you. There are so few reared in Ireland that it's very difficult to source them. Olive Pierce's chickens are so popular they have to be ordered in advance, and could be sold many times over.

You need to scour butchers, markets and country markets in your area. Tell them you want real free-range birds with real flavour, not quick-reared ones from large producers. You may be lucky. We can only hope that demand for them will encourage some more producers to start up.

`Farm Fresh`

This is not a recognised definition, but rather a colloquial term. Unlike with eggs, in the case of chicken it does mean something. It refers to chickens reared in small numbers by farmers; their throughput is limited to 200 per week and they will be sold by butchers in the local area. They are fed standard compound feed and will be just one to two weeks older than an intensively-reared broiler. However, the fact that they are kept in smaller groups may improve both their welfare and their flavour.

Barn-Reared

An EU definition not common in Ireland, barn-reared may sound attractive, but just refers to very slightly better conditions than the standard intensive bird.

The Watery Bird

Another problem with modern, fast-reared chickens is that they release a lot of water in the cooking. If you find a good free-range chicken and roast it in a casserole, you will find that there's just a little juice in the pot when it's done. It has stayed in the bird, making the meat more succulent. Quick-reared birds, on the other hand, whether intensive or 'free-range', end up sitting in a significant quantity of watery juices.

There are strict regulations about the amount of water birds are permitted to take up during wet-plucking, the standard method. Hopefully, the average birds we buy comply with these.

Meat from older animals has a better water-holding capacity. Once again, a slower-grown, slightly older bird scores for eating and cooking quality.

Breaded Chicken

Nuggets, Burgers, Kiev, Tikka Masala, Cordon Bleu, Steaklets, Escalopes, Fingers, Pieces, Fillets . . . is there no end? This, along with yoghurts and margarines, seems to be an area of explosive growth in the supermarket. It's a good deal for the manufacturer: take chicken bits which would be hard to sell anyway, add water and other cheap ingredients, call it a convenience food and sell it for more.

But is it a good deal for you? A Consumer's Association survey and analysis of fifty-seven of these products in 1992 revealed some interesting facts.

■ Breaded chicken with more bread than chicken: total meat content varied from just thirty-seven to seventy per cent.

■ On average almost half the product was crumb.

- Fat content varied, but ranged up to twenty per cent (poultry naturally has five per cent).

- Added water was common. Some added none, but many had over twenty per cent, even up to twenty-nine per cent, nearly one third added water!

- One sixth of the products had ten to twenty per cent less meat than they stated on the packaging.

Turkey

Once an annual treat for the wealthy at Christmas, turkeys have now become as intensively-reared as chickens. All the strictures above apply to turkeys as well, except that turkeys are likely to suffer even more in intensive rearing. They are specifically bred for big, white breasts, and so are even more unbalanced than a broiler chicken. Many are such an unnatural size that they can no longer mate naturally.

Flavour-wise, the same problems apply as for chicken. Every year at Christmas there's a debate: do you really *like* turkey? Why do we have it? It's too tasteless and dry! The reason is in the rearing and the feed. This Christmas, put yourself down on the list at a good butcher or poulterer for a free-range turkey. These, unlike chickens, tend to be 'genuinely' free-range: reared by small producers, 'by ladies who seem to put their heart and soul into it', as Dublin poulterer Peter Caviston puts it. 'Reared on a farm, they eat mash as well as bits of everything when they're out picking. That's where you get the flavour.'

They are often exceptionally good. You'll be surprised by the depth of flavour — and the fact that the bird is succulent, rather than dry and dusty in your mouth.

In addition, a good poulterer or butcher will hang the bird for a week to ten days. This is crucial for flavour. Supermarket birds are not hung at all.

Some prize the flavour of a Cambridge Bronze turkey particularly. This traditional breed is making a bit of a comeback now, though it's likely to remain rare, since it takes so long to mature — almost a full year. The meat is a little firmer than the standard White turkey; since the feathers are dark, they leave a little 'stubble' of pin feathers behind. There is a little less meat on them.

Stuffing Poultry

Standard health advice is now to cook stuffing separately from the bird. This is based on the concern that people may over-stuff the bird. If air can't circulate within its cavity, it is unlikely to cook through well enough to kill off potential salmonella or campylobacter bacteria.

As far as I'm concerned, cooking stuffing separately misses the point: the interaction of flavours between the bird, its juices and fats, and the stuffing mix. If you want to stuff a bird, stuff the cavity no more than one-third full. Check in the cooking that it hasn't swelled to more than a half full. You can stuff the neck end as much as you like.

Duck

A well-reared duck is a treat indeed. And again, there's a world of difference between an intensively-reared bird and a free-range one. Free-range ducks have a rich, gamey flavour which their fast-reared relations just can't match.

There are basically two types of duck available in Ireland: Pekin/Aylesbury and Barbary. Pekin/Aylesbury ducks have quite a flat breast and a softer texture and will only serve two. The flavour is often finer.

Barbary ducks have a much larger breast — this is what the French call a *magret*, and what is called for when recipes specify a duck breast. The breast serves one very generously. Barbary ducks can be very tough and coarse flavoured if not well-reared. The intensively-farmed Barbary ducks reared in Ireland which I have encountered have tended to the coarse and unpleasant, and the smaller Pekin/Aylesbury types are inclined to be bland. I seek out free-range Irish ducks, whatever their breed, or buy a French *magret*.

Guinea Fowl

These birds look scrawny, sunken and rather jaundiced next to the pure plumpness of a chicken. (It's a shame they're sold without their glorious polka-dotted plumage.) However they can, if well-reared, offer the kind of flavour which is all too elusive in a chicken. Ask about their conditions, though. So-called 'free-range' guinea fowl are permitted by EU regulations never to go outside, and to be kept in a perchery instead.

Goose

The glory of a goose at Christmas is something to look forward to. It wasn't always that way. 'My father wouldn't have sold a goose, it was beneath his dignity. It was the poor man's turkey, and turkey was three times the price,' says Donnybrook poulterer Peter Mulloy. The meat is like a deeper version of duck, and then there's all the delicious fat. 'Gallons of grease', people say disparagingly — but don't waste a drop of it. It also means the goose is a self-basting bird. Much less work!

Geese do not take kindly to intensive farming, so you can assume that what you're sold is a true blue free-range bird. It's important to buy from someone who knows his or her stuff — geese can be variable. A goose that has been feeding near the sea can taste fishy, and an old one will be tough. How to tell? 'Check the windpipe,' says Peter Caviston. 'If it doesn't break in your hand too easily, it's an oul' tough one.' I think I'll leave that to the experts.

Like ducks, geese serve fewer people than you'd think from looking at them: they have a large body cavity and a lot of fat on them. When you roast a goose, or a duck, collect every drop of the precious fat and use it to make the best, crispest, most savoury roast and fried potatoes you've ever tasted. And as you tuck into them, muse on the fact that in south-west France, they exemplify the 'French paradox': plenty of fat in the diet, and low rates of heart disease. And pour another glass of red wine.

5

Fish

I don't know what it is about supermarket fish counters. Everyone working behind them seems to end up with the same glazed look in their eyes as the fish on ice below them. And when you ask what's especially fresh today, they *always* say: (a) 'It's all fresh today,' and (b) 'The cod is lovely.'

Getting the very best fish isn't always easy here. This is one of the great mysteries of eating in Ireland. Most of us live within a few short miles of the sea, but do you think anyone would sell us a mackerel a few short hours out of the water, its body still straight and stiff, its flesh still sweet?

Irish people are traditionally rather diffident about fish. Most of the time, we don't demand the best, and that hardly encourages more fish-eating. It's ironic to think that over three quarters of the fish we catch is exported. The French and the Spanish are very keen on the marvellous fish and shellfish they get from Irish waters. Their agents are at the quaysides, prepared to bid high prices for the very best of Irish fish. Just think, we could be eating it days before them!

Still, it's definitely worth persevering. At their best, fish and shellfish in Ireland are magnificent. But, standing at the counter, looking at rows of fanned-out fillets on ice, how can you tell the difference between a fish which will be acceptable but dull, one which has the sour, 'fishy' whiff of spoilage, and a fabulous fillet, sweetly redolent of the briny?

How Fresh Is Fresh?

The fish may indeed be 'fresh' in the shop that morning. But freshness in fish is not just determined by the number of hours it has been out of the water.

Most of us have the idea that fish boats are out at night, land a catch, and bring it in at dawn so we can eat it that day. Not necessarily. You might be surprised to know that the experts reckon that white fish, expertly handled, has a shelf life of an incredible twelve or more days from when it was caught; oily fish spoils quicker and lasts only three to four days. But the simple fact is that edible fish is not at all the same thing as marvellous fish.

If you were really to judge the freshness of that fish on the counter, you'd need to know all sorts of things: whether the crew of the boat which caught the fish took good care of it; how many days the boat was at sea for — just one, or maybe five? which trawl the fish was caught on — three days ago, or last night? You could also do with knowing what the weather was like — were the fisherman tempted to do longer trawls than usual, leaving fish dead in the nets and hanging around at sea temperature for longer than usual? Perhaps the boat has seine nets, which are hauled in every two hours or so, as opposed to a trawler, which leaves its nets out for about five hours. Do the fishermen ice the fish immediately, or does it hang around on deck for a while? And, if they're gutting the fish, how carefully do they do it?

All these factors (and more) affect how the fish will taste — because after fish dies, every minute spent at air or sea temperature, rather than on ice, speeds up spoilage. In addition, fish is quite delicate, so careful handling is imperative.

How can you know all this? Of course you can't. It's the job of the fishmonger and his suppliers. Your task? To find a fishmonger who cares about these things, and to let him know you care.

Assessing the Fishmonger or Fish Counter

First, Take a Sniff

A good fish shop *does not smell fishy*. Fresh fish smells clean and of the sea, like a walk on a breezy beach. If there's a sour smell, buy elsewhere.

Next, Take a Look

Ice

Lots and lots of it. Fish should be on plenty of ice: kept too warm, it will deteriorate rapidly. Pools of water, or no ice, are a bad sign.

Whole fish

Ideally, there should be whole fish, and not just for dramatic display purposes. It's much easier to assess the freshness of whole fish than of fillets. If the fishmonger dealt with the whole fish himself, rather than buying in fillets, he'll be able to tell you which fish is best today.

Eyes and gills

The eyes of fish should bulge and not be sunk in their sockets. The gills of whole fish are a real freshness indicator: they should be bright blood red. As the fish deteriorates, they fade to pink and then turn brown. Turn them back and have a look!

Is there a wide variety?

Don't be deceived. It may look exciting, but it doesn't mean it'll taste great. Expensive exotica such as grouper, parrot fish and others are making appearances at up-market fish counters. A much more thrilling sight would be a sign saying 'fished last night' or even 'live prawns'. In Normandy, you pay more for fish from *petits bateaux*: the smaller boats which fish closer to shore and land their catches each day. It's worth it. If only such signs were a regular feature here.

Don't Be Afraid to Have a Feel

Fresh fish flesh is firm and springy, not flabby; if you press it, it should not leave an indentation. The skin is not sticky, but rather squeaky-wetly-slimy.

And the scales don't fall off easily. The bellies of those oily fish which are not gutted on board boat (mackerel, herring) are still firm when they're really fresh; as they age, they liquefy. If you feel a taut belly on a mackerel, you're in for a treat — and you've found a great fishmonger.

Fillets only?

The sale of filleted fish is on the up, so a display of these isn't necessarily a black mark for a shop. However, it's worth remembering that fillets deteriorate much more rapidly than whole fish. Even fish filleted this morning won't be as good as fish filleted in front of you. And assessing their freshness is much more difficult. You can't really go around poking them. All you can do is look for plump shiny flesh.

Everyone in the business tells me that more and more of you will only take filleted fish home. It's a shame: fish on the bone has more flavour and retains more succulence. But if you want fillets or steaks, ask for them to be cut to order.

Shellfish

These should not be on ice: it kills them. They should be shut, or should close smartly when tapped.

Finally, Ask

A good fishmonger knows what's especially good, because he saw it coming in and filleted it himself. He knows which fish are spawning: when they spawn, they produce roe (the eggs) and the flesh becomes watery. He might, if you're very lucky, know which boat, or even which trawl, the fish came from. At the very least, he should not look bored or indifferent when you ask for a recommendation: he should know instantly, and be able to enthuse about something on the counter. It might even be the cod!

The problem with supermarkets is that, increasingly, the fish are being filleted centrally and sent out in anonymous polystyrene boxes. What hope do the staff have? They know as little about that fillet of fish as you or I. They might as well be selling tins of beans.

How Do Our Fish Shops Measure Up?

Not very well, according to a *Consumer Choice* survey of 1996. Only nineteen per cent of the fish they sampled (from fishmongers, butchers and supermarkets) was stored at an ideal 0°C–2°C; almost half (forty-six per cent) were unacceptably high, over 4°C. Reflecting this, almost half the fish also had unacceptably high bacteria counts. Things are improving a little, I think, but a demanding consumer will speed up that process.

Storing Fish at Home

Ideally, don't. Eat it on the day you bought it. Your fridge, at the recommended 5°C or under, is too warm for fish. If you're going to keep fish, do so at the bottom of the fridge — on crushed ice. (Whack ice-cubes in a heavy plastic bag with a rolling-pin.) Remember, oily fish spoil much more quickly than white fish, so if you're buying fish to keep, pass on the herring and go for the haddock.

Fish fillets can keep very well in vac-pacs. If you buy irregularly from a good fishmonger, see if they can vac-pac the fish for you.

Filleting Fish

Ideally, don't. That's what your fishmonger is there for! And what he should do in front of you. Unfortunately, even when your fishmonger has 'filleted' the fish, you are often left with a row of bones to contend with. That's if your fish was a 'round' fish, i.e. one of the cylindrically-shaped ones like cod or salmon (as opposed to flat fish, like plaice). The bones are called the pin bones, and they run from the mouth of the fish along the centre of the fillet, to about half-way down the fish.

I don't think it's acceptable for fishmongers to leave the pin bones in, but they all do. So if you wish to have them removed you'll have to ask. If you're at home, you can do one of two things.

1. You can cut the pin bones out. Using a very sharp knife, cut either side of the row of bones, almost down to the skin, to form a 'V'. Do this carefully or you'll be left with a gaping hole in the fillet, or in the skin below. Then just lift out the sliver of flesh containing all the bones.

2. More elegant, but more time-consuming, is wrenching them out. Do this with a tweezers or with a fine pliers (reserve the tool for the kitchen only!). Feel with your fingertips for the bones, then pluck them out one

by one. You will, incidentally, need to do this with almost all smoked salmon before slicing it.

Fish and Health

Fish has two main claims to fame in this area. First of all, there's the low-fat, high-protein nature of white fish (the kind that's *not* coated in breadcrumbs or batter and deep-fried).

More recently, nutritional research has shown us that oily fish, once looked down on for being higher in fat than white fish, is in fact a crucial element of a healthy diet.

This came to light when it was discovered that heart disease is practically unknown among Eskimos, despite the fact that they have a very high-fat diet. Long-chain n-3 polyunsaturated fatty acids, found in high levels in oily fish, are thought to be responsible. (They are known generally as omega-3 fatty acids, or omega-3 fish oils.) It is clear that these oils have a number of roles in protecting against heart disease.

Oily fish are the best sources of these fatty acids, as well as being extremely high in vitamins A and D, so they should be eaten regularly. (This applies especially to pregnant and breast-feeding women: the fatty acids have a role in the neuro-development of babies.)

Those fish which are good sources of omega-3 fatty acids are: mackerel, herring, salmon, trout and fresh tuna. Surprisingly, while tinned salmon is a good source, tinned tuna is not. One other factor is worth considering. The diet of farmed fish will clearly affect the omega-3 oils content of the fish. Some farmed fish are fed with vegetable oils which do not contain omega-3 fatty acids (though not Irish farmed salmon, BIM have told me).

However, the impeccably healthy image of fish is disturbed a little by the fact that persistent organochlorine residues (see Pesticides, page 205) such as DDT, dieldrin and lindane are being picked up in tests on body fat and livers of fish and shellfish from various parts of the world. This is a subject about which we could do with a great deal more information. Which fisheries are more contaminated than others? Which fish might be most at risk? Where are the fish we are eating being fished? Unfortunately, the Pesticide Control Service does not test fish and shellfish.

For the same reason, cod liver oil supplements may not be a good idea.

UK government safety advice in 1997 noted that the potential intake by toddlers of persistent chemicals such as PCBs and dioxins was 'undesirably high' if cod liver oil was given, though they said they considered that it was unlikely to pose a risk to health.

When is it in Season?

At some times of the year, when seas warm up, the flesh of fish is rather watery and soft. The plankton blooms, the fish feel well-fed and begin to spawn. Because they are using up a lot of their fat and protein reserves to produce eggs (the roe), the flesh deteriorates. Fish in this condition are called spent fish, and it takes one to two months for them to recover condition.

Spawning times vary with the species and with the area, with the result that fish seasons are a very local matter, varying with the climate. In the days when fishing was local, fish seasons were quite clearly defined. August was for mackerel; in November the herring came in; salmon was a summer treat. But now that fishing is a continental, indeed global affair, with trawlers travelling for days to other waters, the notion of seasonality has become much less clear.

This means that you can, by and large, ignore all those fish season charts which you see in cookbooks. First of all, they're not specific to Ireland, and anyway, they're more or less redundant.

Watch Out for Roe

Fish shops regularly carry spent fish because there are some people who are so wedded to one variety only that they'll eat it no matter what its condition. To get delicious fish all the time, you need to be sure your fishmonger knows you don't want spent fish. Watch out for roe: if a fish is full of it, its flesh often won't be very good. Of course, this won't be apparent if the fish has been filleted, and it's not so easy to see in a whole fish, especially from the other side of a fish counter. So you must trust your fishmonger!

Fish in Summer

Many people still have a feeling that fish is less good in summer. Like notions of avoiding pork when there's no 'r' in the month, this is a concept of seasonality which definitely can be discarded now. Fish (and pork) do deteriorate more rapidly than other meats, but with refrigerated transport and ice, fish can now be just as good in the middle of a heatwave as in the depths of winter. Which is fortunate, since fish's light flesh is very welcome in the warmer months.

A Rough Guide

What follows must be a rough guide, but there are certain times when fish are most likely to be spawning and so may be less good. But don't take this as gospel — ultimately you must consult with the fishmonger over the ice.

Spawning times when fish may be 'spent':

Round white fish
Cod, *haddock*, *hake whiting*, *pollock*, *coley* and *gurnard* may be spawning from March to May. Cod's roe is still a February and March treat — available in those months only.

Flat white fish
In general, spring is the time to avoid; March to May is the worst time for these. *Plaice* can be particularly bad in February, March and April. *Flounder* may be specially poor in March and April, as may *black sole*; it's particularly annoying to spend a lot of money on that luxurious fish to find it watery-fleshed. *Lemon and white sole* may be spent in April and May. Be wary of *brill* from March to June, and of *turbot* in March.

Oily fish
Farmed salmon is of course in similar condition year-round, as are *farmed sea and rainbow trout*. *Wild salmon* may only be caught commercially in seasons permitted by Ministerial order, usually at some stage of early summer, May–July. Line-caught wild salmon and sea trout may appear at times other than these. *Tuna* and *swordfish* should be good year-round, though they are currently fished by Irish boats only in late summer. *Mackerel* should be all right year-round, though always look for it from local boats on short trawls when it will be infinitely nicer and fresher. *Herring* are often spawning in March and April.

Shellfish

Prawns may be soft in the summer, as the prawn takes in more water to extend to its new shell size when it has moulted. *Spider crab*, if you can get this delicacy before it's all shipped to France, is best in late spring and through the summer. *Native oysters* are not available in the summer when they are spawning, and *pacific oysters* are less good but still perfectly edible in August and September (no need to avoid when no 'r' in the month). *Mussels* may lose a little condition in late spring/early summer, but this varies depending on local conditions.

Fish and shellfish often good year-round

Monkfish, John Dory, ray, dogfish, shark, arctic char, halibut, periwinkles, scallops, whelks, prawns, lobsters, brown crab, crawfish and squid.

Farmed Fish

World fish stocks are under pressure. Over-fishing is rampant, and catches are plummeting worldwide. So when fish farming was first developed, it was welcomed as the simple, sensible way to produce more of this wonderful, natural food. But then it emerged that farmed fish, like any other kind of farmed animal, can vary greatly in quality, depending on how it is reared and fed. In addition, the environmental impact of fish farms is under question. And finally, questions are being asked as to whether fish farming is a sensible use of a dwindling global resource: it takes a lot of fish to grow a farmed fish.

Salmon

The vast majority of the salmon we eat is now farmed — though unless you stopped to think about it, you wouldn't know: retailers are under no obligation to state whether the fish is farmed or wild. In practice, unless it trumpets itself as 'wild', you can be sure that the salmon on ice in front of you has come from a fish farm.

Is there a difference between farmed and wild salmon?

Salmon has long been revered. Its long journeys of thousands of miles between spawning grounds upriver and feeding grounds far out at sea are still not fully understood. They lend it an aura of majesty, and its subtle pink flesh is particularly beautiful.

Farmed salmon is a fundamentally different animal. It is caged and lives a cosseted life. It is not a forager, but rather eats a highly-controlled diet which has been compounded by man. Its pink colour comes not from feeding on crustaceans, but from a dye. Chemicals are most likely used on the farm and on the fish.

Can you tell the difference?

That rather depends on what you're looking at. If the salmon is raw or smoked, the difference is quite easily spotted by an expert eye. The farmed fish, having had less exercise, is fattier. A deposit of fat at the belly is a give-away sign, as is even streaking of fat through the flesh. Another give-away is plenty of fish at even sizes, without any blemishes or imperfections: these will certainly be the product of a fish farm. Once the salmon is cooked, even the expert eye has trouble distinguishing between the two. (See also Smoked Salmon, page 75.)

Is the farmed fish as good to eat?

The farmed fish, when cooked, may be indistinguishable from the wild fish. Or it may be fatty, flabby and not much of a treat at all. It depends a great deal on the quality of the farming. The difference can be as great as that between a free-range chicken and its intensively-reared broiler cousins.

Some factors are crucial:

How much swimming has the fish done?

Cages sited well offshore, in water which has strong currents, will mean the fish swim a great deal. If the farm is located in a calm fjord or loch, the fish will be lazier, their flesh flabbier and fattier.

How tightly are the fish packed?

How much space the fish have in the cage will clearly affect how much exercise they get. Stocking densities in Ireland are typically 18 kg per cubic metre (compared with Norway, where they may be 30 kg and more). Exceptionally good salmon farms stock at about 13 kg.

How much fat was in the feed?

More fat means the fish grow faster, so the temptation is to add more. Yet of course this leads to fattier fish. After experimenting with higher levels, Irish salmon farmers are now cutting back. In some countries, vegetable oils are used in the feed, but I'm told that all Irish farmers use feed made with fish oils.

What about the chemicals?

Colour Wild salmon get their colour from feeding on crustaceans, which have fed on plankton, which have fed on algae. Farmed salmon are pink because pigments are added to their feed. Some supermarket buyers point to a colour chart to choose the shade they desire.

There are two pigments used; both are man-made. Canthaxanthin is cheaper. Once banned in the US for use in food, that ban has since been rescinded. It is not totally stable and can lead to colour leaching from the fish, something you may have seen when salmon is on ice in a fish shop. Astaxanthin is considered more natural and is described as 'nature-identical'. It is more expensive, and can now be manufactured by a biological process from yeasts. It is much more rare.

Antibiotics were once used prophylactically in salmon feed. But that practice has given way to vaccination of the young fish. This at least targets them more effectively.

Other chemicals are used to clean up cages and to deal with sea lice (see below). The extent to which these are used depends on the location of the farm — offshore cages in swift currents will need far fewer, if any at all. This is one of the question marks which hangs over farmed salmon.

Sea lice

A sure sign that summer's approaching is the annual spat between the sea trout anglers and the salmon farmers.

Sea trout stocks have collapsed in recent years. The circumstantial evidence linking this to high sea lice levels on fish farms is strong. The fish farmers, however, deny this strenuously, and point to the fact that the link is not scientifically proven.

Various chemicals, also used in land-based agriculture, have been used in an attempt to control sea lice in salmon farms. Their use in, and their effect on, the marine environment is under-researched and questioned by many. Nuvan, or Dichlorvos, an organophosphate, was once widely-used, but has become less effective. Many farmers then switched to Ivermectin, a broad-spectrum parasiticide generally used for land-based farming. It is not licensed for use on fish, though it may be applied under special veterinary licence. Its effect on water is questionable. Some studies suggest that there is no significant accumulation; others that it degrades slowly in sediment and bioaccumulates in shellfish. As a result, Scottish authorities have placed a two nautical mile exclusion zone between shellfish farms and fish farms licensed to use Ivermectin.

Cypermethrin, a synthetic pyrethroid, is under trial licence at present. It is viewed as 'ideal' by some salmon farmers, and studies indicate that it has no significant impact on the environment. No residues have been detected in sediment at trial sites. However, *Leaping in the Dark*, a review of the environmental impact of salmon farming in Scotland, points out that no follow-up studies have been conducted into effects in exposed animals; it considers this particularly important because these pesticides have been identified as hormone (or endocrine) disrupting compounds. It says: 'The adverse effects caused by such compounds, particularly on the reproductive system, can occur at far lower concentrations than would be identified by normal toxicity testing, but can produce long-term and profoundly damaging effects to wildlife, ecosystems and, potentially, humans.'

The jury is still out on the safety of pesticides used to control sea lice. Without random testing of fish on sale, there is no assurance that these chemicals are not making their way into the food chain. Testing by the National Food Centre in Dublin revealed that six per cent of farmed salmon had residues of Ivermectin on them. This is particularly unacceptable in view of the fact that Ivermectin is not licensed.

Meanwhile, farms which are located in ideal sites — far off-shore, in fast currents, cold water and which practise good husbandry by separating stock and fallowing sites — have greatly reduced or negligible sea lice problems. It would be better if all Irish fish farming was sited in excellent locations rather than continuing to take risks with the future of the sea trout and of our waters.

Genetic exchange

All farmed fish are descended from Norwegian stock, selected for its size and growing capabilities. There are worries that escapees from fish farms may breed with wild fish in the area and diminish the ability of the fish to return to their natural spawning grounds. This is an under-researched area of concern.

Finding the best farmed fish

This is not easy, since information about the fish is hard to come by as a consumer. Back to your relationship with your fishmonger. A good retailer or fishmonger will source fish from an excellent farm. They should be happy to supply you with details of their suppliers, their locations, stocking densities, chemical and colourant policies.

'If you want to find the best, look for "Superior" salmon,' a salmon farmer explained. 'There are three grades, Superior, Ordinary and Production. If shops are selling Superior, they really should be advertising that; I've never seen them doing it though. But I suspect a lot of shops are buying Ordinary — and selling it at Superior prices.'

If you have found farmed salmon too fatty, he explains, 'look out for the thickness of the white lines in the flesh. That streaking is the fat. Fish can also have marbling; if the flesh has a whitish tinge, there's fat within it. The most troublesome time for fat is January to April.'

It is time fish farms were named and details of their farming methods made known. One farm which does this, and which produces fish of really exceptional quality, is Glenarm Salmon in County Antrim (its fish can be found in London, in many fine restaurants, and also in Marks and Spencer under their 'Prime' label). Farms in the Republic would do well to follow suit. Meanwhile the summer of 1997 saw the harvesting of the world's first organic salmon from a farm off Clare Island, Co. Mayo. The farm is in a particularly exposed site, stocks at just 10 kg per cubic metre and has a very fast water exchange rate in the cages. The feed is based on organic foods and pigment is astaxanthin. Unfortunately, it is so far available only in Germany but it is hoped that it will become available in Ireland in early 1999, certified by IOFGA.

BIM Quality Assurance

During 1998, the first farms are expected to have been audited under BIM's QA scheme for farmed salmon. This will provide some measure of assurance. For example, stocking densities are set at a fairly low 15 kg per cubic metre, which should allow for reasonably firm-fleshed fish.

However, the concerns regarding the use of chemicals (all licensed chemicals are permitted) remain — although it is reasonable to assume that any farm submitting itself to audit for QA will be careful in their use of them.

Like other State-funded Quality Assurance schemes, this one broadly deals with the status quo, rather than pushing for the best quality possible.

Farmed or wild?

Your ultimate decision about whether or not to eat farmed salmon is likely to be more of an ethical one than one based on immediate health grounds. Good farmed salmon is not awash with chemicals, but neither is it a natural food in the way that a wild fish is.

How to tell a good farmed salmon from a shoddily-produced one is a more difficult question. One ironic factor is that the farmed fish may often be fresher than the wild. This is because, whereas salmon farms handle their fish very speedily and carefully, fishermen of wild fish are often slow to ice them. It's a tragic waste of such a rare resource. BIM has recently begun to work with fishermen of wild salmon to address this.

You may also be surprised to hear that, despite the fact that we all pay more for wild salmon, fishermen often *don't* get this higher price. Indeed, when farmed fish come in supply, the extra fish can even depress the market price.

Sadly, wild salmon catches are now dwindling fast; 1997 was, despite the severe restriction of the number of permitted fishing days, worse than ever. It is increasingly looking as if our choice will not be between farmed and wild, but between farmed salmon and next to no salmon at all.

Are there any alternatives?

Salmon ranching is passionately advocated by many who believe that the farmed fish is inherently inferior but whose livelihoods depend on working with fish, such as salmon fishermen or smokers. This involves stocking rivers with extra eggs in order to boost stocks of fish which will swim out to sea, feed and grow naturally, and later return to those rivers.

It is of questionable benefit. In New England, for example, salmon hatcheries released so many fry into the wild that by 1996, only an estimated 500 Atlantic salmon in New England still had the diverse genetic characteristics of the wild species. Without diversity, a species cannot survive.

Rainbow Trout

Also farmed in Ireland, they are more than likely extremely fresh: harvested, iced immediately and in the shops the same day. But they are pretty bland, and I just can't muster up enthusiasm for them. A good fish for people who don't much like fishy flavours. Not at all the same thing as a line-caught brown trout. Now if you know a fisherman who brings these home . . . there's a relationship worth cultivating.

Sea Trout

This is so widely prevalent in the shops that you'd be forgiven for wondering why the demise of this fish is so keenly mourned by the anglers. The answer is, it may have the same name, but it's not the same fish. The one in the shops is a farmed rainbow trout, taken from the fresh water farm when it weighs a few ounces and grown on in fish farms at sea for another eight months to a year. More flavour than the rainbow, perhaps because of its greater age.

Shellfish

Surveys indicate that fewer than half of you have even tried these! All I can say is, you don't know what you're missing. Irish shellfish is thrillingly good. More than any other food, shellfish depends on clear waters to be good — and we have good clean water to grow them to perfection. Go to smart restaurants in Paris and Irish shellfish is what they're serving.

More so even than fish, the freshness of shellfish is paramount, so much so that they must be alive when you buy them, since they go off very rapidly after they die. For this reason, shellfish, as opposed to fish, should *not* be stored on ice — the freezing would kill them. Look for a careful fishmonger who keeps them cold (2 °C is ideal) but alive.

Mussels

With that wonderful sweet moist flesh, mussels provide the most affordable shellfish sensation there is, and long may they continue to do so. They are one of the exceptions to the general rule that wild is better than farmed. Rope-culture mussels are not raised differently from their wild relations, they're just placed in good locations, then left to get on with their growing. You can recognise them by their smoother shells with hardly a barnacle — much easier to clean. The flesh within tends to be plumper and they're much less likely to offer that nasty surprise which wild ones can: a shell full of silt, which opens in the pan to ruin your broth. If you have wild mussels, watch out for this by weighing up each mussel in your hand as you clean them: a silt-filled mussel shell is noticeably heavier.

Mussels should ideally be tightly shut when you buy them. They may be a tiny bit open, but should not be gaping. But they should close smartly when tapped on a hard surface. Discard any which don't close before you cook, and discard any which don't open after cooking.

Storage

There are plenty of myths surrounding the storage of mussels, including one common one which suggests you put them in a bucket of oatmeal and water overnight to plump them up. Don't. Fresh water kills shellfish just as effectively as ice. Keep them in the coldest part of the fridge, and use as soon as possible.

In Season

All bivalves (mussels, oysters, clams, scallops) are tastier around May and September; these periods see an increase of micro plankton, the stuff on which they feed in the seas.

Frozen mammoth green-lipped mussels from New Zealand are becoming available. When you've got fresh Irish ones year-round which taste better, why bother?

Safety?

Mussels are filter feeders. They are used by researchers to gauge pollution, since they retain toxins in their flesh. So only buy from a reliable source, and only collect them yourself from the shore if you are satisfied that the water in the area is free of effluent. We are fortunate in Ireland that most of our shores are still ideal for clean, wonderful shellfish.

Shellfish — How Clean Is It?

We still put too much raw sewage into our waters. Water from which shellfish is harvested is classified in three grades according to its cleanliness: 'A' is pure and shellfish can be eaten as it is; 'B' must be purified for forty-eight hours before being eaten; 'C' must be placed in clean water for two months. Shellfish purifying procedures do eliminate bacteria — but not viruses. So if you want to eat shellfish such as oysters or mussels, raw or very lightly cooked, be sure they come from an 'A' area. 'B' is fine if they are to be cooked — this kills the viruses. 'A' areas are primarily found in the southwest, west and northwest, but local conditions vary.

Oysters

He was a brave man that first ate an oyster, as Swift once put it. A brave man indeed, who first prised open that clenched shell to sip at those salty juices and probe that slithery flesh.

In Ireland, oysters come in two varieties: edulis and gigas. Native to Ireland is the flat-shelled, rounder-shaped *edulis*. This is the one favoured by raw oyster-lovers. It has a more minerally, intense flavour, and it is the one which is not at is best in the summer months (the months without an 'r'). Not because it's unsafe to eat, but just because it's spawning, which gives its meat a rather slobbery texture.

The *Pacific oyster (gigas)* was imported. This long, craggy, deeper-shelled one is meatier inside, tasty too, though the flavour is less fine than a good edulis. Irish waters don't get warm enough (except in the very warmest of summers) for these blow-ins to feel comfortable enough to reproduce, so they're good to eat twelve months of the year. The Pacific oyster is the one to use if you plan to cook with them. (Ignore people who gasp as if this were sacrilege; hot oysters are delicious.) It is cheaper, it has fewer subtle nuances of flavour to lose, and more flesh to offer.

When buying, accept only oysters which are shut tight. The fishmonger should have them stored cold, with the flat shell uppermost. As should you, once you get them home. Your best bet is to taste one in the shop, since they're a pricey buy if they're not stunningly good. And, in my experience, they're often not up to scratch, even in the best of Irish fishmongers. Perhaps turnover just isn't high enough.

Scallops

These shellfish are sometimes hard to find — restaurants snap them up — but look out for them; they're the sweetest treat of all in the shellfish world. Don't turn your nose up at the smaller Queens, which can be nearly as nice. Look out for scallops still in the shell. Out of the shell, who knows what their history is?

If you're hesitant about removing them from the shell, the fishmonger will do it for you. Make sure he gives you the delicious corals when he does. These morsels are often, inexplicably, left out. They provide such a shot of brilliant colour to a scallop dish.

Frozen scallops

These are something to be very sceptical about. Although nothing can compare to the fresh, scallops do freeze pretty well. But — and it's a big but — most of the time, freezing scallops is an excuse to add water and charge you lots for it. The use of ice 'glazes' (ostensibly to protect the scallop meat) is thoroughly dodgy; you will often find that your frozen scallops have 'melted' away to half their size once defrosted. Worse again, some processors even soak the scallops in water — even phosphate-containing water — to make them gain weight before freezing them. Be warned: it is safe to assume that all frozen scallops have been dipped. Don't buy scallops which don't tell you the weight exclusive of glaze.

Lobster

Lobster provides one of the simplest, most superb eating-in experiences there is. Provided you follow a few rules:

- Look for lively, angry, claw-waving beasts which scuttle across the counter. Listless lobsters, though alive, may have been in a holding tank for days or even weeks; during this time they aren't fed and their flesh shrinks away from the shell.
- To protect stocks, don't buy undersized lobster (less than 8.5 cm from eye socket to end of shell), berried lobster (females with eggs), or lobsters with a 'V' cut into their tails. The latter are part of a restocking programme.
- 1–1½ lb/450–675 g is an ideal weight.

Dublin Bay Prawns

What we call prawns are not what the rest of the world calls prawns. Prawns in Ireland are what they look like, a mini lobster, sometimes called Dublin Bay Prawns. The French (and English) call them *langoustine*.

Dublin Bay Prawns are, when they're good, superlative: firm, juicy, sweet nuggets of shellfish flavour. Their price reflects that. Unfortunately, they're all too often a great disappointment: wet, soggy, disintegrating flesh. Buy them extremely carefully. And if you were landed with a bad lot, make sure you complain bitterly to the fishmonger. At those prices, you deserve better.

Live prawns are only available from boats doing short trawls and short tows — not the norm in Irish waters, although it's well-developed in France and Scotland. Once prawns die, they go downhill quite quickly. First the flesh goes soft and mushy, then it starts to go grey. If you've got mushy prawns, they're too old, or they've been kept too warm, or they weren't washed properly after catching. Greyish prawns are a rare sight, not because too-old prawns aren't sold, but because they are sprinkled with metabisulphates to keep them 'Persil white', as one fishmonger put it. Another good reason to buy from a fishmonger who knows the difference and who won't deal in them. This practice is very common in Ireland.

Look for live prawns, squirming around. If you see these, abandon all cooking plans and buy them instead. They're a rare sight in Ireland, but they will provide you with the most heavenly grub. And keep pestering your fishmonger for them.

Otherwise, check the relative freshness of prawns in the shell by bending back the curled tail. If it springs back into place, they should be all right. If it doesn't, don't buy them.

Cooking tip

Bear this in mind when using recipes from elsewhere: when they say prawns, they mean the flat curled things. This is important if you are given the in-shell weight for a recipe, since Dublin Bay Prawns have such a heavy shell.

Prawns

Just to be really confusing, these are what the Americans often call shrimps. Flat, curled, with a thin translucent shell, they can be a wonderful delicacy. *Can be.* Prawns, which are almost inevitably shelled, cooked and frozen when sold in Ireland, must be one of the biggest rip-offs there is to be found in the world of food. Stratospheric prices are often charged, yet when you taste the things, the only flavour most of them have is wet, fishy salt. Buy with extreme care.

Frozen prawns

Those with the best flavour are raw prawns in the shell, with the heads on. These are rare. The next best are cooked prawns in the shell, with the heads on. These are rare too. Presumably raw, shelled prawns would be quite good, but I've never seen them for sale.

The least successful result is from cooked, shelled prawns, but these are the most common. However, even these vary a great deal in quality. Look for prawns which state 'no ice glaze'; rare, but Dingle processor Ted Browne can do it, so there's no reason why anyone else can't. Failing that, only buy those which state the percentage ice glaze used. You're paying dearly for that frozen water.

Tiger Prawns

These seem such wonderful value: large, meaty prawns from the Far East, usually frozen. Sadly, they promise a great deal more than they offer in terms of flavour; they are usually rubbery and fairly tasteless. Use in spicy stir-fry dishes to hide their lack of flavour.

Another point of concern with these shellfish is that they are usually farmed in the Far East. In many areas, entire mangrove swamps have been given over to these lucrative cash crops of the sea. Unfortunately, they have displaced local fishermen and deprived many of them of an income. And their use of chemicals is unregulated and a matter for considerable concern. Reports indicate that many use large quantities of pesticides, some of which may be banned in developed countries. Bad for the environment, bad for local workers, and not so good for us either.

Crab

They come in late summer. They spawn way up north and spend the summer walking — all the way from the Hebrides, heading straight for Malin Head. Poor little souls. It's rather poignant to think of that long, long journey, which ends in a net and a pot of boiling water.

If you're prepared to do a bit of picking and excavating, a fresh-boiled crab will give you one of the greatest and most affordable seafoody pleasures there is. Crab meat is as sweet as an Indian summer when it comes out of your own pot, or from a good fishmonger who boils it carefully, and who does it just before you arrive. (Another reason to have a relationship with the fishmonger, so he will let you know when the crab will be just done.)

Crab tips

1. It's not just the white meat that's edible. Mysteriously, Irish people tend to scorn the rich brown meat inside the crab shell. Add a little to the white meat and see what a difference it makes to your crab-cakes, salads and crab mayonnaise.

2. When buying whole crab, look for ones whose points are intact. If the tips of the claws are broken, they will 'bleed' through these, leaching flavour.

3. Easiest of all is to buy cooked, frozen white crabmeat. This is very handy indeed, though you will pay dearly for the privilege of having someone else do the picking for you. It also has a great deal less flavour than a fresh-boiled crab.

4. Buy from a reliable source. As with all frozen fish products, rough handling and added water will cut down on the flavour. In addition, buying white meat (or crab claws) alone encourages that truly unpleasant practice where fishermen wrench off the claws and throw back the crab. It's illegal in England. Hopefully it soon will be here too.

5. Worried about what to do with a whole crab? Just get the fishmonger to show you which bits you can eat and which bits you can't.

6. If you're wary of whole crab, having heard that it contains 'Dead Men's Fingers', don't worry. They're popularly believed to be poisonous, but they're not. These greyish fronds inside the body are just the lungs, and simply need to be taken out.

Smoked Fish
Smoked Salmon

Fresh brown bread. A smear of butter. A slice of salmon. A little squeeze of lemon. Heaven. Smoked salmon is one of the Irish greats, a really wonderful treat when it's good. For some time recently, though, I had found myself quietly entertaining the heresy that I didn't much like the stuff after all. Too oily, too flabby, and just not very appetising.

Farmed or wild?

Then I found out why. At a comparative tasting of twenty-one sides, wild and farmed salmon smoked by the same people were presented 'blind'. In all cases but one, the farmed fish jumped out at you. Visually they were instantly recognisable: regular streaks of fat throughout the flesh. And to eat? Time and again, phrases like 'oily sheen', 'off flavours', 'flabby', 'unpleasant', 'very oily' cropped up in my tasting notes. It was the strongest argument I've ever seen for selecting wild rather than farmed fish.

Having said that, one of the best sides of smoked salmon in the room was, to general acclaim, a farmed salmon. Clearly the source of the salmon is crucial. The best smokers, if they use farmed fish, will take care to source the best of it.

A much wider sample of taste buds was used by salmon smoker Jean-Jacques Boulineau just outside Clifden, County Galway. He offered 806 visitors to his smokehouse a taste of his own smoked salmon, both farmed and wild. Ninety-nine per cent found a noticeable difference between the two. Not everyone expressed a preference, but of those who did, seventy-five per cent preferred the wild (before being told it was wild!).

Tips to remember

1. Wild smoked salmon is likely to taste much better than farmed. It is usually less fatty, firmer, with a closer texture than the farmed.
2. But the best farmed salmon, smoked by an expert, may well be superior to indifferently-treated wild salmon.
3. Buy only where you can taste. The variations are so huge, and smoked salmon is just too expensive to make a mistake with. As for the £5 sides which regularly appear at holiday times, they're more than likely to be oily, woolly, over-salted or all of the above.

Watch Out!

Watch out for the labelling. 'Irish smoked salmon' just means the salmon was smoked in Ireland. The fish is unlikely to have been of the best quality. 'Smoked Irish salmon' means Irish fish was used.

Smoked white fish

Smoked haddock and cod can be the basis for some of the most delicious, inexpensive dishes. But beware that their usual appearance in Ireland, that garish yellowy brown, owes nothing to the smokehouse and everything to a tub of dye. Naturally-smoked fish is instantly recognisable: it's a subtle, pale gold tint on the fish. Keep asking for it; it's beginning to appear occasionally.

Kippers

These may also be dyed. Ask for natural-smoked ones.

Cold Smoke or Hot Smoke?

Cold-smoked fish is smoked at low enough temperatures not to cook the flesh of the fish. Salmon, haddock and cod and herring (kippers) are the most common kinds, though sometimes you will see cold-smoked sea trout.

Hot-smoked fish has a cooked appearance: trout and mackerel are almost always hot-smoked. Their biggest problem is over-cooking, which makes them rather mushy — if an oily fish like mackerel — or tough if a drier fish, like trout. A well-smoked, hot-smoked fish should be moist. If you can find a source of freshly-smoked fish, you're in for a real treat, since it tastes quite different from once it has been vac-packed and lying around in fridges for days.

Breaded Frozen Fish

This remains one of the best-loved ways to eat fish in Ireland.

Most mystifying of all, as far as I'm concerned, is the 'quick and easy' reputation that many of these products are currently creating with their advertising, especially the more upmarket, whole-fillet brands. Pre-heating the oven, then cooking a breaded fillet, can take between half an hour and an hour. A fillet of fish is fried in three minutes. Which is easier?

In addition, are you sure of what you're getting? A Consumer Choice test of thirty products (fish fingers, fish steaks and fish fillets) in 1995 made for dismal reading.

- Over a quarter of breaded products had less than fifty per cent fish. Only one sixth contained more than sixty per cent fish. In addition, the use of 'minced fish', water and polyphosphates (E 450) is common; but you don't know what you're getting, since water percentages are not declared on the label.

- The survey was co-ordinated Europe-wide. Except for one brand, the fish content of products other than fish fingers was lowest in the products bought in Ireland.

- The 'Use Before' dates were, in some cases, a year away. That may be all right for industrial-style -30°C freezers, but it isn't for your home one, which should be at about -18°C. Don't keep fish in your relatively warm freezer for that long! Three months is enough.

6

Milk and Other Dairy Products

Milk ▪ **Buttermilk** ▪ **Cream** ▪ **Crème Fraîche** ▪ **Soured Cream** ▪
Yoghurt ▪ **Ice-Cream** ▪ **Butter** ▪ **Margarines and Spreads**

Anyone who has tasted standard milk or cream in other countries will be surprised by the quality which we take for granted here. There is a rich fullness of flavour in even an ordinary glass of Irish milk. Considering this, the surprising thing about Irish dairy products is how few of them we now have. They were, after all, once a staple food in Ireland, eaten with relish and in fascinating variety.

Visitors to Ireland never failed to remark on how important milk and milky foods were. John Stevens in the sixteenth century was typical: 'The Irish are the greatest lovers of milk I have ever met, which they eat and drink in about twenty different ways, and what is strangest they love it best when it is sourest.' Twenty different kinds of milk? And sour milks? No longer. We now have a small range of dairy foods, with a clear bias to sweet rather than soured.

Milk

Once again, we can count ourselves lucky in Ireland to have all that grass. The great flavour of many of our dairy foods, not least the milk, is probably due to this. Compared to cows elsewhere, Irish cows eat a mainly grass-based diet, and are actively out grazing much of the time. The feeding of concentrated feeds, even in winter, is much less common here. This is probably the reason why we escaped with so little BSE here — most cases in the UK were found in dairy herds which are fed a lot of concentrates.

Teagasc's new slogan for dairy farmers is 'cash in on grass'. It's out there and it's the cheapest feed. For once, what's cheapest won't mean a drop in quality.

At the same time, the relentless (international) downward pressure on prices is worrying. It encourages the breeding of cows which yield ever more milk — despite the fact that there are strict quotas because of overproduction, scientists still want each cow to yield more. This can be problematic: the cow's system finds it difficult to cope. Animals bred for large udders may have trouble walking; mastitis (infected udders) is more common, leading to the need for more medication.

Yet still they want more: the genetically-engineered hormone BST is used on cows in the US for even higher yields. It too is associated with more mastitis in cows. It has been reported that even research from Monsanto, the company producing it, associated its use with higher pus levels (somatic cell counts) in milk. However, EU scientists have declared it not damaging to human health. It is banned in the EU until 2000. There is immense pressure from the Americans to have this rescinded, and the World Trade Organisation (GATT's successor) has declared the EU ban unscientific. This must be firmly resisted by the EU.

Antibiotic residues in milk were a problem in previous decades. Those were also the days when antibiotics were freely available over the counter. Stringent testing by the companies is now carried out on milk and it is generally agreed that there is no longer a problem.

Different Kinds of Milk

Milk for sale in Ireland must be pasteurised. This involves a brief heat-treatment to kill possible disease-causing organisms. It is also almost inevitably homogenised. This breaks down the fat globules, making them much smaller so they can't rise up to the top of the milk. It makes whole milk more creamy throughout and also helps the milk to keep for longer. However, it sadly deprives us of that lovely creamy layer which was so useful in the kitchen.

Most cows' milk comes to us from the standard high-yielding milker, that familiar black and white Friesian cow. It is sold by farmers to the Co-ops, who take it away in bulk tankers and process it. There's very little milk of any other variety available, unless you happen to know of a dairy farmer who has, for example, Jersey cows. Their milk is richer than Friesians', and is much prized for its flavour in England and as far away as Japan, but doesn't seem to make an impact here.

And if you're in North Kerry, don't leave without tasting the milk and cream from the area. Long famous for its extra-rich flavour, it has also spawned some of the best farm cheeses which Ireland can offer.

Organic milk

It's surprising this is so underdeveloped in Ireland. In Denmark, for example, a full twenty per cent of their liquid milk sales are organic. In early 1998, Glenisk became the first organic milk on the Irish market. However, it is worth noting that in 1994–7, of 142 dairy products tested by the Pesticide Control Service, 135 had no detectable pesticide residues at all.

Milk — A Fattening Food?

There is a widespread misconception that whole or full-fat milk is a high-fat food. Even health professionals, when surveyed in 1991, were found to estimate the fat content of milk at an average 19.9 per cent. In fact, whole milk contains just 3.5 per cent fat. Low-fat (or 'light') milk contains about 1.5–1.8 per cent; half the fat all right, but still only two per cent less. Skimmed (or 'Slimline') milk has 0.1–0.3 per cent.

Healthy eating programmes like to advise you to drink reduced fat milks. Of course this is up to you, but unless you drink a lot of milk daily the difference to your fat intake will be negligible. There is such a huge difference in flavour between whole milk and low-fat versions that I wouldn't give up proper milk for anything!

This emphasis on low-fat products has led to a common misconception among parents that low-fat milk and milk products are healthier for their children. It is important to know that young children, whose energy requirements differ from those of adults, need whole milk.

Goats' milk and Sheep's milk

These are of interest to those who may have allergies to cows' milk and its products. Goats' milk has about the same fat content as cows' milk; sheep's milk is appreciably higher.

Unpasteurised milk on the farm

In mid 1998, the Food Safety Authority of Ireland (FSAI) issued a warning to farm families about drinking unpasteurised milk — eighty-four per cent of farm families do so, a FSAI survey showed. Once it was enough to know that a herd was free of brucellosis and TB. Now there are new pathogens which can cause human illness without showing symptoms in animals. The emergence of E coli O157 in particular is a cause for concern, and the FSAI recommends home pasteurisation of milk, especially for the very young and the elderly.

This is a sad thought for those who really enjoy the inimitable, fresh flavours of raw (unpasteurised) milk; heating also changes milk's nutritional profile. We must hope that research into E coli discovers ways of identifying affected animals and of eliminating this pathogen. (See also E coli, page 9 and cheese safety, page 95.)

Buttermilk

As it has butter in its name, buttermilk sounds as if it must be very rich. In fact, it's quite the opposite: buttermilk is what was left over in the churn after the butter had formed, so it is very low in fat. It used to be 'ripened' naturally to form its classic sharp flavour. Eaten along with potatoes, it was a vital staple food. And of course, once it encountered baking soda, it was able to create our superb quick soda breads.

Buttermilk nowadays is rarely drunk and is almost exclusively used for bread-making. No wonder, too, when you consider the buttermilk produced by the main dairies: thick and gloopy, it makes good bread but you certainly wouldn't want to put it in a glass and drink it. It's a cultured skim milk, rather than a simple butter-making by-product. Look out for real buttermilk made by producers of country butter. The good ones are quite deliciously refreshing. My favourite is Farmhouse Natural Buttermilk, available in Mayo and some surrounding areas.

Cooking tip

To replace buttermilk for baking if you have none, add one tablespoon of lemon juice to every 200 ml/6–7 fl oz fresh milk.

Cream

Oh luscious and wonderful stuff. Irish cream, like our milk, is still richly-flavoured; again, travel abroad and you will notice how sadly depleted cream often tastes. Let's hope that we manage to hang on to that quality here.

Rich and Thick

Irish cream is also unusual because it's almost exclusively available in just one grade: rich enough for whipping, and everything else besides. In other countries cream comes in several levels of richness. That's why you will see references to single, double, light and heavy cream specified in cookbooks. To convert recipes, you need to know which cream is for what.

Here's how it works. The richness of cream is determined by its fat content. Irish cream is forty per cent. 'Double' cream is not double that — it would be butter! — but forty-eight per cent. In Britain, *double cream* is also forty-eight per cent, but their *single* cream is a thin eighteen per cent, which won't whip. 'Whipping' cream comes in at thirty-five per cent, the minimum necessary to hold air and stiffen. In the US, *heavy cream* is forty per cent and *light* (*table*) is eighteen per cent.

Recipes which call for double, heavy or whipping cream are fine made with Irish standard cream. If *light* or *single* cream is called for, dilute our cream with a little milk — up to half/half.

Meanwhile, just to confuse the issue, Irish 'light' cream is not the same as other light creams — it comes in at about thirty per cent. That's still not enough to whip, though, and as Irish people expect all cream to whip, a dose of stabilisers is added. And — it doesn't taste nearly as good.

If you want lower-fat creamy flavours, use rich and creamy Greek yoghurt (just nine to ten per cent fat) instead.

Cooking tip

There is some superstition about whether cream should be allowed to come to the boil or not. If the cream is fresh, it won't curdle when cooking with it. If you're in doubt about the freshness of the cream, heat it separately first, before risking adding it to a dish.

(Different rules apply to crème fraîche, yoghurt and sour cream — see below.)

Crème Fraîche

Tentatively, sour, tangy flavours are creeping back into the Irish dairy diet. Like yoghurt, crème fraîche and soured cream are slightly acidic and are made with bacterial cultures, though they taste and behave very differently. Absolutely essential for the keen cook.

Crème fraîche is the ordinary cream of France. It's thicker and has a fresh, tangy, nutty flavour, very surprising if you're not expecting it, and quite addictive once you know it. Traditionally, it was made by allowing unpasteurised cream to ripen naturally, by the action of the bacteria found in the cream. Relying on naturally-occurring bacteria was unpredictable, however, so nowadays bacterial cultures are more likely to be used. Crème fraîche available in Ireland is made from pasteurised cream.

Unfortunately there are only imports available at present, but the recent addition of crème fraîche to the supermarket shelves is a great bonus. It is superb for savoury dishes — its flavour less cloying than sweet cream — and unlike yoghurt and soured cream, the other tangy tasting milk products, it doesn't curdle in contact with heat. It is excellent with fruit and desserts. It doesn't whip and should not be frozen. It is dead handy, however, since unlike sweet cream it keeps for a couple of weeks in the fridge.

Real crème fraîche is quite rich, though not necessarily as rich as sweet cream. Yoplait's Crème Fraîche Epaisse is imported from France and has thirty per cent fat; others may have up to forty per cent. If you see a Welsh one called Rachel's Dairy, snap it up — the flavour is good. But I long for an Irish-produced ripened cream to make an appearance. It could be so good.

Yeo Valley do a 'Healthy Organic' crème fraîche with eighteen per cent fat. It's not the real thing, but unlike many low-fat dairy products, it just about sneaks in as acceptable for cooking. Too grainy for eating straight, though.

Cooking tip

For best-flavoured crème fraîche, make it yourself. It's easy. Stir 500 ml/16 fl oz cream with 250 ml/9 fl oz commercial buttermilk. Heat them slowly and gently to 30°C, just below blood temperature, not quite warm to a (clean!) finger. Cover and put in a warm place overnight. Next day it should have thickened. Refrigerate. It will thicken more as it chills and over the next few days. I find that this version tastes better than most of the commercial ones, probably because it's made with better cream to start off with.

Note Many people get confused between crème fraîche and fromage frais. They do both have French names and are thick white creamy things in plastic pots. They're not interchangeable, though; fromage frais is fresh cheese, not cream (see page 104).

Soured Cream

This is not cream that has gone off, but a lower-fat cream (eighteen per cent) 'soured' using cultures to be thicker, with a tangy flavour. It is common in Eastern Europe, and also in America. Excellent swirled into soups just before serving or into savoury dishes such as beef stroganoff. It curdles if heated too high. Avonmore are the only Irish suppliers who make one, although I find it to be thinner and runnier than I would like soured cream to be; bear this in mind if using American recipes which call for it.

Yoghurt

The very word has connotations of healthy eating, conjuring images of grinning nonagenarian Georgian or Bulgarian peasants attributing their longevity to the miraculous bacteria which thicken their milk. So much so that you can add just about any number of spoons of sugar and artificial anything to the pot and still cling to that image. The rise and rise of yoghurt as part of the Irish diet is phenomenal, but much of what's available is pretty awful.

Yoghurt is milk which has been thickened by acid-producing bacteria, usually *lactobacillus bulgaricus* and *streptococcus thermophilus*, which give it its characteristic fresh flavour. The flavour and texture depend on the culture which is used to make it, as well as on the milk. The only difference between set and smooth yoghurts, though, is where the bacterial culture is added. If you add the culture to the milk in the pot, it will set firm (set yoghurt); smooth yoghurt has been made in a large batch, stirred, and then poured into the pots.

Bio-Live — Not So Lively?

Some yoghurts are labelled 'Bio-Live'. This indicates that they contain extra bacteria, usually *bifidobacterium* and *lactobacillus acidophilus* (or *bifidus* and *acidophilus* for short). Unlike the other yoghurt bacteria, these ones can survive in the gut and are thought to help stimulate a beneficial bacterial balance in the body, especially after a course of antibiotics or radiotherapy. Anecdotal evidence is that these can be very helpful. Tests carries out by consumers' associations in Britain and Belgium, however, have found that levels of these beneficial bacteria vary hugely in bio-yoghurts; it is frustrating not to know which are more live than the rest. Don't expect miracles from them. One bonus of bio-yoghurts is that the bio-cultures tend to make for a milder, less acidic tasting yoghurt.

Plain Yoghurts

These vary a great deal in quality and in taste. I have not yet found an Irish-made one which I find satisfactory, much to my disappointment. I find them all too acidic; they often need sugar added, even for savoury cooking, to balance the flavour. Most are rather thin and one-dimensional tasting as well. Two good imports are Yeo Valley Organic (smooth) and Onken (set). I find Glenisk's low-fat probiotic acceptable.

Greek-Style Yoghurt

One of the cook's greatest boons, Greek-style yoghurt is less acidic than most other yoghurts, and it is extra-thick because it has been strained to remove the whey. It is an excellent replacer for cream, since it has a mere nine to ten per cent fat content, yet its thick texture makes it particularly satisfying. Yoplait is widely available country-wide and is pretty good. Use it with fruit desserts, in cooking, and in dressings instead of mayonnaise.

Flavoured Yoghurts

And as for flavoured yoghurts . . . all I can say is, read the label! Of course, there is some 'healthy' yoghurt in the pot. But most of the time there's also a generous portion of preservatives, stabilisers, flavourings, thickeners, artificial sweeteners, sugars, gelling agents, colourings. Low fat, low flavour and lots of extras. Good quality yoghurt with real fruit purées, on the other hand, now there's a pleasure.

> **Stabilisers**
> Many vegetarians were extremely dismayed to discover during the initial days of the BSE crisis that some yoghurts and similar products (custards, desserts, etc.) are stabilised with gelatine, which is of course an animal product (see Gelatine, page 174). It may simply be described as 'stabiliser' on the label.

Cooking tip

Yoghurt curdles at high temperatures (though Greek-style yoghurts are less prone to this). This can be counteracted by mixing it with a little cornflour, which has been stirred to a paste with a little water, before cooking with it.

Ice-Cream

The taste of our childhood it may be, but the fact is that a lot of ice-cream in this country doesn't deserve the name. 'Iced vegetable fats' would be a more honest description, 'with added guar gum, carrageen, skimmed milk powder, lecithin, and artificial vanilla flavouring'.

There's one other ingredient you won't find listed: air. This is called 'overrun' in the trade. Luxury ice-creams may have very little, or up to about twenty per cent. Cheap ice-creams reach a much higher over-run. But you can't know, because you're buying the ice-cream by volume, not weight. Of course some air is needed, or eating the ice-cream would be like sucking on a milky iced lolly. But if the manufacturer can persuade ice-cream to hold more air without collapsing, profit goes up.

Emulsifiers and Stabilisers

That's what all those emulsifiers and stabilisers are there to do: keep the air in, and keep water from separating out. And to allow the use of no cream, or next to none. They wouldn't be allowed to call it ice-cream on the Continent or in the US, where it's felt — understandably — that if something is described as cream, it ought to contain some of the stuff.

The curious things about the stabilisers is that they thicken rather than relax as the ice-cream gets warmer. This means that if you leave it to melt, you get a dollop of shaving foam. After a taste test, I left some behind at room temperature. The Carte d'Or, marketed as a luxury product, kept its shape for days. (Of course, if you read a recipe for ice-cream, or look at the label of one of the luxury ones, you will see that the only emulsifier ice-cream actually needs is a bit of egg-yolk. Which also happens to taste rather good.)

Luxury Ice-Cream

The market for luxury ice-creams is increasing; terms like 'dairy', 'premium' and 'super-premium' abound. They are unregulated, so they are no guarantee of anything. 'Dairy' in particular can mean very little in terms of quality; there may be other fats present as well. And most ice-creams, even those with pretensions to grandeur, continue to use very synthetic-smelling and tasting flavourings; vanilla is the biggest offender here.

The super-duper premiums have in recent years created a whole new image for ice-cream: what was once pure and wholesome is now unutterably decadent. A good piece of marketing which allows companies to get away with whopping mark-ups. Certainly good ingredients cost more — anyone who has made ice-cream at home knows it isn't cheap. But one business magazine estimated in 1984 that the super-premium manufacturers were paying twenty-two per cent extra for ingredients, and then charging 400 per cent extra for the product.

Regulation

The percentage of air in the ice-cream should be listed on the ingredients panels. In addition, terms like 'dairy', 'premium' and 'super-premium' should be regulated.

> **Soft Ice-creams**
>
> Not surprisingly, these are made just as other ice-creams are, with plenty of stabilisers and emulsifiers added to fats and skimmed milk. Indeed, they may contain more additives, to help them hold even more air than a brick of ice-cream.
>
> A Consumers' Association test in the summer of 1994 was carried out on soft ice-creams. They found a poor standard of hygiene in some outlets; both shops and vans were selling ice-creams with excessive numbers of bacteria. Choose your outlet carefully!

Butter

Poor old butter has been given such a hard time in recent decades. Clearly, it is not wise to overdo the fat intake in your diet. However, it baffles me to see healthy eating advice focusing time and again on low-fat spreads, suggesting they are a healthier alternative to butter. (See Margarines and Spreads opposite.)

Meanwhile, let's not lose sight of the fact that butter is absolutely delicious. You don't want to drench every potato you eat in it, but if you want the best flavour for sauces, or the most fragrant cakes and tarts, butter is the only thing. In addition, butter is a simple, minimally-processed food. As time goes on, the value of this for our health is becoming more apparent.

Country Butter

This is ripened, which standard Irish creamery butter is not. Country butter varies a great deal; some are just about as mild as standard butter, while others are full and ripe, with a flavour and aroma of blue cheese. Watch out, though, that it isn't rancid — be careful where you buy it.

Used to the mild flavour of Irish butter, many people find country butter quite shocking; from a good producer it's superb. A favourite for wonderful flavour is Holyhill country butter, which comes with the added bonus of being organic.

Unsalted Butter

Unsalted butter is often specified in European recipes. Irish unsalted butter has a very mild flavour. In Europe, their butters are made with cream that has been ripened a little with lactic cultures, giving it a fresh, tangy flavour. Look for French Beurre d'Isigny — particularly good.

Margarines and Spreads

For years, margarines basked in 'healthy' glory. So much so that the very words 'vegetable fat' or 'polyunsaturated' still have the power to confer an aura of wholesomeness. Yet it has since emerged that the issue of 'good' fats and 'bad' fats is much more subtle than we imagined.

The notion that margarines should be a healthy food is a curious one, since they are the end-product of a highly complex industrial process and are full of flavourings, emulsifiers, stabilisers, colourings and preservatives.

What is Margarine?

Margarines are based on vegetable oils, which are derived from seeds. They are commonly extracted by petroleum-based solvents. They are then typically de-gummed, refined with caustic soda, bleached with Fuller's earth, and deodorised by steam distillation. Next, the liquid oil needs to be hardened. This is done by hydrogenation. Under pressure with hydrogen gas, the oils react in the presence of a metal catalyst and become hard.

Usually, water is blended in to the hard hydrogenated oil. To keep it there, emulsifiers are used. Stabilisers are also often necessary. Preservatives are needed; usually, potassium sorbate is used. To make the stuff palatable, various additions may be made. The spreads which claim butter-like flavours will contain some buttermilk or milk-based proteins. There may be lactic acid, or lactose (milk sugar), or artificial flavourings. To give the spread the yellowness we expect from a butter imitation, a colouring is added. Vitamins A and D are also added, because they are naturally present in butter.

And you call that healthy?

Margarine versus Butter

The great margarine war is fascinating to watch. The margarine/olive oil/butter debates are the battleground of two of the all-consuming food issues in the developed world in the late twentieth century: the fight for market share of huge food corporations, and the struggle to define a 'healthy' diet in these days where most of us eat more than we need to.

Confused? It's hardly surprising. Every couple of years, a new research report changes the goal posts. First, butter and other saturated fats were the out-and-out villains and polyunsaturated vegetable fats could do no wrong. Then along came the benefits of monounsaturates and olive oil, the Mediterranean diet in its wake.

Next, trans-fats reared their heads and hydrogenated vegetable oils became the new villain. Hydrogenating vegetable oil creates trans-fats. These are mono- and polyunsaturates which have been twisted out of shape. They have been implicated in research studies with a higher risk of heart disease. Although most people have the impression that they should reduce butter and red meat intake, Irish people take more 'unhealthy' fats in the form of hydrogenated vegetable fats in biscuits, confectionery and cakes.

It has also emerged that an ultra-low-fat diet can be dangerous. This is because it can reduce the levels of 'good' (HDL) cholesterol in the blood, the cholesterol that protects against heart disease. This effect is particularly pronounced in women.

At the moment the competition seems to be between margarines striving for butter-like flavour with butterlike names and some buttermilk in the tub, and ever-'lighter' spreads with plenty of water blended in. Olive oil in one is creating an interesting diversion.

At this stage, dieticians are recommending that you get your fats from a variety of monounsaturated, polyunsaturated and saturated fats, and that you don't eat too much of them. This is a sensible variation on the old dictum of everything in moderation.

What concerns me about standard 'healthy eating' advice is its emphasis on low-fat spreads. At this stage, not enough research has been done on the cocktails of chemicals we are taking into our bodies daily in the processed foods we eat. It makes sense to stick to foods in their most unrefined states.

Tips to Remember

1. Try butter spread thinly, rather than butter served with water, caseinates, emulsifiers, preservatives, flavour, colour and an acidity regulator.

2. Go for unrefined extra-virgin olive oil, rather than refined olive oil with added water, vegetable oil, hydrogenated vegetable oil, salt, stabiliser, emulsifiers, whey powder, preservative, lactic acid, colour and vitamins.

7

Cheese

We're still a little cautious when it comes to cheese. Except for familiar old Cheddar, Irish people tend to think of cheese as a slightly exotic, foreign, smelly item. Something to be saved for the end of a big dinner (when everyone's too full to eat anyway). Definitely not for the lunchtime sandwich. Perhaps this has to do with the fact that many of us first encountered cheese by sucking on the corners of squishy foil triangles.

In fact, cheese couldn't be less exotic. It's just a simple farm food, once a necessity wherever a milk-producing cow, goat, or sheep was to be found. In the days before refrigeration, precious extra milk had to be turned into something that would keep.

Cheeses of all kinds are certainly not foreign to Ireland, in any case. Cheese was once a mainstay of the Irish diet — and no wonder, with the natural dairying climate that we have. Along with other milky foods like soured milks, buttermilk and curds, cheese was devoured in great variety by the Celts. Yet by the early nineteenth century, cheese was almost gone from this island. Economic changes and the suppression of Gaelic ways of life were the culprits.

Thousands of Flavours from Milk

The fascinating thing about cheese is that simple, bland milk can be transformed into so many thousands of flavours — and so many different textures. Anything from a white, floppy cream to a proud, hard, sweetly-aged

Parmesan, with any number of textures, smells and flavours in between.

Milk may seem baby-bland and innocuous. It can vary hugely, though; and its character affects how the cheese will taste in the end. We're used to the notion of the land, the climate and the grape variety affecting the flavour of wine. In the same way, the soil, the pasture, the weather and seasons, and the breed of animal, all affect the way milk tastes. Nowhere is this more evident than in cheese. But only if the cheese is made in a way that allows the flavours of milk to emerge.

Factory or Farm?

Nowadays, cheese broadly divides into two categories. There's factory-made, and there's farm cheese. Factory cheese is churned out in vast quantities and aims to offend as few people as possible. It can vary from execrable to pretty good. Hand-made farm cheese, meanwhile, has burst back onto our tables. It's one of the most exciting things that has happened to food in Ireland this century.

Factory Cheese

With all those delicious variables, it seems a shame to lump vast quantities of milk together and aim for identical year-round mousetrap. But that is the goal of factory cheesemaking. Like factory sliced pan, baked with a no-time dough, mass-produced cheese is fairly uninteresting. The milk enters the factory at one end and the wrapped cheese emerges at the other. The process is entirely mechanised, and no person lays a hand on the cheese at any stage. The result is pretty dull.

There are some exceptions — see the list below for a couple. But generally, the vast majority of cheese churned out in Ireland is a commodity aiming to be inoffensive, not a food aiming for delicious flavours. Advertising gives it different names, but there's precious little to choose between any of them.

Farm Cheese

Something very exciting happened in Ireland in the early 1970s in furthest West Cork. On their small farm in Allihies, Veronica Steele and her husband Norman began to experiment with making cheese, to use up surplus milk.

Little did they know it, but they were setting something momentous in train. At last, Ireland's rich dairying pasture was once again to yield cheese with character. These cheeses have become the toast of international awards, the exciting harbingers of the revival of a food culture in Ireland. They are one of the most precious foods we have.

But is it Irish?

Some people are a bit doubtful. What's so Irish about a Dutch or French-style cheese, just because it's made in West Cork?

A good hand-made farm cheese is a product of its place — of all those factors described above which combine with the cheese recipe to make the cheese taste the way it does. The same recipe made in another country would taste different. Our damp climate, for example, has meant that washed-rind cheeses (such as Milleens, Croghan, Gubbeen, Ardrahan and Durrus, which smell stronger than they taste) have really flourished here.

There's another more intriguing thought. It's possible that many of those European cheeses were originally Irish! The Swiss certainly believe that it was Irish monks who brought cheesemaking skills to Europe, after the Dark Ages.

What's so special about farm cheese?

Sometimes you might wonder. Most of us expect a farmhouse cheese to have lots of flavour, but most Irish farm cheese in Ireland is sold terribly under-ripe. As a result, it can be distinctly under-whelming, especially when compared to French and other European cheeses, which may be fundamentally less tasty but are often ripened properly before being imported.

In addition, not all cheeses with 'farmhouse' attached to their names are worthy of the name. There are some pretty large operations which have taken to calling themselves farmhouse cheeses just because they're not a mega-sized factory, or because they mature the cheese a little.

Great Cheese Depends on Two Things

Firstly, the cheesemaker. The best cheesemakers are dedicated people who set out to make a cheese with layers of flavour, one which reflects the character of its origins. One which you can sit back and savour, rather than just munch without noticing.

Secondly, the cheesemonger. If cheese is sold before it's ready to be eaten, before its flavours have had a chance to emerge, much of the cheesemaker's work is lost.

The Thrill of Raw Milk — Or Is It Dangerous?

Raw milk is special. As we've seen, milk is not just a neutral white liquid; it's a delicate mix of flavour compounds, all of which are sensitive to heat in varying degrees. Heat the milk — which is what pasteurisation does — and you change it. Some of its essential, exciting, local character is removed. A good cheesemaker can make good cheese with pasteurised milk. But raw milk, in the hands of a skilful cheesemaker, gives cheese a depth of flavour which can't be matched.

Irish health authorities appear to be fearful of raw milk cheese. Warnings about it are issued with such regularity that you'd think it was a high-risk food. In fact, cheese is a very low-risk food. See the safety note below.

In 1989, the Food Safety Advisory Committee (FSAC) actually went so far as to recommend that all milk in Ireland, for all purposes, be pasteurised. This caused consternation among lovers of great farm cheeses. The recommendation was rather grudgingly amended a year later, when it was pointed out to the FSAC that people wanted to eat raw milk cheese, and that we couldn't stop the importation of raw milk cheeses since they would remain legal in the rest of the EU.

This fear of raw milk cheese seems to be most prevalent in countries which don't have a long tradition of producing it. Time and time again, an episode occurs where it becomes clear that the authorities in Ireland don't understand the point of using raw milk. 'So much of our time,' said Breda Maher, Chairperson of Cais, the Farmhouse Cheesemakers' Association, 'goes into fighting for a right which is there for the rest of Europe. Why do they keep coming on and threatening us? I think they should be trying to nurture the cheeses rather than kill the damn things off.'

Cheese Safety
Very few foods have warning stickers attached to them, but

unpasteurised cheese is one such. Is it dangerous? And what about pasteurised cheeses?

Although we still have no figures for Ireland, comparable figures for other countries indicate that cheese is one of the safest foods there is. It is important to retain this sense of perspective, since unpasteurised cheese is so often cited as a risky food. For example, just three per cent of confirmed outbreaks of food-borne disease found by the Communicable Disease Surveillance Centre in England were linked to milk and milk-based products; cheese was a sub-group of these. Not what you would categorise as a high-risk item. In addition, good cheesemakers take a great deal of care with their milk supplies. Pure, clean raw milk makes the best cheese. However, there always remains a possibility that pathogens (disease-causing bacteria) may be present in raw milk (unpasteurised) cheese. Since the advent of E coli O157 (see page 9), which can be present in raw milk without having shown illness in animals, this has become a matter of greater concern.

Those vulnerable to infection (the very young, the elderly, the ill and pregnant women) should take the precaution of avoiding all soft cheeses, whether pasteurised or unpasteurised, which have a small chance of carrying listeria (as do pâtés, ready meals and prepared salads).

Labelling of cheeses is extremely patchy — some unpasteurised cheeses indicate this; others, especially pre-cut wedges, usually don't state that they are made with raw milk. And I've never seen a pasteurised soft cheese with a warning for sensitive groups, despite the fact that it would be just as appropriate — nor for that matter a pâté, ready meal or prepared salad. (See also Safety Note, page 104.)

Buying Good Cheese

What to look for in a good cheese shop

1. A good cheesemonger is a rare thing. The same rules apply as for butchers and fishmongers. Search out someone who knows about the food and its origins.

2. A huge selection of cheese may look imposing, but it doesn't mean it is

going to be any good. Three well-matured cheeses would be better than thirty under-ripe ones.

3.   Look for well-tended cheese. No dried-out ends, nor a whole counter swathed in cling-film. You should see whole cheeses, ready to be cut to order.

4.   Above all, look for someone who knows a bit about the cheese. Ask them which cheese is particularly good at the moment. If they look blank, don't expect too much!

5.   And taste the cheese. Farm cheese varies, so you need to know what you're buying.

Fortunately there are some shops which sell great cheese. See Where to Buy, page 240, for the special shops.

The Supermarket?

Some supermarkets now have huge ranges of cheese, but they just aren't ideal places for cheeses. They tend to chill the flavour out of them, wrap them in too much cling-film, pre-cut everything, and the staff know nothing about them. Some do try. Superquinn, for example, will cut fresh from whole cheeses and wrap in waxed paper.

Supermarket cheese strategy

Buy, wherever possible, whole mini cheeses and then store them for up to three weeks before eating. There'll be more flavour in the cheese.

Maturing Cheese

The French even have a special name for this skilful job, which is done by the *affineur*. It's a time-consuming, painstaking skill and all too rare here.

Peter Ward of Country Choice in Nenagh is one man who takes great care to sell cheese when it's delicious. 'It's almost bordering on the immoral, selling unripe cheese,' he says, 'like a butcher who couldn't be bothered to hang his meat. A ripe Irish farm cheese, bubbling full of life, is unlike the imported cheeses. Those are technology cheeses, made with stabilisers. They're always reasonable, but they'll never be exciting.'

Farm cheeses in Ireland are usually sold weeks, even months before they're ready. It's such a shame to think of all the work which has gone into making a potentially fantastic cheese, which is then eaten long before it has developed its flavours.

Irish factory Cheddar, our most-consumed cheese, is no longer matured in cloth as traditional Cheddar should be. It is matured in plastic, as is almost all Cheddar made the world over. This suits the processors since there's less wastage — no rind, and no weight loss through evaporation. But it means the cheese can't breathe as it matures. You end up with a rather rubbery, squidgy thing, with no hint of Cheddar's characteristic firm bite. Plus more water for your money.

Cheeseboard?

Here's a good idea. Obviously, cheeses of contrasting textures and flavours are nice. But often it's much better to choose just one cheese which is marvellous, then serve a single large piece of this. Much better than lots of bits which aren't ripe.

Cheese is Seasonal

If the animals aren't producing milk, there's no cheese. Many goats' and sheep's milk cheeses aren't available all year round.

'Vegetarian' Cheese

This is cheese made with non-animal rennet. (Vegetarian rennet is either derived from a genetically-engineered process, or from moulds.) It's really a marketing gimmick, since almost all cheeses these days are made with non-animal rennet. Whether cheese itself can ever be truly vegetarian is another question, since calves (and kids and lambs) die anyway so we can have milk and all its products.

Cheese 'For Cooking'

Ever found yourself adding more and more cheese to a white sauce, and yet it never gets a cheesy flavour? The usual advice is that the cheapest cheese will 'do' for cooking. Clearly, it makes sense not to sacrifice a superb specimen for macaroni cheese. But cheap cheese in cooking is a false economy — you need to use so much of it to get any flavour. Use a well-flavoured cheese and you'll need less.

Fat in Cheese

We're often advised to choose low-fat cheese. The problem is, it tastes awful. Choose a cheese which is naturally low in fat — eat Brie rather than Cheddar. Or eat a bit of a great cheese, and savour it, and don't eat too much!

Sixty per cent fat?

Fat levels in cheese are calculated in rather an odd way, not as a percentage of weight, but as a percentage of the *dry matter* in the cheese. This means that a cheese may state a whopping-sounding sixty per cent fat on the label. Yet count in the water, and the true fat level is just a little over twenty per cent.

The paradox is that creamier-textured cheeses are usually lower in fat than hard cheeses. This is because they contain more water than hard cheeses.

Storing Your Cheese

Fresh cheeses (white, curdy, unripened ones): keep in the fridge.

Oozy cheeses (non-technical term for those which go very soft, such as Cooleeney or Cashel Blue): in the fridge. They should be in the warmest, moistest part, so the vegetable drawer is best.

Washed-rind cheeses and farm-made hard cheeses love cool cellar temperatures — try your garage or spare room (in winter). Keep it in a cardboard box to prevent it drying out. If you're unsure, store in the fridge, but wrap very well, since the fridge dries out cheese.

Keeping a whole cheese? Turn it once a week to stop the bottom going soggy.

Serving Cheese

Bring it up to room temperature if you possibly can. Clearly this is not practical if you're just rustling up a quick sandwich, but if you have a beautiful farm cheese it's worth doing this for several hours. You'll be surprised at how many flavours emerge once again.

Some Irish Farm Cheeses

Washed-rind cheeses

These are the ones which smell stronger than they taste. They often have pinkish rinds and they flourish in our damp, salty climate. Durrus and Gubbeen are the milder-mannered of these.

- **Milleens** Look out for Veronica Steele's little 'dotes'; more chance of containing Milleens' characteristic rich, farmyardy flavour.
- **Durrus** Jeffa Gill's cheese has a delicate, gently fruity milky sweetness and a pliant texture.
- **Ardrahan** is made in Kanturk by third-generation dairy farmers Eugene and Mary Burns. One cheese which I like young (milky) as well as mature (smelly).
- **Gubbeen** A peachy-pink rind on Tom and Giana Ferguson's cheeses alerts you to a lively one. A mild taste and silky texture.
- **Croghan** is, unusually, made from goats' milk. The best of Luc van Kampen's cheeses are superlative.

Soft mould-ripened cheeses

To be less technical, Camembert-types. Don't scorn a firm centre — that's how many French Camembert-makers prefer their cheese. But chalky all the way through? They just won't have reached their potential. Nor should they stink; this is an indication that the second, ammoniac fermentation has set in.

- **Carrigbyrne** is the most familiar. It's a little one-dimensional, but can develop pleasing mushroomy scents.
- **Cooleeney**, made by the Mahers in County Tipperary, is richer than a Camembert, with a thicker rind; it ripens to a strong ooze.
- **Abbey Brie** and **Dunbarra** are both popular.

Moulds work on soft goats' cheeses too:
- **St Tola** has a wonderful aroma of pears when riper.
- **Mine Gabhar** is a delightful turret of soft goaty flavour from Luc van Kampen.

Hard cheese

■ **Desmond, Gabriel** and **Mizen,** from Bill Hogan have bracing flavours and a lingering glow. Awarded the Ballygowan/Irish Food Writers' Guild Supreme Award for 1997. Excellent for cooking, wherever Parmesan would lead the way.

■ **Coolea** is made by the Willems family. Mild when young, it is caramelly and butterscotch-like when matured, though hard to find like this in Ireland.

■ **Killorglin** is, like Coolea, a Gouda-style cheese, made at the foot of the MacGillycuddys Reeks by Wilma O'Connor; also with garlic, cumin or cloves.

■ **Cratloe,** a sheep's cheese made in Clare by Sean and Deirdre Fitzgerald — tastes superb, minerally when matured to about eight months.

■ **Lavistown** is a favourite from County Kilkenny, a lovely, simple, curdy cheese with a fresh lactic flavour, made by Olivia Goodwillie.

■ **Brekish** and **Kilshanny** are two simple Gouda-style cheeses, very appealing in a milky sort of a way, to be found in the Galway and Limerick markets respectively.

■ **Poulcoin** also has Gouda-like origins but is made with goats' milk by Anneliese Bartelinck on her farm in County Clare. A masterful cheese, especially if ripened a little.

■ **Bandon Vale Cheddar** is a farmhouse Cheddar which is matured modern-style in plastic. Cheddar graders (who must remain nameless!) were most enthusiastic about it. 'Now that's the flavour we're looking for, but it's just not there in the creamery cheeses,' one said enthusiastically.

■ **Ring** and **Baylough** are not Cheddars but are hard farmhouse cheeses which many people who want a little more flavour are keen on.

Blue cheese

■ **Cashel Blue** is one of the old venerables of the Irish farm cheese scene, and the first blue, made by Jane and Louis Grubb in County Tipperary. Delectably, voluptuously creamy when ripe, yet it's almost always sold upright, stern and chalky. Which would you prefer?

■ **Chetwynd Blue** is the preferred blue for some; from Jerry Beechinor's farm in Cork.

Cheeses in oil

These are indispensable store cupboard stand-bys. Serve in a salad, enrich an omelette with them, or spoon straight onto crusty bread.

■ **Boilie**, from the Brodie family in County Cavan, is particularly delicious in its goat's cheese version.

■ **Knockalara**, fresh lemony sheep's cheese in olive oil, is excellent.

Some Irish Factory Cheeses

Doolin

This is sometimes described as a farm cheese, but it's made by Waterford Co-op. The brainchild of Dutchman Sid Walsweer, it has an Irish name, a Dutch recipe, Irish milk, and is matured by Walsweer in Holland. A real Euro-cheese! When good, the black-rind one can be wonderful: flaky, resonant flavours. A salutary reminder that factory cheese need not mean boring cheese.

Cheddar

Cheddars are, as we've seen, made for uniformity rather than flavour and most of the creamery cheeses — especially the mild ones — are hard to tell apart.

■ **Wexford Co-op's Extra Mature** is pretty tasty and has won many awards for factory 'block' Cheddar in recent years.

Sadly no-one is maturing Irish-made Cheddar in cloth anymore. If you want to know what Cheddar is really about, you'll have to find a cheesemonger who has some English farm Cheddars (see below).

Regato

A Parmesan style cheese, which curiously is the no. 1 selling cheese in Greece. Unlike good Parmesan, it's not nice enough to savour by the sliver. However, it is much less awful than 'Parmesan' in cardboard tubs, and is useful for grating on pasta. Keep it in the fridge for a few weeks and it will be less wet, with a more concentrated flavour.

Irish 'Mozzarella'

It's a shame they couldn't have invested some of that vast technology to come up with a cheese that actually displays some of the attributes of mozzarella, rather than a tasteless, stodgy brick. Don't try to use this wherever mozzarella is called for cold, though you can get away with it on a pizza.

Processed Cheese

This is made with the lowest-grade cheese. Mixed with water and emulsifiers, it is heated and extruded. It has more water and a lower nutritional content than natural cheese. I fail to understand why it is considered suitable for children. But I do remember being very fond of the stuff myself . . .

Some Imported Cheeses

Parmesan

I always thought I hated Parmesan until I tried the real thing. The stuff ready-grated in little drums smells putrid. True Parmesan is sweet, hard yet crumbly; when not too hard, it's lovely after dinner, eaten in thin slivers.

Buy Parmesan in the piece. It should still be moist and you should be able to see the characteristic name on the rind: Parmigiano Reggiano. If the Parmesan is too expensive, try Grana Padano; made in a similar way. Store, well-wrapped, in a cool place or in the vegetable drawer of the fridge.

Mascarpone

An Italian soft cream cheese, very rich indeed; really it's just a thick, thick cream. Usually used, often flavoured, for desserts — most famously in Tiramisu. You can substitute with a thick crème fraîche if serving it cold, or with cream cheese softened with some cream.

Ricotta

An Italian fresh cheese most used for cooking, as a pasta filling and for cooked desserts. Traditionally it is made with whey rather than milk, so is relatively lower in fat than many soft cream cheeses. It is rather like a drier form of cottage cheese.

Fromage Frais

This is a French fresh cheese, sold in tubs (sometimes referred to as Jockey, since that was once the most common brand). It is hardly drained of whey, so is nearly as soft as yoghurt and low in fat. *Fromage blanc* is essentially the same, only the curds are more separate.

Mozzarella

Traditionally made with rich buffalo milk, this should be a tender ball of delicate cheese stored in water. Cow's milk versions are bland; slice and marinate in olive oil for a few hours to infuse some flavour.

Camembert and Brie

After Cheddar, these must be the world's most copied cheeses. Danish and German ones are pretty grim. Look for a French one which doesn't have too jellied a texture (this comes from using stabilisers). For ripeness, see Soft Mould-Ripened Cheeses above.

Stilton

A traditional treat for many at Christmas, though it's great year-round. The ripeness of good Stilton is judged not by blueing, but by how creamy it has become. For best flavour, buy a piece of a large cheese rather than a mini.

Cheddar

For the real flavour of great Cheddar, look for English farm Cheddars in Iago in Cork, Sheridans in Dublin and Galway, and the Big Cheese Company in Dublin (see page 244).

Safety Note

As we go to press, sources tell me that research under way in France is demonstrating that E coli O157 dies out rapidly during the cheese-making process in raw milk cheese. It is very poor at competing with rival coliforms. If this is proven, it may even be an argument for more — not fewer — bugs in cheese! Further research is due to be carried out by Professor Hugh Pennington in the UK at the end of 1998. One to watch!

8

Eggs

At the Food Forum in Kinsale in 1995, Irish members of Eurotoques, the European association of chefs, pondered the parlous state of the egg. 'Most of us,' Aidan McManus of the King Sitric in Dublin said, 'can remember what an egg once tasted like. It had a substantial white, and a strong-coloured yolk. It used to take two egg yolks to make a pint of mayonnaise. Now we need four.'

Then Darina Allen stepped forward with two bowls and a whisk. She whipped up two mayonnaises, one made with her own free-range eggs, one made with 'ordinary' eggs from a local shop. I had been expecting some difference, but what I saw shocked me. The free-range mayo was stiff and thick as sticky custard, and rich buttercup yellow. The battery-egg mayo? Sickly off-white and rather runny. No contest.

The battery egg is one of the prime examples of what industrial-scale food production can do to our food. When the price on the packet is all that counts, the quality of what we eat deteriorates. We think we have saved a few pence, but we are all losers. We also lose out on good nutrition: free-range eggs have been shown to have more vitamin B 12 and folic acid than battery eggs. We lose out on a simple pleasure, the rich taste of a good egg and all those good foods it can produce. The hens which produce these inferior eggs, however, are much greater losers than we are.

Battery Eggs

Think of a standard A4 sheet of paper. Cut off about a third of it. That's how much room a battery hen has to exist on. Stuck in a wire cage with four or five other hens, she can't stretch her wings out and can't lift her head up high — a quarter of her natural head movements are restricted. She can't do any of the things which come naturally to her — foraging, dust-bathing, or even just preening, stretching, turning and exercising. As a result, her bones are weak and are prone to break, even in the cage.

Not surprisingly, many have condemned this cruel way of arriving at cheap eggs. The European Commission's Scientific Veterinary Committee has concluded simply that the battery cage contains 'inherent severe disadvantages for the welfare of hens'. Still, nearly ninety per cent of eggs produced in Ireland come from hens in cages, about 1.76 million hens.

What hens eat is probably the determining factor in the quality of the egg. In cages, they cannot avail of their natural diet of foraged grass, seeds and other nibbles. Battery rations may be made up of grains and soya; or poultry offal meal (chickens re-processed into feed) may be used. A fat source could be soya oil, or it might be an animal-based tallow fat blend. Vitamins and minerals are needed to make up for what a hen would naturally pick up in foraged feed. A colorant is necessary to make the yolks yellow. This may be from a natural source such as grassmeal or marigolds, or it may be an artificial colour. Finally, the hens' feed may be medicated with growth-promoting antibiotics.

How do you know what you're getting in that egg? You don't.

Not surprisingly, battery egg producers don't want to draw your attention to the fact that their eggs come from caged hens. EU labelling laws make it easy for them: they don't require producers to state that eggs are from batteries. Words like 'farm fresh' and 'country' are very misleading. They have no definition, and they give the false impression the hens roam free. So do pictures of farmyards and hens pecking the ground. Unless it specifically states 'free-range' on the box, the eggs will be from an intensive system. Misleading terms and illustrations should be banned from egg boxes, and battery egg producers should be required to state the origin of the eggs prominently on the label.

Free-Range?

We all have an image of free-range hens scrambling about the farmyard, pecking at grass and other delicious foraged scraps. The reality may be very different. EU free-range regulations allow a very low standard indeed. The hens must have continuous daytime access to the outdoors, mainly covered in vegetation; each hen must have ten metres square to run in. Indoors, they may be packed even more tightly than battery hens: twenty-five hens per square metre. (The logic is that they will mostly be outside, so need less space indoors.)

However, the regulations say nothing about the pop-holes through which hens gain access to the open. If there are too few, many hens may rarely make it out. Nor do they prescribe better feed for free-range hens. Above all, there are no restrictions on flock or group size. It's possible for many thousands of hens to be kept in one group, which means they are unable to establish a natural pecking order — this may lead to aggression, feather-pecking and even cannibalism. As a result, de-beaking is actually more common in some free-range systems than in batteries. Yet it poses even more of a problem for an outdoor hen, since it prevents her from pecking properly.

Many 'free-range' systems simply stock hens too densely and keep them in groups that are too large. Compassion in World Farming, in a welfare charter for egg-laying hens, has pointed out that problems arise when management techniques suited to intensive systems are carried over to extensive free-range systems. It has called for free-range hens to be stocked less densely (no more than 650 per hectare, preferably 375 per hectare, as opposed to the current 1000 per hectare) and to be kept in much smaller group sizes (no more than 500, preferably 100; several distinct groups may make up a flock).

The Better Option

There are free-range producers who keep hens carefully, in reasonably-sized groups, who feed them well and do not de-beak them. The result is that the hens, less stressed and better fed, produce better eggs. But how can you know?

Irish Free-Range Egg Producers' Association (IFREPA)

Look for the logo. This association represents about 80 small family-owned egg-producing and packing units around the country. Their Code of Practice requires its members to comply with British RSPCA guidelines for 'Freedom Food'. These address some hen welfare problems, requiring that the hens be free from hunger, thirst, discomfort, pain, injury, disease, fear and distress, and that they have freedom to express normal behaviour.

They also go further than Freedom Food requirements. Animal proteins are not allowed in feed; nor are antibiotics or colourants. Above all, the IFREPA insists on small flocks. The maximum is 1500 birds (though many members choose to stick to smaller flock sizes of around 400), significantly smaller than the Freedom Food maximum, for example, which is 6000. 'It's better for the welfare of the bird,' says Pat Kenny of the IFREPA. 'They really are getting out into the open air, not just poking their heads out. They keep their feathers right through the year that way.' James O'Brien of Valley View Free Range Eggs of Bandon, also a member of the IFREPA, adds, 'The birds are more stress-free in smaller numbers. People are always welcome to come and see the hens and the farm. I think that would convince you to buy my half dozen, rather than ones from hens in a flock of thousands and thousands.'

Otherwise, take a look at the box. A good producer will be delighted to tell you about themselves: there should be a name, address and phone number. A guarantee that the hens' diet contains only vegetable proteins, for example, doesn't mean everything, but is at least an indication that care is being taken about the feed. Ask your retailer for information about the way the hens are kept and the food they eat. Does their feed contain growth-promoting antibiotics? Colourants? Poultry offal meal? Animal fats? How large are the flocks? Or ring up the producers and ask them. Good, conscientious producers will be proud to tell you what they do.

Why Use Free-Range Eggs?

Even if you don't much mind about how the hen is kept, there are very good reasons to favour free-range over battery eggs.

Free-range eggs perform better. Cooks everywhere will tell you this. The yolks are likely to have a higher lipid content and higher emulsification capabilities. That makes for better mayo, and better sauces. They also make better pasta, cakes, scones and other foods. Good free-range eggs are more natural, with better nutritional contents. The hen has led a normal life. And for all that, the price difference is only a few pence per egg.

The Q Mark
This looks like a reassuring guarantee of good food, doesn't it? Don't get too excited. It is a quality scheme administered by Excellence Ireland, which audits a system — not the quality of the food it produces. A Q Mark means the system has been vetted. It doesn't necessarily mean the system produces a wonderful egg.

Quality Assured Eggs
This is not the same as the Q Mark. A new Quality Assured Scheme administered by An Bord Bia was due to be launched in October 1998. The Irish Egg Association estimated in mid-1998 that approximately seventy per cent of Irish egg production would be participating. The scheme covers both free-range and battery production. Above all, QA guarantees eggs from premises with rigorous control for salmonella (more rigorous than the Q Mark), and it also precludes the use of antibiotics in feed.

In all other respects it follows standard EU guidelines for egg production. A QA battery egg is still a battery egg, and a free-range egg may still come from very large flocks.

'Fresh' Eggs

A really fresh egg is quite different from one which is several weeks old. Crack it open and the white will cling like clear jelly close to the yolk; the yolk will sit up high. A less fresh egg spreads far and wide, with a watery white and a thin yolk. This matters if you want to poach or fry an egg and don't want it to drift all over the pan. A very fresh egg is *most* important if you want to use it raw or lightly-cooked (see below). Less fresh eggs are best reserved for baking.

Eggs may have a variety of dates on them, such as packing dates, selling dates and so on. Unfortunately, laying dates, though they may be shown, are not compulsory. However, you can work it out, since the Best Before date must be no more than twenty-eight days after laying.

Extra, or Extra fresh, may be added to the label; this date will extend only to the ninth day after laying.

Storing eggs

Store eggs in the fridge to slow down the deterioration in freshness.

Buttered Eggs

In Cork, buttered eggs are still available; you'll find them in the English Market. The still-warm just-laid egg is rubbed with butter to close the pores. This prevents air being absorbed into the egg, keeping it fresh for much longer, and they have a distinct buttery flavour.

Egg Sizes

Egg sizes have changed; the new size bands are wider than the old numbered sizes. There are now four sizes, where once there were seven. Straightforward conversions are not possible, since the new bands cut halfway through the old sizes.

- Very large = 0 and 1.
- Large = 1, 2 and 3.
- Medium = 3, 4 and 5.
- Small = 5, 6 and 7.

Does it matter? Of course not, if you're frying an egg. You will, if you love a soft-boiled egg, have realised there is a minimal adjustment to be made in the cooking time. However, for bakers the issue is more complex, since amounts should be really accurate for best results. Most bakers will have used egg sizes 1–3:

- If you used size 1 eggs, use smaller Very Large, or larger Large.
- If you used size 2, clearly Large is the one.
- If you used size 3, choose the smallest Large or the largest Medium!

Eggs and Food Poisoning

Department of Health advice is not to eat food with raw eggs, and to be wary of lightly-cooked eggs.

That means the end of: soft-boiled eggs; real mayonnaise; chocolate and other mousses; soft meringue; soft scrambled eggs and tender omelettes; fried eggs if the yolk isn't set rock-hard; egg nog; spaghetti carbonara; Caesar salad; tiramisu; and many cake icings, including royal icing on the Christmas cake. Plus that time-honoured family tradition, licking out the bowl of cake mixture once the cake is in the oven. Are you prepared to give them all up? Do you need to?

The Food Safety Authority, in one of its very first public pronouncements, advised the same. It helpfully added that we should use pasteurised egg instead. Pasteurised egg is not available in the shops (and anyway, you wouldn't want to use it; it's most likely to be produced with lowest-common denominator eggs).

The reason for this advice from health authorities is that eggs may contain salmonella bacteria. These may cause illness if the egg is not cooked stone hard. How big is the risk? You'd think it was huge, since this advice is stressed so often, but it's absolutely miniscule. Eggs in Ireland are not generally contaminated with salmonella. 1996 Department of Agriculture testing found no salmonella in eggs, or raw egg-based products, from the Irish Republic.

It makes no sense for our health authorities to be recommending we eliminate all these delicious foods from our diets. They should instead be focusing their energies on assuring, as far as possible, salmonella-free eggs for us to eat. (In Sweden, where they measure salmonella levels at well below one per cent, they are proud of the fact that 'you can eat raw eggs, no problem', as Yvonne Anderson of the Swedish Institute for Infectious Disease Control put it.)

In that respect, the salmonella outbreaks traced to eggs, which occurred in summer 1998, may prove to be a blessing in disguise. There is now public pressure for salmonella-free eggs and hopefully this will not wane.

The importance of salmonella-free eggs is underlined by studies conducted at the Public Health Laboratory in Exeter in 1994 by Professor Tom Humphrey. After cracking open, mixing and making batter with salmonella-infected eggs, he later found salmonella bacteria on washed kitchen utensils and even on work surfaces 40 cm away. Bringing salmonella-infected eggs into any kitchen under any circumstances is just not wise. Caterers should insist on sourcing all eggs from salmonella-controlled flocks. So should we. Cooking eggs and egg foods thoroughly — as standard safety advice recommends — is not good enough if they may leave salmonella in our kitchens in the process of preparation.

When asked in mid-1998 if their eggs were sourced from salmonella-controlled flocks, Super Valu, Superquinn, Roches Stores and Dunnes replied that they were. Tesco replied that their eggs were 'packed in the Republic and conformed to all EU and Irish regulations'.

In mid-1998, attention was focused on eggs from the North of Ireland because some salmonella outbreaks were traced to there. While there are salmonella-free flocks in the North, the level of salmonella contamination of eggs there and in Britain is considerably higher than in the Republic. In the UK, they have decided to live with the problem. Levels of salmonella enteritidis have risen twenty-five-fold in the last fifteen years in England and Wales. Fortunately, the Department of Agriculture here has for some time had a policy to slaughter infected flocks.

It is worth noting that it is a legal requirement to state the packing station, but not the location, of the flock, on egg boxes; so read the label very carefully if you are looking for eggs from the Republic. I look forward to the day when egg boxes will carry the sign 'From salmonella-controlled flocks'.

Is a free-range egg safer?

That would depend. Both battery and free-range systems offer eggs from salmonella-controlled flocks and this is the basic guarantee to look for. Some authorities suggest that free-range eggs cannot be guaranteed disease-free, since rodents and wild birds may spread salmonella. I feel happier eating a free-range egg from a well-run, small flock, than a battery egg, because I would expect free-range hens to be healthier and less stressed — and thus more disease-resistant — and because spacious, free-range conditions mean there is less likelihood of passing on disease.

However, choose your free-range supplier carefully. *Where* they source their birds is just as important as *how* they keep them, since infected hens lay infected eggs. Members of the IFREPA monitor very closely for salmonella through an independent contract with Teagasc, and do not allow new hens onto farms without a salmonella clearance certificate.

If you want to eat a food with raw or lightly-cooked eggs

- Use eggs from a certified salmonella-controlled flock.
- Both IFREPA and Quality Assured eggs are required to meet this standard.
- Don't use cracked eggs.
- Keep eggs refrigerated.
- Do not serve it to people for whom the very small risk of a bout of salmonella illness is still too high a risk. These are: the frail elderly, babies, infants, pregnant women and the ill.
- Use the best free-range eggs. A well-produced egg tastes better!

9

Bread and Flour

Bread

'**B**read is similar to wine in that it is often understood to evoke something larger than itself, the regional soil, the character of the place and people who make and eat it.'

(Paul Bertolli, *Chez Panisse Cooking*)

So what does our bread evoke of us in Ireland? We have wonderful breads in this country, a tradition of home baking of which we can rightly be proud. Our quick soda breads and other baked foods are a product of the simple hearth, using local ingredients and minimal equipment, which was the norm in most Irish houses until so recently. Yet we flung these excellent foods aside for the mesmerising attractions of the industrial loaf. This bread also evoked plenty about the people who baked and ate it. It spoke of our eagerness to embrace a new identity. To be modern and progressive, to produce food quickly and cheaply.

What was the result? Being 'modern' has given us a foamy bread which squelches and rips when spread with anything but the softest butter, bread which turns brittle and dusty when toasted, bread which curls up its edges in disdain if left out in the air. The bread is produced using more water and much, much less time. It is now typically produced in minutes rather than hours, and is untouched by human hand, from first ingredients to sliced-and-wrapped. The bread has no substance, no savour.

Nothing expresses more clearly the disadvantages of clasping intensive food production in an enthusiastic embrace than the white sliced pan.

It's a supreme irony that it should have taken a French-style bread, centrally-fabricated in Dublin with French bread flour, distributed nationwide to be 'baked off' in petrol stations and corner shops around the country, to re-introduce the Irish to the pleasures of a truly crusty, white yeast loaf. Yet that is just what Cuisine de France has done. 'Whatever about it, it got people's palates accustomed to a real crust again,' one small baker said.

This bread too speaks of our character: uncertain of the value of our own foods, we turned instead to the foods of other countries in the search for better flavour. At the moment, we stand in uneasy balance. But slowly, good bread is becoming more available again, and alongside the ciabatta and the sourdough, we can increasingly be sure to find fresh soda bread too.

A great white yeast bread is still a rare creature, though. A bread which has body and savour in the crumb, which is chewy without being tough, which has a tasty crusty crunch.

The White Sliced Loaf: 'Water Standing Up'

We have a few things to thank for the woeful quality of the white sliced bread so widely on sale today.

No time? No flavour

The aptly-named 'no-time dough' was the first culprit. Unlike soda breads, which are naturally fast-acting, the true process of baking bread with yeast involves one crucial ingredient which is never listed: time. Time in the mixing, time in the fermenting (or rising), time in the baking. With time, flavours develop and texture can emerge.

Once, bakeries needed fifteen minutes or half an hour just to mix the dough. It took six to twenty-four hours for the bread to ferment. Bakeries had a dough, or fermentation, 'loft', where hundreds of vats of dough were left to rise. During this time, natural by-products of the fermentation gave the dough its character and body.

All this was dispensed with once the no-time dough arrived, a process developed in England in the early Sixties. High-speed mixers mix the dough in three minutes flat, after which it is ready for 'processing'. The fermentation period has gone altogether.

Time was once needed in the baking too: anyone who has baked a loaf of bread knows it takes about an hour. But modern plant bakeries can do the job in less than half that. Time is money. So now our bread can be cheaper to buy. But time is what adds flavour to bread.

Bread wars

Then came the bread price wars of the early Eighties, which finished off many of the small bakeries of Ireland. Intense competition between Irish supermarkets saw the price of a sliced loaf drop to levels unsustainable for smaller operators, who couldn't set losses off against profits elsewhere. '1987 was our hundredth anniversary, and about a hundred bakeries went out of business,' Esther Barron of Barron's Bakery in Waterford remembers. With the loss of smaller bakers went many who still produced bread on a smaller scale using that secret ingredient, time.

More water in the bread

These days, bread may come with less time and flavour, but it comes with more of something else: water. About a gallon to a gallon and a half of water is incorporated for every sack (280 lbs) of flour. This is possible due to modern milling methods, which can make flour with a smaller particle size, so it is able to absorb more water. Why is this deemed desirable? Because the bakeries reckon we want it.

The 'Squeeze Test'

'Ask anyone what they want from bread,' said an industry source who wished to remain nameless, 'and they'll say, "I want a well-baked crusty loaf." But observe them in the shop, and what do they do? They go along the shelf, and they squeeze. And then they choose the softest loaf.'

Esther Barron echoes this. 'The one that squelches the most is the one they buy.'

What's the significance of this? Once again, it means more water in our food. Industry has discovered that we attempt to judge freshness of bread on supermarket shelves by giving it a bit of a squeeze. Resistance is judged to mean stale bread, not a nice bit of crust. So the bakeries bake bread which is more amenable to the squeeze test. (They even design the wrapping material to aid this.)

Better Bread

Good bread is available in a few places. It is rare, though. If you're stuck with the products of the big 'plant' bakeries, buy a batch loaf rather than a sliced pan any day. They don't have a whole lot more flavour, but the texture is usually much better.

There are some smaller bakeries which make an initial ('sponge') dough, a method which increases flavour. They ferment the bread for several hours, and bake it more slowly. (Day-long fermentations are no longer likely, since we import wheat from Europe now rather than North America, and it is less strong. But several hours will still lend bread good flavour.)

Barron's of Waterford is one such bakery. Esther Barron is the third generation to preside over baking there, and she is proud of their batch bread, and the time involved in baking it. 'The dough takes two and a half or nearly three hours,' she says. 'It depends on the weather. In wintertime it takes longer to make; when you make the dough, it's the boss.' Barron's still hand-shape the loaves, which is considerably more labour intensive, but which helps the bread's quality, Esther Barron says. 'That adds a flavour to bread, believe it or not,' she laughs. 'It's like caring for something. Otherwise it's without any feeling or spirit in it, if it's just all done by machine.' The bread takes a full hour to bake, 'unlike others, which can do it in seventeen minutes', and a critical part of the bread's flavour is the old brick oven. Once wood-fired, it was converted to oil in the 1940s. The licking flames, Ms Barron says, contribute to the taste.

Markets

Sometimes a local market is the best place to source good bread, if there happens to be a gifted baker in your area.

Exciting flavours?

One new trend of recent years has been flavoured bread. It really took off with tomato and fennel bread from Cooke's (see below), now widely-emulated. The problem is that you can't disguise the abominable quality of fast-baked breads just by throwing in a handful of walnuts or some tomato purée. They still have a pappy texture and no flavour. Exciting-sounding flavours don't mean the bread is any better.

Restaurants enter the fray

Cooke's of Dublin was the first, and now has a substantial separate bakery business supplying shops and supermarkets. Its tomato and fennel bread is a delicious new classic, and its ciabatta is pretty good. Other breads in the range are, to my mind, not as successful. But Cooke's was also responsible for re-awakening taste buds to the flavours of real, slower-baked bread.

Just because it comes with the imprint of an upmarket restaurant doesn't mean it'll be satisfying. Dublin's Restaurant Patrick Guilbaud sells bread through Tesco/Quinnsworth stores. Crisp on the outside, I found it disappointing within.

Soda bread

It remains a puzzle (and a great frustration to tourists) that great soda breads are hard to come by. In many parts of the country, it's not even to be found at all in the shops. I think this is because it's a bread which doesn't take well to large-scale production. It needs to be baked in relatively small quantities. And above all, it needs to be eaten fresh. Nothing goes stale faster than soda bread (with the possible exception of a French baguette). This means that it must be locally-made. In recent years, health authorities made it difficult for home producers to continue baking, requiring them to have entirely separate kitchens. If the Department of Health finally introduces new guidelines which it has formulated (now promised for the end of 1998), a resurgence of home-baked, locally-supplied bread might be possible.

The best thing since sliced bread?

If you want your soda pre-sliced, you'll find the quality diminishes. There are two reasons for this: first, sliced bread stales more quickly; this is a particular issue with soda breads which stale so speedily anyway. In addition, the texture of bread changes when it's baked to be suitable for automatic slicing. It loses some of its soft, crumbly, cake-like qualities, the very ones which make it so delicious.

Storing bread

Bread stales fastest at fridge temperatures. Either freeze it, or store at room temperature.

Breads from Other Countries

Breads from so many cultures are arriving on our shelves now. (It's ironic that we venerate the peasant food of other countries while still neglecting our own . . .) Although some derive their true character and appeal from different recipes, many are just standard dough moulded into different shapes.

Baguettes

These hardly need an introduction — as described above, they've become a national staple. However, the quality of many of them leaves a lot to be desired. Most 'French sticks' are just Irish no-time dough in a long stick. Meanwhile, bake-off varieties, such as Cuisine de France, vary a great deal in quality from location to location. All too often they are doughy and stodgy — underbaked. The smaller, narrower Cuisine de France baguettes are much more successful than the large ones.

Focaccia

This bread comes from the Italian for 'hearth', and is a flat, white yeast bread. It should be dimpled and drizzled with olive oil; flavourings such as herbs, olives and more may be added. Often expensive, considering it's really just bread in a different shape. At its best, focaccia is fragrant, crisp and chewy. All too often here, it's stodgy and greasy from too much, inferior, oil.

Ciabatta

Another Italian bread; the word ciabatta means 'slipper', and refers to the low-slung, elongated shape of the loaf. It should be crusty outside, very spongy and chewy within, with plenty of holes. Most versions are underbaked and benefit from ten to twenty minutes in a hot oven to restore the crispy crust and freshen the flavour.

Pitta

This bread has been around now for so long that it hardly qualifies as exotic any more. It would be lovely if someone made a tasty one. Most of the long-life packets generally available have so little flavour and an unappealing mealy, gritty texture. Asian stores sometimes stock slightly better brands. Freeze pittas as soon as you have opened the pack — they go very stale in the fridge.

Nan (or Naan)

A north Indian flat bread, nan is made with yeast and white flour, and used instead of cutlery to eat the sauced dishes of the region. Traditionally, some yoghurt is used in the dough, which makes the bread delectably tender and aromatic. Again, the quality of the pre-packs leaves a great deal to be desired; I have yet to find one which gives the pleasure of a freshly-baked nan. Sometimes I use them, but I've never enthused about them.

Rye

Rye bread refers to any bread which contains rye flour. Since rye flour is very low in gluten, it is almost always lightened with some wheat flour, to give the bread a good raise. Often, the rye ends up as just a token few ounces in the loaf, contributing colour, but very little flavour.

Sourdough

This can mean anything from a fantastically deep-flavoured, crusty, satisfyingly chewy, appealing loaf, to a wet, sour, dense brick. It depends on the baker's skill, the method and the kind of flour used.

Sourdough itself is a way of rising bread by using a 'starter' instead of bought, cultured yeast: the natural wild yeasts in the air ferment flour and water. Some parts of the world, such as Germany, Scandinavia and San Francisco, are particularly renowned for it.

Sourdough doesn't necessarily mean the bread is yeast-free; apart from the wild yeast content, baker's yeast may also be used to give the bread more of a rise. Rye or wheat flour, or a combination of the two, may be used; wheat gives a milder taste. The quality of the starter is critical. Usually, a portion of each dough is kept back to make the starter for the next baking. This means that with time, the flavour of the starter can evolve, and can give the bread a marvellous depth of flavour which a yeast bread can't rival.

However, sourdough in Ireland has generally been given a bad name by many 'health-food' versions available, which are unpleasantly leaden and sour. If these are all you've ever tasted, think again — they don't need to be that way.

Tortilla

The soft tortilla comes in half-way between a bread and a pancake, a Mexican staple used for wrapping food. (Not to be confused with tortilla chips, or with the crisp tortillas sold for piling mince into.) Again, the long-life versions on the Irish market are a great convenience, but very flat in flavour. They are all wheat tortillas, though corn is the more common Mexican one. To get the best from them, toast on both sides in a *dry*, hot frying pan on both sides before serving — black speckles will appear. They taste best fresh from the pan, but can be stacked in foil and kept hot in the oven. There are several brands available; I find Discovery to be significantly better than others.

Flour

Wheats are very different from one country to the next, and this accounts for many of the differences in international bread-baking habits. It's not just wheats, but also flour blends which vary a great deal from country to country. This makes translating baking recipes the trickiest of all.

Is the Flour Hard or Soft?

The basic distinction between flours is not just brown versus white, it's also 'hard' versus 'soft'.

We grow wheats in Ireland's mild climate which make great soft flour. This is the one you need for tender pastries, cakes and breads such as soda bread; soft flours have a relatively low protein content, which means they develop less gluten in the dough when they are handled. Hard flour is necessary for bread-baking with yeast. It develops lots of gluten, which makes doughs springy and stretchy; it's also good for pastries which will rise, such as puff pastry. Hard flours, usually referred to as 'strong' flours, are grown in Europe and particularly in North America.

Pesticides in Flour and Bread

We often think of pesticide residues as being simply a fruit-and-veg issue, but this is not the case. We may receive much of our pesticide loading from dietary staples, and bread is one of them.

There is considerable chemical use in the production of much wheat and other grains, in the pursuit of the highest possible yields. Yet it appears that this is largely unnecessary. In Sweden, thoughtful policies have been developed in the last decade to increase confidence in food. One result has been a seventy per cent drop in pesticide use since 1985; the biggest area of decrease was in herbicide use in grain fields. This was done by changing the perceptions of farmers, built up over forty years, that fields must be completely free of weeds and pests in order to be efficient.

Another concern is the practice of using chemicals to dry grain for storage, and applying organophosphate 'grain protectants' after harvesting to aid storage. These remain on the surface of the wheat. Ironically, this means that brown flours, despite their healthier associations, are likely to carry more pesticides than white flours, since the outer bran layer of the grain will contain most pesticides. Testing by the UK's Working Party on Pesticide Residues has shown that wholemeal breads in the UK contain more residues than white breads — twelve per cent of white breads tested contained residues, whereas twenty-seven per cent wholemeal breads did. Unfortunately our Pesticide Control Service does not test bread for pesticide residues.

White Flours

These are made from the starchy interior of the wheat berry. The outer layer, the bran (which contains most fibre) and the little germ (which contains many nutrients) are removed in the initial milling; the rest is then ground down into white flour. Some health-food advocates are fanatical about the evils of white flour. Although there is more nutrition in some brown flours, and more fibre in all of them, white flour does have some fibre (a third to a half of brown flours) and also nutritional value. It also has the great advantage of making superb cakes and breads.

It's true that fast modern roller-milling methods, in removing all the wheat germ from white flour, remove much of the nutrition available; these have to be added back in the form of B vitamins and iron. However, synthetic vitamins are often found not to replicate the nutritional advantages of trace elements in food in its natural state.

White flours may also have been bleached, and may have 'improvers' added to them. These make a maturation period of several weeks unnecessary; during this period of exposure to oxygen, flour traditionally became better for baking. There are heated debates about the merits of these bleaches and improvers.

Many advocate unbleached flour as being the best for bread-baking. Odlums is reducing the bleach in its white flours now. On the other hand, American cake expert Rose Levy Berenbaum (she wrote her Masters dissertation on whether sifting the flour improves a cake!) is emphatic that bleached flour is essential for the best cakes. Experienced bakers also report that bleached Irish white flour is the best for soda breads, though whether this is due to the bleaching or the small quantity of raising agents in the flour is not clear.

Wheat Germ

Unpromising as the word sounds, the germ of the wheat is actually its heart. The germ contains much of the protein, vitamins and oil found in wheat. Millers say it is not expedient to return wheat germ to white flour, since it would affect the keeping quality of the flour — the natural oils in the germ do not keep for more than a couple of months, and should be kept cool. However, it is difficult to understand the logic of this, since one hundred per cent wholewheat flours, which contain all the germ, are stamped with one-year shelf-lives, just as the white flours are.

If you bake your own white breads, you can add wheatgerm back to white flour. It is, food writer Elizabeth David reports in her masterly *English Bread and Yeast Cookery*, 'apart from its valuable nutritional qualities and its good savour . . . a most useful dough "improver", helping to produce loaves with nice open crumb, good volume and excellent keeping quality'. She recommends 2–3 oz/50–75 g wheat germ for every 18 oz/500 g white flour.

Plain or Cream

This is the name usually given to white soft flour, ideal for cakes, pastries, scones, biscuits and soft breads. Plain flour in Ireland, apart from being made from very soft wheat, also has a very small proportion of raising agents added to it which gives it particular rising properties.

Self-raising

Self-raising flour is plain flour with baking powder added; it's usually used for quick cakes and scones. Keep an eye on 'best before' dates, since raising agents lose their power over time. If you have no self-raising, add two teaspoons baking powder to every lb/450g plain flour.

Strong

Essential for yeast breads if they are to rise well. It's also advisable for puff pastry, if you are committed enough to make it yourself!

Brown Flours

Terminology is confusing here, with similar-sounding words for very different types of flour. Brown flours also vary a great deal from one country to another, and from one miller to the next. Many brown flours, contrary to popular impression, do not contain one hundred per cent of the wheat grain. They may be missing much of the bran and, most perplexingly, the nutritious wheatgerm too.

Wholemeal (or one hundred per cent wholewheat)

This is the entire grain, simply crushed. This means it contains all the nutrition and fibre that wheat has to offer (but unfortunately all the pesticides too, if these are present). The best-tasting ones are stoneground: ground between slow-moving stones, rather than the faster rollers of modern milling which heat and change the flavour and nature of the flour. Irish wholemeals are usually particularly coarse by the standards of other countries and this contributes to the wonderful nutty flavour and texture of our brown soda breads.

One hundred per cent flours are not good for kneaded yeast breads, since the bran interferes with the gluten developing its full springy powers. This is part of the reason why many wholefoody breads are so depressingly, worthily stodgy.

Wheatmeal, or brown

Most 'brown' flours are simply made by returning part of the bran to white flour. This means it is much finer than wholemeal. But it may also mean that the nutritional advantage thought to be found in such brown flours is illusory, if the wheat germ is not returned to the white flour as well.

Rye

Rather unpromisingly grey in appearance, rye flour makes a much harder-to-handle dough than wheat flour, since it contains a different kind of gluten. Some wheat is necessary in the mix, or the result tends to be leaden. However, when well-baked it creates particularly tasty breads. It's often used in conjunction with sourdough starters to make tangy breads.

Best Flours?

Every baker has absolute opinions on this matter. For Irish soda recipes, Irish plain or cream flour gives best results. I also favour Odlums Coarse Stoneground wholemeal. Esther Barron of Barron's bakery (see Bread above) recommends Odlums Strong White flour. Some organic flours are superb. Look out for: Ballybrado for wholemeal and rye, Lifeforce for wholemeal, and Dove's for white and strong white (these are available in health food shops).

Oats

The oat is a grain, which once was most commonly available ground, as oatmeal — like a coarse oat flour. This has become quite rare nowadays. You tend to find either *oatflakes*, oat grains steamed to soften them, then flattened with rollers (whether Jumbo or ordinary, they make quicker porridge because they are already partially cooked); or *pinhead oatmeal*, the grain cut into three. It is hard to imagine that there is machinery which can do this so neatly, but it can. Pinhead oatmeal makes for wonderfully-textured porridge, since the little niblets of grain swell, yet retain their shape.

Sadly, almost no-one roasts oats any more before making oatmeal or pinhead oatmeal. Roasted oats have a heavenly, delicately nutty flavour and smell. Making porridge with them, you suddenly understand that it can be a fragrant, flavoursome food and not just a gluey good-for-you breakfast. There is one mill I know of which roasts its oats: Macroom. Their oatmeal makes the only porridge I want to eat. (It is, unusually, ground.) Donal Creedon at Macroom also roasts and grinds organic oats for Ballybrado.

Cornmeal

Now here's a minefield. There is a host of different words for this simple food. Cornmeal, originally an American staple, is also used in parts of Europe for cooking and baking, most famously to make polenta and some breads, like delicious American southern corn breads.

Cornmeal has had a chequered past in Ireland; brought in during the Famine as emergency relief, some supplies were insufficiently treated and inadequately cooked, and as a result some people became ill. This earned it suspicion and the name of Peel's brimstone (its yellow colour and spitting bubbles when cooked as a mush made people associate it with the sulphurs of hell). It was also known as yellowmeal, and is still used to bake soda breads in Dingle and Cork.

Cornmeal is ground corn. It may be ground *coarse* or *fine* (sometimes medium too). When coarse, it's quite gritty; when fine, it's nearly as soft as flour. It may also be called *maize meal*, and I have also seen the fine version referred to as *maize flour*. Since *polenta* (an Italian savoury corn mush) is made with cornmeal/maizemeal, they are also sometimes called *polenta flour*. (This is where the confusion really begins, since although polenta flour is made from corn, it is not at all the same thing as cornflour — see below.) Either fine or coarse cornmeal may be used for polenta. The coarse takes longer to cook, but has more texture. For baking, fine or coarse corn/maize meal may be specified; if it is not, using a coarser one is usually the safer bet.

Finally, corn/maize meals may either be yellow or soft white. The difference in flavour is marginal, if any.

Cornflour

This is not the same thing at all — it is a corn-extracted pure starch (also known as *cornstarch*) which is used for thickening sauces.

Cooking tip

Always dissolve cornflour in a few tablespoons of cold water or other cold liquid before adding to a hot sauce, to prevent lumps forming.

Raising Agents

Yeast

For best flavour and aroma, use *fresh yeast*. This is becoming very difficult to find; if you have a baker in the area, you may be able to beg some from him. Fresh yeast keeps well in the fridge and, surprisingly, freezes very well too. Older recipes may, confusingly, refer to it as 'compressed yeast'.

Dried yeast granules work very well too. Use half the weight of fresh yeast. *Fast-action dried yeasts* come with various brand names. They have been treated so the dough only needs to rise once. Quicker bread may sound like a good idea, but as we saw in the bread section, less fermentation time with yeast doughs means less flavour.

■ Keep a watch on the best-before-date on dried yeast packs. The yeast may become less effective if this has expired.

Yeastless Breads and Batters

These are raised with the aid of bubbles of carbon dioxide, created when an acid and an alkaline compound react with each other.

Bread Soda

Alkaline soda is what made Irish soda bread possible. Combined with acidic buttermilk, it created enough fizz to rise a loaf of bread. Elsewhere, its association is not specifically with bread, and so it's known as *baking soda* or by its proper name: *bicarbonate of soda*.

Store bread soda in a dry place, watch its best-before-date, and sieve it when using; lumps will show up as green spots in the bread. Using more will not make the bread rise more, it just makes it taste bitter or soapy.

Cream of Tartar

As it is acidic, cream of tartar may be combined with bread soda to make the batter rise. Combined with milk, it can replace buttermilk as the acidic ingredient with which the bread soda reacts. Use two and a half teaspoons cream of tartar for every pint/600 ml milk.

Baking Powder

This raising agent is a mix of an acid and an alkaline compound. (If you have none, you can combine a quarter of a teaspoon bread soda with half a teaspoon cream of tartar; this is about the equivalent of one teaspoon baking powder.) It loses its power with time, so watch its best-before-date.

10

Fruit and Vegetables

Most of the vibrancy, colour and sheer seasonal fun to be had at the table comes from the fruit and vegetables we buy. What would high summer be without a punnet of fragrant Irish strawberries? Or the first green shoots of spring without a scruffy bundle of tender, purple sprouting broccoli? Would you do without the first of the year's new Home Guard potatoes, thin-skinned and smelling of fresh dug earth?

Unfortunately, a system of growing and buying food has evolved which denies us many of these pleasures. It's quite daft. Progress in the fruit and vegetable world is not measured in taste. Shelf-life, visual perfection, storage, ease of transport, yield and an obsession with conquering the so-called 'problem' of seasonality is what matters nowadays. As for the flavour . . . well, that comes so far down the list that it's hardly relevant.

The result is that much of our fruit and vegetables are grown in unsustainable ways which deplete the soil and degrade our land. They also leave residues of chemicals on our food. The effects on our health of some are suspect and of most are unknown.

Finding the Best

If you want the fruit and vegetables which taste the best, you need to buy carefully. Much fruit, for example, is picked when green and rock-hard. That way it can be mechanically harvested, graded and packed. It will also have been bred for a nice tough skin to help in this process. It is expected to last during transport, to last in the shops, and to last when you get it home. Being left on the vine or the tree until it has developed enough flavour just isn't compatible with these requirements.

In addition, to make them available for as much of the year as possible, some fruit and vegetables are grown in artificial glasshouse conditions. The roots grow into soil substitutes, the plants are fed liquid nutrients and fertilisers . . . Not all glasshouse produce is poor in flavour, but much of it can be extremely bland for these reasons.

EU Grading

Ironically, this doesn't really help in the search for quality. 'Class 1' produce sounds good, until you learn that these classifications are all about appearance and nothing to do with taste. Classes are defined in millimetres, in lack of blemish and lack of deviation from the bureaucrats' norm. This encourages growers to aim for beauty and uniformity, at the expense of flavour, and to over-use pesticides.

Labelling

This is no help either. Information on fruit and vegetable varieties would help to identify the better ones, but this is only required in the case of oranges, grapes, plums, cherries, some apples, pears, apricots, peaches and nectarines, and potatoes.

To Buy the Best

1. Buy with the seasons wherever possible.
2. Try to identify the flavoursome varieties. Ask!
3. Look for ripe fruit and just-picked vegetables. Don't expect them to last forever in the fridge.
4. Be sceptical of 'ready-to-eat today' stickers; they're usually out by several days.
5. Search for local growers, markets and small shopkeepers who care enough to tell you about the provenance of the fruit and veg. This is where the real pleasure is to be found, from the most vibrant produce, which actually entices you into the kitchen.

Are They Safe?

Fruit and vegetables have not been exempt from food scares of recent years.

Pesticide Residues

Pesticides are used the world over to protect crops and keep up yields. We are often told that the world would starve without their aid. This is a questionable assertion when you consider that US farmers have increased their pesticide use tenfold since the 1940s — yet crop losses have not reduced. In UK trials, pesticide use was cut by fifty to seventy-five per cent, and yet yields were only very slightly reduced. And Sweden has already reduced pesticide use by fifty per cent, yet still manages the same food yields.

The problem with pesticides is that they leave residues on the food we eat. About half the fruit and vegetables tested by the Pesticide Control Unit of the Department of Agriculture each year have detectable residues of between one and six pesticides. These are, we are assured, almost all within safe limits. Unfortunately, every now and again high levels are discovered. One year it's cucumbers, then it might be carrots, next it's apples . . .

High residue levels are not the only problem. The entire concept of 'safety' is a dubious one. Chemicals considered safe in previous decades have since been banned. What will be discovered about the pesticides being used now? Many don't even have safety limits set for them, and are not tested for. Nobody knows what the consequences will be of ingesting small quantities of these chemicals over decades — our generation is participating in a worldwide, uncontrolled experiment.

Pesticide levels have recently been found to vary a great deal from one fruit or vegetable to another, within the same batch; single fruits may contain up to twenty-nine times the average level (the average is what testing can detect). This calls into question standard testing methods and current safety standards.

The biggest question mark hangs over children. Their smaller body weight means they consume proportionately more. Their faster rate of development means they are still more vulnerable to damage. Yet 'safety' limits are calculated not for them, but for the average adult. Even more at risk is the developing foetus, yet this area is hardly researched at all.

For more information on these aspects of the pesticide problem, see Chapter 14 Pesticides, page 205.

Post-Harvest Treatments

Most questionable of all pesticides are post-harvest treatments. These are applied to make food keep better during transport and storage. While pesticides should, in theory at least, have mostly dissipated by the time the food is harvested, post-harvest treatments have nowhere to go but into you.

Post-harvest treatments are used on nearly all citrus fruit, and on some stored apples, potatoes and wheat. Bananas, pears, cherries and grapes are also routinely treated.

Although many of these chemicals carry E numbers (E 230–233), and would have to be declared on other foods, there is no requirement that fresh foods be labelled. This is quite unacceptable, especially since this group of preservatives are suspected carcinogens and mutagens — that is, they may cause cancer or foetal damage. In France or Germany, you might see this label on a lemon: 'Preserved with Diphenyl, Orthophenyl-phenol and Thiabendazole; waxed; skin not suitable for eating.' No such labelling exists here. It's about time it was introduced.

Nitrates

High nitrate levels are of concern because they convert in the body to nitrosamines, which are highly suspect carcinogens. Since 1997, EU regulations have set maximum levels for spinach and for glasshouse and outdoor lettuce.

Nitrates are not directly added chemicals in fruit and vegetables (though they may be used as preservatives in meat products). They can occur naturally, when plants are not able to convert all the nitrogen in the soil. This can happen when there is too much nitrogen in the soil, or too much added as fertiliser, or when growing conditions are poor — with insufficient light, the plant cannot metabolise properly.

Winter glasshouse crops of green vegetables are most likely to have high nitrate levels. This is because of excessive levels of fertiliser; combined with shorter days, the plants' nitrate conversion is low. A Consumers' Association test in 1993 found particularly high levels in winter lettuces, spinach, celery and cucumber (Irish and imported), levels at which a 60 kg adult would exceed recommended limits by eating just 100g or less.

Department of Agriculture testing in 1997 revealed that nine per cent of butterhead lettuce samples and nineteen per cent of spinach samples exceeded EU maximum levels. These levels are set fairly high, so any samples exceeding them is a matter for concern. At present several countries, Ireland included, are permitted to go on selling home-grown lettuce and spinach which exceed EU levels. In Holland, the food information service has advised consumers to limit their intake of winter glasshouse vegetables. They also monitor nitrate levels and warn the public when they are particularly high.

So far in Ireland, we have been told nothing.

Waxes

These may be applied to prevent fruits and vegetables from drying out, or they may also incorporate fungicides. The waxes themselves are considered to be edible. They are usually insect- or palm-derived. They are applied mainly to citrus fruits, apples, cucumbers and pears and occasionally to turnips and swedes. Opinions vary on how easily these are removed. Some sources claim that they can be removed by warm water, others that this is not the case. Even after scrubbing with soap and hot water, I find most waxed fruits still feel sticky.

What Can You Do?

In the absence of hard information on pesticide residues, nitrate levels or anything else, the answer is: very little. Pesticide residues cannot be removed by washing or scrubbing. Peeling is the only answer, and even this does not remove them all.

Can you wash it off?

In general, water is not successful at removing pesticide residues from the surfaces of foods. This is hardly surprising, since pesticides are formulated to resist being washed off by rain. Tests report 70–95.7 per cent residues remain after washing.

In 1997, the UK-based Pesticides Trust reported in its newsletter *Pesticides News* that a new washing aid, Veggi Wash, was available in health food stores. It was reported to remove between 12.5–95 per cent of surface residues of a number of pesticides. I have not seen the product on sale in Ireland. Of course, a washing aid cannot remove pesticides which are within the flesh of fruits and vegetables.

To minimise possible pesticide consumption

1. Buy organic. This is particularly important if you are going to use citrus peel for cooking or preserving.
2. Buy potatoes which have been stored in cold-storage (they are less likely to have received post-harvest treatments; find out from your retailer, and tell him why you want to know); or buy organic potatoes. Otherwise, peel them before eating. The same applies to apples.
3. Demand information on post-harvest treatments on fruit and vegetables sold in your shops. (This is particularly important for fruits which you would certainly not expect to peel, such as grapes.) Remember: consumer demand is powerful. Let your retailer know that you want to know. It is the only way things will change.

To minimise possible nitrate consumption

1. Limit your consumption of out-of-season green vegetables. This applies to organic produce too, which may also have higher than ideal nitrate levels out of season, although organic methods of cultivation are unlikely to produce the highs which can result from chemically-assisted farming.
2. Eat frozen spinach in winter — it will have been harvested at optimum growing times.
3. Discard outer leaves of vegetables which may have high levels.
4. Eat with the seasons.
5. Demand information on nitrate levels in Irish and imported vegetables, so that you can make an informed choice.

Fruit
Apples

The notion of a dessert apple being sweet and scented seems almost shocking. Yet that is just what a classic eating apple should be: perfumed, aromatic, rich in natural sugars, a real juicy fruit. Many years of Golden Delicious (was there ever such a misnomer?) stupefied our tastebuds and our memories, while the EU actually hastened the demise of native varieties by grant-aiding the grubbing up of orchards. The tragedy is that there were many older varieties in orchards and walled gardens around the country which are now lost to us.

The full loss that this represents only came home to me when I tasted a range of apples from the Brogdale Horticultural Trust's orchards in Kent, where a fruit collection including over 2300 varieties of apple is preserved. The subtle variations in flavour were astounding and exciting.

However, things have taken a few tentative steps in the right direction in recent years. While there is still no sign of any effort to preserve classic older varieties, at least newly-bred varieties are now being grown in Ireland. For flavour, amazingly enough. Oddly, however, the varieties are seldom advertised: 'Irish eating apples' is a common and utterly useless description. Pester your retailer to tell you what you are being sold!

Eaters and cookers

Britain and Ireland are the only two countries to make this distinction. The rest of Europe cooks with dessert apples, which is why a French apple tart is a very different thing from an Irish apple pie. It's important to remember this when cooking dishes from other countries: use well-flavoured eating apples, not cookers.

Varieties

Cox's Pippin A good one still has my vote for the best flavour: complex fruitiness, with a tart refreshing bite. It varies hugely in quality, though, depending on how it was grown, and whether it was picked green and stored or picked fairly ripe. Dutch and New Zealand specimens rarely taste as good as an English or Irish one. To maximise your chances, buy Cox's in season, which means autumn. Southern hemisphere Cox's are in season during their autumn, which means our late spring.

Elstar One of the new Irish-grown varieties, this is the one to look out for; it can give Cox's a run for its money, with a fruity perfume.

Jonagold This can be good too.

Braeburn I've only seen this as a French apple, despite the sound of its name, but it can be outstanding.

Bramley . . . Well, it does its job, collapsing easily to lovely fluff. But it can't be accused of being high in flavour, and it needs a mountain of sugar to make it edible. If you want to use less sugar and have more flavour, use tart eating apples instead.

Storage
Keep apples in a cool place, but not the fridge.

Safety?
Apples are one of the crops on which most pesticides may be used. They are consistently heavily tested by the PCS and often contain residues of two to five pesticides. In 1997, very high residues were discovered on English apples, and consumers were advised to peel them before eating. Washing is good hygiene, but does not remove residues. Apple juice may, as a result, be high in residues. The pity of it is that there are some conscientious growers out there who keep pesticide use to a minimum. But who are they?

Bananas
We have to make do with just one variety here. Go to the Far East and you will know what you've been missing. Some are as small as your finger. The flavours can be complex, caramelly, wonderfully sweet. Bananas available in Ireland will have been picked and shipped green, then ripened with ethylene gas in Cork. There's nothing sinister about that: bananas in hot countries are cut green too, and ethylene is the gas which the ripening fruit naturally gives off.

Storage
Never in the fridge, which turns them black.

Safety?
See Post-Harvest Treatments, page 131. At least bananas are peeled before eating, so this isn't a great problem, but wash your hands well after handling them.

Blueberries
These are just delightful, with their fragile, dusty bloom, and are so welcome for being in season in August and September, just when the soft fruits of summer have bowed out. Cultivated ones are creeping into the Irish shops, marked 'Exotics', with a price to match. This seems odd, since their wild cousins, the fraughans, grow freely, and cultivated blueberries flourish where little else will grow, on acid boggy soil. However, the bushes are, I'm told, expensive to establish. Let's hope that as they become more common, the price will come down.

Storage
Blueberries keep well in the fridge for a few days.

Berries: Raspberry, Blackberry and Other Relations
These delicate soft fruits of summer really need to be picked ripe and eaten that same day, which doesn't marry with most large-scale selling. Raspberries in the shops tend to be under-ripe and green-tasting, picked a little early so they will have a few days' shelf-life. Your best bet is to pick your own, or buy from a local country market. They are in season July–September (or later, depending on variety).

Look for
Carefully-packed berries which are not damp, squashed or sitting in a pool of juice at the bottom of the punnet.

Storage
Try not to! They quickly go mouldy in the fridge, and their glorious flavour is deadened. If you must keep them, spread them out so they don't squash each other — every bit of damp encourages them to go off.

Citrus Fruits: Oranges, Lemons, Limes, Grapefruit, Satsumas . . .
These are all, of course, imported from warmer climes. Generally, this involves picking them green and giving them a blast of ethylene gas to 'ripen' them to the expected colour before selling. Unfortunately, citrus fruits don't have starch stores to convert to sugars, so the colour is deceptive: what they picked is what you get. In general, the quality is OK, but rarely exciting.

Varieties
At least oranges are required to be identified.
Blood oranges Look out for these just after Christmas: fantastically dramatic magenta interiors.
Seville or Marmalade These oranges are those lumpy, baggy, scruffy ones in the shops for a few short weeks in January: indispensable for marmalade.
Lemons These are invariably dull. If you've ever had the pleasure of tasting a sweeter **Meyer** lemon, you'll know what I mean.

Storage
At room temperature. In the fridge, they will get brown spots. However, I store organic lemons, which I always buy (see below), in the fridge — without waxes and chemicals they soften and mould much more quickly.

Safety?
See Post-Harvest Treatments, page 131. Citrus fruits are routinely treated with these before being waxed, both treatments in order to make them last longer. You can't wash them off. If you use citrus peel — for desserts, baking, drinks, preserving, Asian cooking and so on — look for fruits which have not been treated. You are highly unlikely to find them here (unlike in France or Germany, where they are common), so your only option is to buy organic. Keep pestering your retailer for them.

Currants: Red, Black and White
An essential part of summer, yet a rarity in supermarkets. Often the only ones available are outrageously priced imports. For jam-making, or Summer Pudding, or beautiful jewel-like compotes, go to a local country market. They are in season July and August.

Storage
Best used fresh, but they will keep in the fridge for a day or two.

Cooking tip
To string currants, strip them off with a fork. If you are freezing them, don't bother: they fall off the strings when defrosting. And it's not necessary if you're making a jelly which will be strained.

Grapes
Varieties
I've rarely encountered excellent grapes in Ireland, they usually just have a pleasant crunch.

Muscat We are unlikely to see the wonderful fragrant Muscat grape in Irish shops — look out for it if you're holidaying in the south in summer. It has big pips, but fantastic, sweet perfumed flesh (and makes superb raisins). Green grapes should be a soft yellow, and black ones purple!

Safety?

Grapes are a much-sprayed crop — wash carefully and hope for the best.

Melons

The sweet, yeasty perfume of a ripe melon is hard to better for sheer pleasure. So often, though, they are hard and unappetising. Look for a melon with scent. Pick it up. Sniff. If there's no aroma, put it back down again. To check for ripeness, press oh-so-gently at the stem end, which should 'give' noticeably. (Don't overdo this and squelch the end, ruining it for the next person.) It should also feel heavy for its size — compare a few and take the heaviest.

Varieties

Honeydew This is the cheapest and usually the least tasty; it's pale green or yellow, and shaped like a rugby ball. Hardest to gauge for ripeness. A good one will have a semi-liquid honey centre; poor ones are about as good as a turnip.

Ogen These are greenish yellow with green stripes, and green flesh.

Galia This variety has similar green flesh, but a net-like skin. Both can be very tasty if ripe.

Orange-fleshed melons tend to be the most fragrant. Look for **Charentais** which has a greenish yellow skin and green stripes, and **cantaloupe**, which can both be just glorious.

Melons are in season late summer in Europe.

Storage

At room temperature. In the fridge once cut, or if it's ripening too quickly, but cover it tightly with cling film : the smell is incredibly penetrating, and soon your eggs will be melon-flavoured.

Peaches and Nectarines

We all have memories of southern summer picnics, the juice of a peach leaving a sticky trail of bliss down your chin. Once again, we rarely encounter that bliss here. Peaches and their smooth-skinned cousins the nectarines come in punnets, rattling against each other, picked when you could have played a game of tennis with them. Often they don't ripen at all, and just go straight from hard as rock to mealy and mouldy. Nor are we often offered the haunting delicacy of the white peach or nectarine, which both have pale ivory flesh and make their custardy yellow relations seem a touch vulgar by comparison.

Look for peaches and nectarines sold in trays, not punnets: they're likely to have been treated with more care, though they are, of course, more expensive.

Storage

Treat these fruit with kid gloves, even if they are hard when you buy them. Store at room temperature. If you've bought a punnet of fruit, remove it from the punnet and place in a shallow bowl to ripen, so that a damaged one which starts to go mouldy doesn't infect the rest.

Cooking tip

A punnet of recalcitrant, rock-hard peaches is best poached. Halve them, remove the stones, and simmer for a few minutes in a syrup of equal quantities of sugar and water with a few strips of lemon peel. Lift out the peaches and the skins will slip off, having transferred glorious blazing sunset colours to the fruit.

Pears

These are one of the few fruits which should be picked still hard, and which can ripen on to perfect succulence and aroma after picking. Patience! Bring them home and ripen at room temperature for several days. However, many varieties are just plain dull and will never develop much interest. They are in season autumn and winter.

Varieties

Anjou are large, sweet and succulent.
Comice and **Beurre Hardy** can be melting and exquisite
Conference is measly and uninteresting (and very poor value with its small proportion of flesh).

Safety?

Peel pears before eating, especially if giving to young children. They are consistently found to contain multiple pesticide residues.

Rhubarb

Rhubarb is not a fruit, no more than the tomato is a vegetable, but since we view it as a thing for sweet eating, this is where it belongs.

Rhubarb should be pink and slender. When it reaches the tough stringy stage, it has lost much of its pinkness and most of its charm. There's nothing very nice about a bowl of greenish, swampy goo. The time to snap up rhubarb is early in the year. Best of all are the finger-thin stalks of forced rhubarb, so tender it cooks to little pieces of bright pink jelly, not a string in sight.

Still, it is very welcome during the 'hungry gap' in April, one of the only home-grown crops to see us through until the earlies of May start the fruit and vegetable year going again. In late spring, look for the thinnest stalks possible, and trim the green parts. Never peel off the pink skin.

Cooking tip

Always cook in a single layer if you want pieces rather than mush. And leave it to cool in its juices for half an hour or so after first cooking. This intensifies the pink colour.

Strawberries

Strawberries spell the soft luxury of northern summers. Sweet-berried perfume and a dollop of cream. Like just about every other crop, though, strawberries have been forced to succumb to our late twentieth century demands: shelf-life, transport, out-of-season availability.

Varieties

The result? Older varieties have all but vanished from the shelves. The classics of Irish strawberry growing were once **Cambridge Vigour** and **Cambridge Favourite**, tasty, soft little berries which tire overnight. They are still grown for jam, where appearance doesn't matter, but we won't be offered them in the shops anymore.

Elsanta, developed by the Dutch in 1981, has all but taken over. It's bright, it's glossy, it travels well, it has several days' shelf-life . . .

Look for Irish strawberries. They have been grown in soil, unlike the Spanish, which grow in sand, are fed artificially and have spent time in trucks before they even get to our shelves. *Smell* the punnet: if there's no perfume, there's unlikely to be flavour. And be conscious of the weather. Elsanta can taste very good if it has just had a burst of sun; but picked in a cloudy week it tends to be rather turnipy, with a hard green nose.

Storage
Like all soft fruit, don't. If you must, keep in the fridge, but beware: strawberries will lose flavour and tend to mouldiness.

Cooking tip
Tasteless strawberries are much improved by macerating in slices in freshly-squeezed orange juice for a few hours.

Exotic Fruit
This gives many a supermarket display the semblance of wonderful variety, but often the quality of the fruit on offer leaves a great deal to be desired.

Mangoes Almost always a travesty of the real thing, tough, stringy and tasteless. A really ripe mango perfumes a whole room and has juicy, sweet flesh; even if you keep the mangoes we're offered they never reach this stage. Look out for Alphonso mangoes in season in Asian shops, if you want to experience the true pleasure of this seductive fruit.

Pineapples are picked so green that they will always be fairly sour, even when the greenness fades.

Papaya is hard as a turnip. And so on . . .

Storage
Tropical fruits should be stored at room temperature, in the hope that they will ripen as much as they are able.

Safety
This is always a question, since accounts from developing countries regularly report over-use of pesticides.

Vegetables
Asparagus
It's a curious thing: beans flown in from Kenya are no oddity, nor mangoes

from Brazil . . . but just-picked Irish asparagus? A rare sight indeed. Spanish imports dominate the market for several months of the year. They are pleasant, but not special.

For the sweet, grassy delight of asparagus, the only answer is spears which were picked on the same day as you buy and eat them. This is not an affectation, but chemistry: with every hour out of the ground, the natural sugars in asparagus convert to fibrous matter. A day later, it's not the same vegetable. Asparagus is in season in May and June. Imports are available many other months.

Look for firm stalks without a hint of droop about the head. The flowering tips should be tightly closed. Comb markets for Irish asparagus, picked that day, and when you find it, cook it the same day too.

Storage
Don't! Eat the same day! (In the vegetable drawer of the fridge if you must.)

Cooking tip
The asparagus may have cost a lot, so every bit of trimming hurts, but you must be ruthless. The fibrous base of the stalks must go. Then peel the thicker stalk bases with a swivel vegetable peeler, so they cook more evenly and are less chewy.

Aubergine
Lustrous, and the purple of darkest night, the aubergine is a rather magical vegetable. Its interior is a blank sponge until it meets heat or oil, which transform it to silk. Look for shiny, taut skin: the aubergine should seem about to burst out of it. No wrinkled, squashy specimens.

Varieties
Sadly, we only ever see the dullest of aubergines on sale in this country. Asian varieties are narrow, elongated and absorb less oil, and there are myriad other types, including the little round white one from which it derives its alternative name: eggplant.

Storage
In the fridge.

Cooking tip

You are usually advised to salt aubergines to remove bitter juices. It's actually not necessary with the varieties cultivated for our shops. (Beware, though, that if you're cooking on holiday, this step may still be essential. I learned this to my cost a few years ago in Spain: a stunning dish of fried aubergines was bitterly inedible.)

Salting has another useful purpose, however: it breaks down the cell walls, which means the aubergine absorbs much less oil when fried. Another tip to reduce its thirst for oil is to roast in the oven after a brief initial frying; or roast whole in the oven, over a gas burner or on the barbeque. With this last technique, you lose the beautiful lustre of the skin, unfortunately.

Avocado

Varieties

Although varieties are rarely specified, they vary a great deal. Smooth-skinned green ones are usually slippery and rather watery even when ripe. You will recognise *Hass* by its near-black, warty skin; inside, it is the richest, butteriest of them all.

Ripeness is something the supermarkets don't believe in; eating an avocado almost always entails advance planning. Ripen in a drawer with bananas, which give off ethylene gas to help that process. They may need up to a week. Store at room temperature — they will darken and fail to soften if stored below 7°C.

Beetroot

A much maligned vegetable, probably because of all those years it spent puckering in jars of pickle. Beetroot has a rich sweet flavour which no other vegetable can match, and its jolt of lurid colour is very welcome in winter. If you can't find it fresh, the vac-packed variety is a reasonable substitute, although it always tastes rather more watery than beetroot which you have cooked yourself.

Look for beets with leaves attached, a sure indicator of freshness, since the leaves wilt rapidly. If the stems have been cut, look closely. If the root itself is sliced into — and this is terribly common — the beets will bleed and lose flavour when cooked.

Cooking tip

Best of all, wrap in foil and roast in the oven at a medium temperature for about an hour. The flavour is concentrated and intense.

Broad Beans

Another vegetable to eat as fresh as possible. In early summer, look for young pods which can be eaten pod and all: slice into chunks and cook for a real treat. Frozen broad beans are a reasonable substitute at other times of the year.

Cooking tip

For a true labour of love, peel the tough white skin from each bean to reveal the brilliant green tender bean within.

Broccoli

There was a lot of furtive snapping off of the chunky stalks of calabrese (the big, ubiquitous broccoli) in my local supermarket, until the management decided to legalise the practice by providing a hacksaw. They clearly don't know what they're missing. Those stalks, quickly peeled with a vegetable peeler, then steamed to a jade-like translucence, are juicy and flavoursome without any of the deadly wet squelch which the florets can offer up.

Look for firm stalks and stiff florets. Reject any with the merest hint of yellow. Available year-round, though broccoli is traditionally a winter vegetable. Purple sprouting is available in April and May.

Varieties

Calabrese This all-purpose variety is fine, but resolutely unexciting, bred to be tough, not tasty.

Romescu Imaginative growers may try their hand at this variety, lime green with stunning, tight, pointy florets.

Purple Sprouting Broccoli One of the first new vegetables of spring, it has slender stalks, furled leaves and dusty purple tips which look, when cooked, as if they had been dipped in fresh indigo. And it tastes fantastic: crunchy and delicate.

Storage

In the fridge. But not for long — like asparagus, broccoli's sugars convert to more stringy fibres with every hour after being cut.

Cooking tip

Like all brassicas — broccoli is a member of the cabbage family — it can tend to a sulphurous whiff. Quick cooking (steaming or stir-frying) and assertive flavours (chilli, anchovy, garlic, ginger) are its best allies.

Brussels Sprouts

I can't pretend to any great enthusiasm for these mini-cabbages: they seem to me to have all the disadvantages of cabbage (rather smelly and squelchy) with none of its compensating flavour. They should be tight and firm. Shredded finely and stir-fried (see Cabbage below), they're rather nice — tender and crinkly. In season in the winter; aficionados say they're sweeter and nuttier after frost.

Cabbage

Fully deserves its dodgy reputation, but only because of the way it has been abused by generations of cooks. Like all brassicas, long-cooking destroys its fresh, sparky, mustardy flavours and develops its woeful sulphurous ones. So cook it quickly!

Look for squeaky greens.

Varieties and Seasons

Spring or **York** cabbages are fresh and welcome at Easter; dark green, all leaf and no heart.

Savoy, with its crinkly tasty green leaves, matures mid-autumn and into the winter.

'Coleslaw' cabbages are winter types; little flavour.

Red cabbage is a good source of winter colour.

Storage

As cool a place as possible — the fridge, if you have room.

Cooking tip

Stir-fry cabbage. Shred it finely, then cook in a large pan or wok, either in oil, with chilli and/or garlic; or in butter, with chopped streaky rashers, finished with a little cream. You will be amazed at the reaction: slave over an entire meal, and everybody will be oohing and aahing at the stir-fried cabbage.

Carrots

Sad that they are generally so flavourless; it's rare to find ones which give the sweet intensity which marks out the best carrots. Varieties are rarely specified. Organic carrots are usually, though not always, definably sweeter. They are indisputably less watery though, and make for noticeably better roasted carrots. Baby carrots are a pointless affectation. Some vegetables taste better young, but carrots need to grow to develop flavour. They are in season most of the year, so with storage they're available year-round.

Look for carrots from a named source, so that if you find really tasty ones, you can buy them again. Carrots with green tops attached don't necessarily taste any better, despite their high price, but they will be very fresh.

Storage

In a really cool place or in the fridge. If the carrots had leaves attached, remove them immediately, or the roots will soften.

Safety?

The UK government issued a health warning on carrots in 1995. High levels of organophosphate pesticides had been found. Consumers were advised to top them generously and peel. In both 1995 and 1996, carrots from Ireland tested by the PCS were found to exceed MRLs for the pesticide Chlorfenvinphos.

Cauliflower

Look for fresh-looking green leaves on the outside. The flower nestling within should be compact and curdy, and not at all gritty. A real tell-tale sign is a 'shaved' head of curds (they were doubtless going brown) or outside leaves completely trimmed, since they are the first to wilt.

Cooking tip
Tender leaves and stems add excellent colour and texture to cauliflower dishes: just cook along with the curds.

Celery
Look for smooth, pale green stalks with vivid, fresh-looking leaves in the centre. Celery keeps well in the fridge for several days.

Safety?
See Nitrates, page 131.

Courgettes
Small is beautiful. Turn-of the century Ulster cook Florence Irwin tells how an American woman despairingly described the then-common Irish marrow: 'solidified fog'. With every bit that courgettes expand, they become more foggy, as they increase in water and decrease in flavour. Courgettes are in seson midsummer to autumn; imports available year-round.

Look for the smallest you can find, with bright tight skin. They have more crisp flesh and a nuttier flavour.

Cooking tip
Simmer small courgettes whole in water; while still firm, slice lengthways and dress with olive oil, lemon juice and lots of herbs.

Cucumber
Most glasshouse cucumber these days is pretty neutral and tasteless, although its crunch can be agreeably refreshing. Cucumber was at the centre of one of the early food scares in Ireland, when people became sick after eating cucumbers contaminated with aldicarb, a pesticide not authorised for use on them.

Cucumbers are usually waxed, so scrub well before eating.

Safety?
See Nitrates, page 131.

Chicory

Some years ago, this conical winter vegetable always slumbered in boxes, chaste and pale under flimsy sheets of purple tissue. There was a reason for this: any light develops chicory's tendency to inedible bitterness. Look out for the tell-tale tinge of green in the leaf; the tips of chicory should always be palest yellow. Avoid cling-filmed pre-pack chicory for this reason: it has been exposed to light, and will be bitter even if it's not very green-tipped. Supermarkets should know better than to display it this way.

Cooking tips

1. If you find it untainted, chicory makes a wonderful crunchy base for winter salads.
2. Cook it by halving it, steaming until not quite done, then turning in butter in a frying pan until golden and melting, finishing it with a few tablespoons of cream.

Fennel

Fresh and crunchy, with a mild aniseed flavour, this white bulb deserves to be better known. Its crisp bite cuts through rich flavours; particularly good with porky things. Look for pearly bulbs, small and squat and not too stringy. Avoid brown-tinged ones which are no longer fresh.

Cooking tips

1. Trim the tough base and all the green stalks; keep any feathery green bits for garnishing.
2. Excellent raw and crispy in salads, as well as braised.

French Beans

A neat line-up of these, ready-trimmed in a polystyrene tray like a little coffin, flown in from Kenya, sums up all that is wrong with the way we buy our vegetables today. Maximum air miles, minimal flavour. The fruit of a cash crop in a developing country, grown with the aid of plenty of chemicals by workers who aren't even supplied with the basic protective equipment necessary to safeguard their health . . .

Look for French beans grown in Ireland in season, in late spring and summer. The pods should snap, not bend. Enjoy them. Then wait another year.

Garlic

Look for large cloves (less work peeling). Above all, they must be firm. There's still far too much soft garlic sold in Ireland, with shrivelled, yellow, sprouting, or mouldy cloves. Don't accept it in that condition. New season garlic, or 'wet' garlic, is available in May/June. Snap it up for its fresh, light flavour. Woodland areas in spring yield wild garlic: garlicky leaves and pretty white bell-like flowers.

Storage

At room temperature; not in the fridge, where it will go mouldy.

Cooking tip

The more you break the cells of a garlic clove, the more of its pungency is released. Left whole, cloves become subtle and nutty, like beans, with long cooking.

Ginger

Look for thin-skinned, plump-looking pieces of this rhizome. When too old, it shrivels and becomes very stringy.

Storage

At room temperature; or, if you use it less frequently, in the freezer. It can be grated from frozen.

Cooking tip

Recipes usually tell you to chop ginger, which is hard work. Much quicker and easier is to grate it on the large holes of a grater. This also filters out the stringy bits, if you're stuck with an ancient piece.

Jerusalem Artichokes

These knobbly, inexpensive tubers lead a double life. Raw, they're crisp, crunchy and fresh — very welcome in midwinter. Cooked, they become nutty and mysteriously musky. Look for the least knobbly ones — much less work peeling. They're not nearly as widespread as they ought to be — they're terribly easy to grow.

Cooking tip
Once peeled, they discolour quickly, so drop into a bowl of water acidulated with lemon juice as you work. Superb for soup.

Leeks
Look for slender leeks. They taste much less coarse. All leeks should have stiff leaves and no yellowing. They are in season almost all year, except early spring. The slender ones are most common in summer.

Storage
In the fridge, where they will keep reasonably well for a few days.

Lettuces, Other Salad Leaves and Herbs
Where once there was just shy flopsy butterhead lettuce, a profusion of frills and bronzed beauties now reigns. Much of the credit — as so often where more unusual varieties of fruit and vegetable are concerned — goes to organic growers, who have brought magnificent variety to the salad bowls of Ireland.

Look for vibrant, vigorous leaves without a hint of sagging. They should look alive.

Lettuces and leaves are grown year-round in tunnels and glasshouses, but are naturally in season in the brighter, warmer months of the year. Winter glasshouse lettuces, usually from France and Spain, may look vibrant, but usually spectacularly fail the flavour test. This probably has more to do with the soil and fertiliser they're using, since the best Irish organic growers produce magnificent salad crops year-round.

Varieties
Oak leaf Looks like its namesake, gently undulating leaves which may be green or tinged with mauve at the tips. A beautiful lettuce.

Cos This is the classic lettuce for Caesar salad: crispy, long, upright elegance, each leaf bowed and pointy, rather like the shape of a currach.

Lollo rosso Probably the most common of the glamour lettuces, with tight frills like the layers of a can-can dancer's skirt. It wilts particularly quickly, and can trap a lot of grit in those frills, so wash very carefully. It is tinged red at the tips.

Lollo Biondo Sister to Lollo rosso, this lettuce is green all through.

Frisée may also be called **Curly endive**. A slightly bitter taste from the leaves (pale green to yellow at the centre), which are tangled like fine seaweed. Refreshing mixed in small amounts with others.

Four Seasons It has a generous, broad-petalled spread.

Radicchio Looks like a mini red cabbage. A few slivers add fabulous colour to a salad bowl — but go easy, it's very bitter.

Butterhead The old classic, and not to be scorned. When grown well in good soil, it has wonderful flavour. However, the stuff produced by large commercial growers is just plain boring.

Iceberg Crunch, but no taste.

Other leaves

Watercress Why is this not available everywhere? This lovely peppery leaf ought to be ideally suited to Irish conditions, yet almost invariably the only watercress available is (wildly expensive) imported French.

Rocket Another peppery leaf, fiercely trendy of late in the US and Britain, but still rare here. Grab it when you can — or grow it yourself; it comes up in weeks.

Herbs These are usually sold in ludicrously small amounts. The plastic box may weigh more than the contents. Herbs should be used by the handful, not the leaf. If you've ever bought bags of herbs in wholesale markets, you will appreciate the outrageous mark-up that you are being charged. Find someone who sells herbs in reasonable quantities.

Modified Atmosphere Packaging

Cellophane 'pillows' of prepared lettuces and/or herbs are usually in a nitrogen and carbon dioxide atmosphere which slows down their deterioration and gives a false impression of their freshness. They tend to be low in flavour, though whether this is because of the storage or because the contents were indifferent to start off with is hard to say.

Storage

Eat as quickly as possible; flavour evaporates from lettuces, herbs and leaves quickly. To store in the fridge, keep slightly moist and store in a 'ziploc' vegetable bag in the vegetable compartment. To restore tired lettuce leaves, wash and spin dry, then place in the fridge; a good chill usually perks them up.

Safety?

Lettuces have two safety questions hanging over them. Nitrates is one. Glasshouse lettuces are one of the crops which have tested highest for nitrates, which are suspected of having carcinogenic effects. Organic produce is lower, but not exempt, so the best advice is to eat seasonally. See Nitrates, page 131.

Pesticides are another safety issue. Lettuces are specially targeted by the Pesticide Control Service and each year several fail. In 1996, nearly half of all fruit and vegetables which exceeded Maximum Residue Levels (MRLs) in testing were lettuces. And in 1997, two Irish and one Spanish lettuce exceeded MRLs (see page 130).

Mushrooms

Look for moist and plump-looking specimens, nothing shrivelled.

Varieties

Button, **Cup** and **Breakfast flats** are all varieties of the same white mushroom, at different stages of maturity. They are, at their youngest, mild and inoffensive; the large flats can have a reasonable amount of flavour and are wonderful grilled with a knob of butter or a touch of olive oil.

Brown caps A different strain of the same mushroom, with a gentle, earthy fragrance — well worth looking out for.

Oyster Usually soft, pearly grey, furled, with their gills exposed. They don't have a great deal of flavour, but look beautiful and have a superb, meaty texture.

Shiitake An Asian mushroom, with a chestnut-coloured cap. An inimitable rich woodsy flavour, they are the cultivated mushroom which approaches most closely the aroma of the wild.

Wild mushrooms A rare sight in Irish shops, since we don't much value them. When they are available they are usually imported from France. Use wherever you'd use the cultivated ones, for bags more flavour.

Storage
More than any other vegetable, mushrooms need to breathe during storage. They will go slimy in plastic, so store in a covered bowl or a paper bag.

Onions
Look for hard onions without a trace of 'give' to them. It's astounding how often squashy, second-rate onions are on sale. Available year-round from storage. Fresh onions are a summer and autumn crop; it would be nice to see them celebrated in the shops.

Varieties
Onion varietal names are never offered.
Yellow The standard brown-skinned ones.
Red These onions cut open to reveal delightful magenta stripes, and are good for salsas and other raw uses as they're less pungent; cooked, however, they're not as sweet as yellow onions.
Spanish Enormous and mild. Useful because there's a lot less peeling than with smaller types, but they are much more watery, so allow for that in the cooking.

Storage
In a dry cool place, but away from other vegetables, such as potatoes, as they can pick up moisture from them and go soft.

Parsnips
Look for medium-sized parsnips. Large ones have very woody cores which need to be cut out; weeny ones are fiddly to peel. Tradition has it that parsnips are best after the first frost has touched them. I'm not quite convinced, but they are much more welcome in cold weather, with their mealy, rich pungency.

Cooking tip
Don't just keep them for traditional pairings with roasts, carrots and cream.

They are superb — better, I'd say — with spicy Indian flavours. Good in a curry and wonderful boiled, then fried with fresh root ginger and a little turmeric.

Peas

Peas lose up to forty per cent of their sugar in six hours at room temperature, so freshness is all. This is one of those rare occasions where frozen is often better than 'fresh', if the fresh aren't really fresh. Look for shiny, bright, squeaky pods, with no yellowing, in late spring and early summer.

Cooking tip

Cook them the day you buy them.

Peppers

Sweet peppers come in hundreds of varieties, but we generally only see one in Ireland. Green peppers are just unripe versions of the red ones, and are particularly indigestible. Peppers are one of the quintessential vegetables of the hot days of late summer in southern Europe; glasshouse cultivation from Holland to Israel means we get identical, reasonable but not stunning, specimens year-round. A shame.

Look for: smooth, shiny sheen with no soft spots.

Cooking tip

Roasted, they taste best of all; it chars them slightly and intensifies their sweetness. Don't roast green ones, which just end up looking dirty. Roast red and yellow peppers whole in a hot oven (or cut into segments and grill skin-side up), until the skin is blackened and blistering. Place in a bowl, cover with cling film and allow to cool; the skins will lift off easily. They can now be used in cooking, or for Mediterranean salads.

Potatoes

I hear more complaints about potatoes than I do about any other food — except perhaps rashers. You'd think that in Ireland, of all places, we'd be able to get the potatoes right. What has gone wrong?

Modern methods of cultivation are to a large degree the culprits. Relying on artificial fertiliser does two things to the potato. Firstly, soil which lacks natural humus (because it has been fertilised chemically, rather than with compost or farmyard manure) has less flavour and aroma to contribute to the growing tuber. In addition, using chemical fertilisers on the plants encourages the tubers to absorb lots of water. More water in the spud means the grower gets a higher yield per acre. It also means you get less flavour per potato, and a wetter, 'soapier' spud.

The problem is being recognised by some enterprising potato growers, who now grow without the aid of chemical fertilisers, to considerable acclaim. Perhaps others will sit up and take note, if they don't want us all to convert to pasta instead.

Quality

Rather tasteless potatoes are one thing. Discovering your potatoes are black and blue all the way through as you prepare them for cooking is quite another. This is bruising, pure and simple, and it just shouldn't happen. Potatoes are delicate, believe it or not, and should be treated as carefully as eggs, both by suppliers and by you. So don't toss them gaily into the boot of the car. If your potatoes are bruised, complain. Your retailer should be told.

What if your potatoes are green instead? Potatoes exposed to light can develop alkaloids, which are toxic at high levels. They reveal themselves as green patches. Since they aren't destroyed by cooking, they must be removed. Green potatoes are becoming much too common, the result of displaying washed potatoes in see-through plastic, or loose under bright supermarket lights. If you see them, complain.

Washed potatoes are, it seems, here to stay. This is a mixed blessing, as they keep much less well. 'Washed potatoes are like milk,' says Angus Wilson of Wilson's Potatoes. 'Treat them carefully, keep them cool, and don't expect them to last for more than a few days.'

Floury potatoes are still a particularly Irish passion. I've never heard that disparaging term 'soapy' applied to spuds anywhere but here. English cookbooks, for example, describe Cara (a waxy potato by Irish standards) as floury, so bear that in mind when using potato recipes from elsewhere. True waxy salad potatoes are not failed floury spuds, but a different thing altogether: they should be nutty, aromatic and slightly sticky when cooked. Irish people are suspicious of them, so they are extremely hard to come by here. That accounts for the abysmal quality of most Irish potato salads. Floury potatoes disintegrate to a gritty mush if you try to toss them in a dressing, whereas waxy potatoes hold their shape — and absorb infinitely less dressing.

Varieties and Seasons

First earlies The first of the year's new potatoes: usually **Home Guard**; **Colleen** is another variety, not nearly as good.

Second earlies Appear in summer: **British Queens** are the most common.

Maincrop Potatoes which are harvested in autumn and stored for the rest of the year:

Golden Wonder A tremendously floury, very well-flavoured old-fashioned potato.

Kerr's Pink Floury too, with an attractive pink tinge in the skin.

Records Also high in dry matter — and in flavour when they are good.

Pentland Dell Appreciated by the trade because it washes well; less floury and more popular with younger people, I'm told.

Cara A reasonably waxy, new Irish-bred variety.

Rooster The newest potato, bred here and launched in 1993. Pretty floury and a reasonable all-rounder. It's less likely to be poor, but I've never tasted a superlative one either.

'New' potatoes From Italy and Cyprus, available from very early in the year. They are waxier than any common Irish variety and so are good in salads, but almost invariably lack flavour for simple boiling.

Salad potatoes **Pink fir apples** (long, pink-skinned and knobbly) French salad varieties such as **Charlotte, La Ratte** or **Roseval** are rarely spotted in Ireland.

Storage

Potatoes should be stored in a cool, dark, humid place. The fridge may be too cold and is certainly too dry — they will wrinkle. Never store in plastic. If they're washed, don't expect them to keep for long.

Cooking tips

1. Irish floury varieties are best never boiled. Steam them instead. That way, if they crack, they can still cook through without turning to sludge.

You don't need expensive equipment: a petal steamer fits into any size pan.

2. Beware recipes from other countries which suggest you peel potatoes before boiling or steaming. Irish floury varieties aren't suitable for this. Always steam in their skins, then peel.

3. If you can't get true, waxy, salad potatoes, immature 'baby roasters' are the best substitute for a potato salad: they're a good deal less floury than their larger brothers. Alternatively, use Italian or Cyprus new potatoes, again selecting the smaller ones.

Safety?

Potatoes may be given sprout suppressant post-harvest treatments to help preservation. Because we eat a lot of potatoes, some commentators have suggested that treated potatoes could be a significant source of pesticides in our diets. However, most distributors are switching to cold-storage facilities, in which potatoes keep well without having been treated.

There is no requirement for retailers to inform you whether or not potatoes have been treated. Potatoes sold early in the season are unlikely to have received treatments, since sprouting problems only really begin in January. After January, you might prefer to check if the potatoes were treated; if no information is forthcoming, opt for potatoes from cold storage, or buy organic.

Radishes

Very refreshing, sparking with crunch and peppery heat: odd that they are so rare here, since they do well in our cool climate. Most of the time, all you can find are tired little red bullets in plastic cornets from Holland. When you spy a truly fresh bunch, leaves still on, snap them up.

Cooking tips

1. They make a wonderful hors d'oeuvre, just with fresh-baked bread and a pat of butter.

2. Radishes add an excellent touch of spice sliced into a salad.

Shallots

These narrow, elegant relatives of the onion have a more delicate flavour, excellent for delicate sauces and for using raw. As with onions and garlic, they should be rock hard, not at all spongy. Store as onions.

Spinach

Look for bright green leaves which should, as Jane Grigson memorably put it, squeak as you stuff them into your string bag. Younger leaves are smaller, arrow-shaped and much more tender, good enough for salad. Remove stalks quickly by holding the stalk in one hand and ripping the leaf off with the other, along the length of the stalk.

Spinach is one of the very few vegetables where frozen is nearly as good as fresh. Frozen spinach in leaves or individual portion clusters is a much better option than the more common bricks, which take an age to defrost.

Safety?

See Nitrates, page 131. Eat spinach in season — summer. Or use frozen, which will have been harvested in season and thus have much lower nitrate levels.

Tomatoes

A good tomato is a wondrous thing. The bitter scent of the vine clings to its ruddy skin. The flesh is red and sweet. Inside, seeds quiver in a delectable, wobbly jelly . . .

Sound familiar? No? How could it? Most tomatoes on sale nowadays bear no relation to this. They are, you understand, not *meant* to be tasty. Often as not, they are not even grown in soil, but conjured up in soil substitutes (rather like anorak filling), with a liquid feed of fertilisers and other nutrients. They grow fast. They have damage-proof skins. They are picked green and rock-hard, so that they can be mechanically harvested and selected, transported easily, and poured into supermarket display boxes with little more care than a skip-load of rubble.

Quality

The result is a wan, watery copy of the real thing. Even if you take it home and keep it for a week to let it turn red, the age at which it was ripped from the umbilical vine means it can't get any tastier. Shoppers have to bear some responsibility for this situation. If you want a cheap tomato in January, that kind of a tomato is what you will get.

However, all is not lost. 'Grown for flavour' is an extraordinary label to see on food (what are they growing the rest for? you wonder). Still, its appearance in the last few years is no less welcome for that. Tomatoes, like almost all other fruit and vegetables, are rarely graced with varietal labelling, which doesn't help the search for flavour. All is not lost, though, since growers agree that a vital factor in tomato flavour is where and how it was grown. Tomatoes need to struggle a bit in order to taste good; and they need sun.

Varieties

The range of types available now increases your chances of finding good ones:

Dear little **Cherry** tomatoes are the tastiest of them all, gelatinous and tartly sweet. They also cost a bomb, sadly; but for flavour, they can't be beaten.

Plum tomatoes are the ones used for canning. They have much less jelly inside (which is where a tomato carries its flavour, not in the flesh), so they can often be rather disappointing taste-wise. Good for cooking, though, because of that bulk.

Vine tomatoes burst on the scene a few years ago. They look beautiful. They are always much riper than the ordinary ones. They smell heavenly; the scent of the vine really does cling to them. Do they taste better? Not necessarily, so buy cautiously.

Beef tomatoes may be good for stuffing, but they're rarely great for eating. As for the **'ordinary'** tomato, there's nothing wrong with it in principle. Buy in season, which means mid- to late summer, and from southern sunny countries with less sophisticated growing techniques (e.g. the Canaries rather than Holland). They can be good. And if they are, tell your shopkeeper!

Look for varietal labelling. Any shop which cares enough to tell you what they're selling is likely to care about how it tastes. (Best cherry tomatoes: **Gardener's Delight, Sweet 100**. Best others: **Delice, Melrow, Ailsa Craig**.)

Tomatoes should be reasonably red, firm but not hard, and certainly not squashy. A red tomato is no guarantee of flavour, because you can't know when it was picked and how it was grown, but it's more hopeful than a green one. Ignore 'tomatoes for tomorrow' signs, which really mean 'tomatoes which will be red in several days but won't have much flavour anyway'.

Storage

Not in the fridge, which stops them ripening and deadens the flavour. At room temperature. If they need a little ripening, normal indoor light is better than the oft-quoted sunny windowsill.

Cooking tip

Many recipes specify fresh tomatoes for sauces, but with the watery tasteless ones usually on offer, it's better to opt for tinned for most of the year.

11

Convenience foods

onvenience or hype? The freezer and the chill cabinet are booming. Packed to the gills with ready meals, their promise is seductive. Lusciously photographed, lovingly described, they hold out the prospect of eating delicious foods we'd find so difficult to cook.

Much of this promise turns out to be false. There's an amazing amount of junk in the freezer and chill cabinet these days. But even among the better foods, most lack fresh, direct flavours. The reason for this is simple. Cook-chill foods may be brilliantly packaged. But underneath the attractive box they really are only yesterday's — or last week's — dinner, prepared on a vast scale, portioned out and chilled until you heat it up. Don't expect too much!

Methods and ingredients have to be changed to allow for the scale of the cooking. That's why you may see a string of ingredients on the list which you don't recognise, like modified starch, emulsifiers and so on. They are there for the convenience of the processor, not because they do the food any favours. Even where preservatives are not used, the food often has a 'samey' flavour: that reheated taste.

Which Ones to Buy?

What these foods *definitely* do, however, is clear space in your head. No cooking to think of. At times, this is bliss!

Unfortunately, giving you guidelines on where to go for these is difficult. An extensive taste test which I conducted for the *Sunday Tribune* in early 1998, with some ready-meal enthusiasts, revealed that no one retailer produces reliably good food across the board. Food from each retailer was found in both best and worst categories. Getting good food from these meals entails trawling through an awful lot of indifferent gunk before you happen on something which tastes fresh out of a kitchen.

These were some of the tasters' conclusions:

1. *The less they do for you, the better it tastes.* Meals with raw ingredients usually came out better than fully pre-cooked grub.

2. *Stews and curries should all be delicious. Should be.* A stew lovingly prepared on a large scale, and reheated days later, should be absolutely delicious, with flavours having mingled and matured in the interim. All too often, though, the flavours are thin and nasty.

3. *Avoid anything calling itself a stir-fry.* It's not a stir-fry; you can't stir-fry, except in small quantities. It's a stew with bits cut small. And Chinese stir-fry flavours don't usually work well on reheating anyway.

4. *Pasta is a no-no.* While lasagne and cannelloni may be all right, steer clear of simple pasta dishes at all costs. Re-heated penne is just horrid.

5. *Don't expect these foods to save you time.* They claim to be time-saving. But many of these dishes are at their best reheated in the oven. Preheating it, plus twenty minutes for heating the dish? 'I could cook pasta in ten minutes, and it would taste so much better,' was a constant refrain. Or take a frozen, crumbed fillet of fish. Baking it, plus heating the oven, comes to about forty-five minutes. You could fry the fresh fish in three minutes flat.

6. *Don't believe their cooking times.* Time and again, we found food would have burned if cooked for the time recommended on the pack. Time may need to be adjusted up or down for your oven.

7. *Look for assembled but not fully-cooked versions of dishes.* This saves you the work, but avoids that dreaded reheated flavour. Fish en croute which hasn't yet been cooked, or marinated meat which you will stir-fry yourself, and so on.

The unanimous winner in the taste test was a dish from Superquinn's Seafood Kitchen: cod in cheese and mushroom sauce, the sauce from the kitchens of the King Sitric in Howth. The uncooked fillet of fish looked most unpromising in a puddle of beige-coloured sauce. But when baked for twelve minutes in a hot oven, it revealed itself to be fantastically-fresh fish in a delicious, finely-balanced sauce. It showed that the problem with most prepared food is not the idea itself, but the way it's done.

Some other dishes popular with tasters were Wild Boar Stew and Veal Stew with a cream sauce from Morton's of Ranelagh; and all-butter pastry Quiche, Orange-glazed chicken breasts and Mini chicken fillets with creamy white wine and grape sauce from St Michael.

Yet nine out of ten dishes tasted were rated 'disappointing' to 'inedible', and tasters said they wouldn't buy them.

Quick yet Tasty Cooking

The galloping ready-meal phenomenon can leave the impression that cooking is a difficult, time-consuming process. Of course it can be. But cooking can also be ultra-speedy. Dinner, prepared from scratch, can be on the table in ten or twenty minutes. And preparing food can be so restorative, a chance to smell a few smells, to do something tactile after a day at the desk, in the car, or being harried by the kids.

I would say that, wouldn't I? Well, yes, I would, because I love to cook. There's a more fundamental issue underlying all this, though. It concerns me that if we buy these foods on a regular basis, we have surrendered control over what we eat. Now, it's up to the manufacturer to choose the ingredients. How much do we trust them? They will need to assure quality of course. But also to ensure themselves a profit. And that means choosing the cheapest food available.

Labelling is no comfort here. We have no way of knowing where they have sourced their ingredients. A pre-pack lasagne, 'product of Ireland', could have bought its ingredients from anywhere.

Healthy Meals?

Be wary of 'healthy' claims, which are becoming more common. Many of these meals when analysed have been reported to contain too little vegetable, carbohydrates and fibre and too much salt. 'Ninety per cent fat free!' sounds encouraging. Until you think that this means ten per cent fat, which is quite high.

Tip to Remember

Go for the least processed version of a meal. Take the example of a chicken curry. Best results come from cooking meat and spices fresh yourself, but there mightn't be time for that. Next best? A jar of spice paste, a tin of tomatoes or coconut milk, and some uncooked chicken and an onion into the pan. Bottom of the list, with least immediacy of flavour, is usually the pre-cooked meal itself.

Keep them cold!

Cooked chilled foods have been linked with food poisoning from listeria. It is very important to keep them well-chilled: don't shop for them at lunch time and leave them in the boot of the car until you get home from work. Be sure that the place you buy them from keeps them below 5°C; be sure your fridge is below 5°C too; don't eat them after the best-before-date; and above all reheat them until piping hot all the way through.

Convenience from Fridge and Freezer

The fridge and freezer do, of course, supply some really great convenience foods. But you'll eat better if you use them as a place to put handy ingredients for fresh ten-minute meals, rather than a storage depot for a week's dinners. Top of the list are the following.

Fridge

Eggs, crème fraîche, rashers, sun-dried tomatoes packed in oil, olives, black olive paste, pesto, scallions, fresh herbs, fish fillets, pork, beef or lamb mince.

Vac-pac is an option not considered nearly often enough, except perhaps by people bringing two weeks' worth of sausages and rashers to Alicante with them. Yet it works very well indeed with meat, and even with fresh fillets of fish, keeping them fresh for many days.

Freezer

Buy packs of *spinach* which have single portions, not the bricks, which take forever to thaw. *Peas*, especially petits pois; they're often much sweeter than fresh, unless the fresh are only a few hours old. *Frozen vegetables* do not lose their nutritional value — indeed they may be better than ones which have been hanging around the shops for a few days, provided they have been frozen within a short time of picking. However there's a great loss in texture with most.

Berries Keep raspberries, black currants and blackberries in the freezer, but not strawberries, which go foamy.

Filo pastry — I can't enthuse about puff and shortcrust pastries, which are made with cheap, nasty vegetable fats. Why doesn't someone make them with butter?

Plenty of *ice-cream*!

Meat and fish? In general, meat and fish don't freeze very well. However, there are exceptions. In the fishy world, scallops and squid can be good, and smoked fish freezes better than fresh. Where meat is concerned, the smaller the better. Mince freezes very well; slivers for a stir-fry too; stewing meat is good; a roast would suffer.

Although we all prefer to set eyes on the fresh item, you're better off letting a good butcher or fishmonger do the freezing for you. The quicker the item is frozen, the less fibre damage it will suffer.

To thaw foods

Always thaw in the fridge, especially raw foods, whose texture can deteriorate if they defrost too rapidly.

See also Breaded fish, page 77, Breaded chicken, page 50, shellfish glazes, page 229. See also Chapter 12 The Larder, page 167.

`Convenience´?

The market for convenience foods is insatiable now, and anything which describes itself as saving you trouble seems to be fair game for the supermarket shelves. Again, in theory, this should pose no problem. But unfortunately food manufacturers all too often use the 'convenience' tag to dress up shoddy food laden with additives and cheap ingredients and sold to you at a huge mark-up. It may also be used to sell you a product which doesn't save you any time at all, yet means you use fewer fresh foods in your cooking.

Pesto sauces are a good example. At their best, they are a wonderful convenience, enabling you to have a fragrant plate of freshly-cooked pasta on the table in no longer than it takes to boil the pasta and grate a little cheese. But most taste very unpleasant. Why is this? Because the true ingredients of good pesto: basil, pine nuts, olive oil, parmesan cheese, don't come cheap. So cheap substitutes are used: tasteless oils, rancid nuts, bitter cheese, and all sorts of additives (see Chapter 16 Labelling, page 220 for more on this).

Don't be fooled by the hype. True convenience foods are those which have bags of flavour, so you don't have to do much to them.

12

The Larder

In this chapter I have listed many of the foodstuffs I consider essential ingredients for a well-stocked larder. And some which you should avoid!

Baby Food

Commercial, prepared baby foods are a brilliant convenience. They are an expensive way to feed a child, but can be a lifesaver for a harassed parent. However, what's in it for the baby? Studies show that you need to choose the brands of baby food very carefully if you don't want to be giving your child a lot of unwanted stuff with her meal.

Gluey 'Fillers' and other Unwanted Extras

Ever wondered why most jars and dried baby foods taste so peculiar? It's not just because of the processing, although that can contribute. The main reason for the strange flavours and gluey textures of most commercial baby foods is their liberal use of low-nutrient 'fillers' — ingredients which bulk out food and have no nutritional value. Very handy for the manufacturer, not so good for the baby.

The strange flavour that these fillers impart is all the more unfortunate because there is emerging research that at the age of four to seven months, babies are setting a 'library' of tastes in their brains. Feeding them the unnatural flavours of processing aids is not conducive to developing good eating habits later!

A survey in 1997 by the London-based Food Commission included most baby food brands on Irish shelves. It concluded that parents should scrutinise labels very carefully before buying commercial baby foods.

These are the areas of concern:

Low-nutrient fillers

These starches and gums are used to thicken, to absorb added water and increase bulk. They are not a direct health hazard, but they replace genuine nutrient-rich food. Maltodextrin is the most common. This highly-refined starch forms a gluey paste, which is why it is also used to make envelopes and stamps sticky. It is devoid of vitamins, minerals and proteins. Some manufacturers have shown that such fillers are unnecessary. Most others still use them, however. Of baby foods surveyed, these contained low-nutrient fillers: Milupa dry packs (one hundred per cent); Farley's dry packs (ninety-four per cent); Heinz jars and cans (eighty-four per cent); Cow & Gate and Olvarit (seventy-three per cent); Hipp (twenty per cent); Baby Organix (nought per cent).

Too much sugar

Added sugar is not recommended for babies. It damages their teeth and gives them an even sweeter tooth than they already have naturally. It is not recommended to add sugars which aren't milk-based, or which don't already exist in a food (e.g. within fruit) to baby foods. The technical term for these is non-milk extrinsic sugars (NMEs). While they may have a place in desserts, they are particularly unacceptable in savoury products. Yet they were found in the following savoury baby foods: Cow & Gate and Olvarit (forty-six per cent); Farley's dried (thirty-six per cent); Milupa dried (twenty per cent); Heinz jars and cans (ten per cent); Hipp and Baby Organix (nought per cent).

Sugar may appear as: sucrose, dextrose, glucose, fructose, lactose, maltose, honey, fruit syrups, corn syrup and glucose syrup.

Gluten

Not recommended in foods before six months of age; babies find it difficult to absorb, and may develop allergic reactions to it. To prevent coeliac disease (rates are unusually high in Ireland), there should be no gluten in baby foods.

It was found in Farley's dried (thirty-seven per cent); Milupa dried (twenty-four per cent); Heinz jars and cans (thirteen per cent); Cow & Gate and Olvarit (two per cent); none of the others.

Gluten is found in wheat, rye and barley.

Misleading names

Misleading names for baby foods often trumpet nutritious ingredients on the front of the pack, yet include them in small quantities in the recipe. For example, Heinz Yoghurt dessert strawberry has more water in it than yoghurt. The water is thickened with cornflour and rice starch to give it the thick texture you would expect from a yoghurt.

Unsavoury additions

Often made to disguise a lack of flavour. Steer clear of anything with meat extracts, hydrolysed vegetable protein, yeast, vegetable extract and 'flavourings'. These don't do much for the rest of us, but they're particularly inappropriate for babies.

Read the label with great care when buying baby foods!

Pesticides

Although baby foods are exclusively made for consumption by an extremely vulnerable population, tests both in the US and UK regularly reveal that about fifty per cent are contaminated with pesticide residues. This is hardly surprising, since baby foods are made from foods grown by common methods, with standard levels of pesticide residues. See Children Are Most Vulnerable, page 204.

At the end of 1997, the European Parliament voted for pesticide-free baby food. It is now up to the Commission to implement this. Germany has led calls for zero levels in baby food. However, Commissioners from other countries, Ireland included, resisted; they want varying residue levels to be permitted. They have deferred the item from the Commission's agenda as a result.

Commission officials meanwhile say that variable levels would be extremely difficult to administer, since baby foods contain residues of up to 200 different pesticides, very few of which are harmonised at EU level. One official has said that it could take years to set different residue limits for every pesticide.

The question is unresolved as this book goes to press. It is unedifying to see authorities reluctant to implement proposals designed to protect the most vulnerable members of our population. It is *most* unedifying to see Ireland's green, clean food image being tainted by such a stance on the part of our Commissioner.

The only advice? Feed your baby organic baby food. Hipp, Baby Organix and some Cow & Gate are three brands currently available in Ireland — albeit sporadically.

Baby Formula Milk

Infant Formula Regulations, intended to support breastfeeding, mean that formula milk companies may not advertise, so the differences between baby formula milks are not widely perceived. However, if you plan to bottle-feed your baby, it is worth knowing that the current state of scientific thinking suggests that long-chain polyunsaturated fatty acids (LCPs) are essential for brain, eye and nervous tissue development in babies. Two in particular are considered important, AA and DHA; these LCPs are found in breast milk. Previously, they were found only in formulas intended for premature babies, but evidence now suggests that full-term babies may benefit from them too, in the first few months of life.

At present, these LCPs are not a required ingredient in baby formula milks, although the WHO, the British Nutrition foundation and COMA, the UK Department of Health's advisory body, recommend their inclusion.

As this book goes to press, the only baby formula milks in Ireland which include both LCPs (derived from egg lipids), in the proportion in which they occur in breast milk, are Aptamil First and Aptamil Extra. (Milupa, the company which makes these milks, uses the term 'Milupan' to cover these two LCPs in an attempt to simplify the issue.)

Farley's formula contains LCPs (derived from fish oils), though in slightly different proportions, using an AA precursor instead. Some nutritionists suggest that the proportions are crucial, others that this difference is not significant. Meanwhile, Cow & Gate and SMA say they are not yet satisfied that the scientific evidence justifies adding LCPs. If you are not breastfeeding during a baby's first few months, seek current nutritional advice.

Chocolate

The addictive flavour is only part of its appeal. The other is the unique melting quality of cocoa butter. (Treating chocolate in order to create a smooth bar was a process only discovered in the nineteenth century.) It melts unusually slowly, and does so at human blood temperature, which is why chocolate is literally, lusciously, melt-in-the-mouth.

The right balance of cocoa for flavour and cocoa butter for texture is one of the crucial factors of good chocolate. These two ingredients together are described as *cocoa solids*, and are given as a percentage of the chocolate. Other ingredients in chocolate: *sugar* is essential to make this bitter food palatable. Milk chocolate contains *milk solids* (dried or condensed milk). *Lecithin* is an emulsifier (considered safe). Chocolate may be flavoured with a little *vanilla*. Look for ones with natural rather than artificial vanilla flavouring.

But is it Chocolate?

The bar of chocolate has divided European nations into two bitter camps for a quarter of a century, with no sign yet of resolution.

Those EU nations with a long history of fine chocolate-making (such as France, Belgium, the Netherlands, Luxembourg and Spain) don't allow any fat other than cocoa butter in chocolate. As we saw, cocoa butter is what gives chocolate its unique smooth, melting texture. However, it's expensive, and there are many European countries, Ireland included, which consider five per cent vegetable fat an acceptable addition. Unsurprisingly, they are not impressed with the thought of being forced to describe their long-standing favourites as 'chocolate-flavoured confectionery with added vegetable fat' or some such Euro term.

Vegetable fat makes for cheaper chocolate — and for a somewhat stodgier, stickier bar. Chocolate without vegetable fat snaps more crisply when hard, and melts more smoothly on your tongue or in the cooking. Whatever your preferences for eating, you should always seek out chocolate with no vegetable fat for cooking with — it works better.

Chocolate Terms

Unsweetened chocolate is utterly bitter. Often used in American recipes, it is hard to find in Ireland.

Plain, *dark*, *semisweet* and *bittersweet* are more or less interchangeable and are the ones most used in baking and desserts.

Couverture (or *coating* or *dipping*) chocolate has more cocoa butter; it melts and flows most easily and is best for chocolate coatings.

'*Cooking chocolate*' is, you may have noticed, no longer called chocolate. This nasty stuff is best avoided. It is just flavoured vegetable fat, and has none of the attributes of chocolate.

Best Buys

For baking and desserts, buy a *dark chocolate* with at least forty-five per cent cocoa solids, preferably more. Up to seventy per cent is available; most chefs generally use fifty-five per cent. The seventy per cent is pricier, but delivers a wonderful intensity of flavour for real chocaholics.

Price is no guide to quality, however. Large 500g bars of Belgian chocolate are often the best value. Lindt Excellence (seventy per cent) is good; Cadbury's 1848 Poilane Noir (sixty-four per cent) is generally available. It does have a slightly synthetic flavour for eating, but marks a great improvement for the Irish cooking chocolate scene — preferable to Bournville, which contains a mere thirty-four per cent cocoa solids.

The best *milk chocolates* have about forty per cent cocoa solids and no vegetable fat; Irish milk chocolate bars only have around twenty per cent cocoa solids. *White chocolate* has only cocoa butter and thus no chocolate flavour. Avoid ones which use vegetable oils or fat.

To store

In a cool, dry place. Chocolate may develop a slight white 'bloom' on it but this, although not pretty, is not a problem.

Safety?

The production of cocoa crops uses very high levels of pesticides. The residues left in chocolate are minimal, but the ethical issue for workers with poor conditions is, as with all such food production for the developed world, immense. See Chapter 16 Labelling, page 220, on Fairtrade brands.

Cooking tip

To melt chocolate, heat away from direct heat — in a bowl set over simmering water, or in a very low oven, or in the microwave. Wipe the inside of the microwave dry first. Droplets of water can cause the chocolate to 'seize' and harden.

Condiments and Sauces

Some favourite brands:

Soy — Kikkoman.

Mayo and Ketchup have to be Hellmann's and Heinz, though Maille do a pretty good mayonnaise too.

Mustard: Dijon — Maille or Champs. English — Colman's. Other favourites are West Cork Herb Farm Tarragon and Green Peppercorn.

Indian, Thai and Chinese spice pastes and sauces — Pataks, Amoy, Lee Kum Kee.

Dried Fruit

Your Christmas baking will taste very different if you pay attention to the fruit you buy. Some is shrivelled, gritty and sad. The best is plump, sweet and promising.

Look for named varieties, such as Lexia raisins, Agen prunes, Hunza apricots.

Agen Prunes

French Agen prunes are particularly tasty, with an almondy flavour around the stone.

Hunza Apricots

These are from a valley between Pakistan and Afghanistan. They look most unpromising, like wrinkled pebbles. They need soaking and very gentle cooking; a delectable, intense honeyed flavour results.

Safety?

Much dried fruit is treated with sulphur dioxide to preserve it; this common preservative is used in particularly high concentrations in dried fruit. It can cause allergic reactions, including shortness of breath, and can even be fatal.

Unfortunately, it is this preservative which keeps the fresh colour in dried fruits, so unsulphured specimens are darker and also have a more caramelly flavour. The sulphur dioxide is removed in cooking or baking, but if eaten raw, dried fruit should always be of the unsulphured variety. This is particularly important for children and pregnant women, who are often recommended dried fruits as 'healthy' alternatives to sweets. Check the label. If it just says 'permitted preservative', it's likely to be sulphur dioxide.

Candied Peel

The chopped stuff in supermarkets tastes worlds apart from the real thing. It should have an intense and identifiable flavour of citrus rind. Look in good delis at Christmas for real peel in recognisable wedges. Ideally, this should be made from untreated citrus fruits (see Post-Harvest Treatments, page 131). You're unlikely to find this, though. Making your own, with untreated fruit peel, is an option — but a small quantity of the stuff once a year isn't going to do much harm.

Gelatine

Pure animal protein, used to make jellies and set other puddings, as well as the occasional savoury aspic. A lot of people don't really want to know this, but the base for those wobbly fruit-flavoured bowls of dessert from our childhoods is derived from meat bones and other tissue. (This came as an alarming surprise to many who weren't aware of the origins of this clear, tasteless food at the time that BSE first appeared; vegetarians were especially dismayed to discover that yoghurts were often stabilised with gelatine without its necessarily being listed on the ingredients panel. (See BSE, page 10.)

Much gelatine nowadays is derived from pigskin. Clearly this is not desirable if you are a vegetarian. Omnivores, however, might as well stop being squeamish: if you love crispy crackling on a pork roast, what's the problem with eating a different form of the same food in a jelly? (Consider yourself lucky. If you were a nineteen-century cook, you'd have to boil calves knuckles to extract the stuff . . .)

Vegetarian alternatives to gelatine are *agar-agar* and *carrageen*.

Grains and Pulses
Couscous

Just to be difficult, couscous is not really a grain at all, but rather the finest pasta imaginable, made from durum wheat and rolled into grain-shapes. However, it's cooked like a grain. The word refers both to the pasta and also to the Moroccan dish on which it's based, an aromatic and highly-spiced meat or vegetable stew. There are two types of couscous: *traditional* requires lengthy, careful cooking; *instant* or *quick-cooking* is very easy: just soak in boiling water, then fluff with a fork. A bland, background food to dishes with lots of sauce.

Bulgar (or Burghul)

A Middle-Eastern staple, bulgar is a tasty, nutty grain, and one all busy cooks should get to know. You may have encountered this cracked wheat in tabbouleh, a salad with parsley, tomatoes and mint. It cooks particularly quickly, since it has been par-steamed, so all it needs is soaking in boiling water. A very good substitute for rice.

It is most important to buy dried pulses in a shop which has a speedy turnover and which buys only from the most recent harvest. Otherwise you may be boiling them for many hours and find they still aren't soft.

Herbs and Spices

There are only a few herbs which retain some of their character when dried; most are quite hopeless.

- Good dried are: bay, oregano and thyme.
- Basil, coriander, tarragon, sage, chives, parsley, mint and lemon grass are particularly pointless dried; if you can't get them fresh, use something else instead.
- Look for whole spices where possible, grinding them yourself just before use in a pestle and mortar, or an electric coffee grinder, for most aroma.

To Store

All dried herbs and spices should be stored in airtight containers away from heat and direct sunlight. Keep those you use frequently near the cooker in small containers.

Honey

Check the label carefully. Honey can be fantastically fragrant, redolent of wildflower pastures, or just quite flat. 'Produce of more than one country' means you are getting a blended commodity. Perfectly fine, but nothing to set the world on fire.

Honey from specific flowers can be very tasty, although the accuracy of these claims is something I've always wondered about — how can you control where the bee sucks?

Safety?

It is recommended not to serve honey to infants under a year old, since it can sometimes contain tiny quantities of botulism spores.

Jams and Marmalades

Here's a minefield. The EU spent years trying to come up with laws defining recipes in this area, and seems to have given up — and moved away from 'recipe law' to do with foods generally. Part of the problem is harmonising the culinary habits of so many different countries — the Portuguese, for example, are fond of jam made with carrots, which led to all those 'EU says carrot is a fruit' headlines.

So far, however, they have laid down three different types of jam: standard, extra and reduced sugar, and the laws refer to percentages of fruit and sugar permitted. Jams must show on the label how much fruit and how much sugar they contain per 100 g. If you've ever wondered why these often add up to more than 100, it's because fruit itself contains sugars.

Standard Jam

This one must have at least thirty-five per cent fruit and at least sixty per cent sugar. Sulphur dioxide is a permitted preservative, so check the label (see Dried Fruit, page 173).

Extra Jam

Must contain at least forty-five per cent fruit and at least sixty per cent sugar — whole fruit, not purée or juice, both of which are allowed in standard. No colourings or flavourings are allowed, but sulphur dioxide is (though the maximum is one-tenth of that permitted in Standard).

Reduced Sugar Jams

Must have less than sixty per cent sugar.

The above are the only terms which have any legal meaning. *Traditional*, *conserve*, *preserve*, *home-made* and *hand-made* are all rather dubious; nice-sounding, but with little significance.

Quality Jam

The most important guidance to quality jam is information which is not provided on the label. What volume was it cooked in? Was the pan open or closed? When was it made?

The problem is that large-scale processing is the very opposite of the processes which make for the best jams. Modern techniques boil up jams in vast quantities. They get less evaporation, but not usually better flavour. Rapid boiling in open pans is essential if flavour is not to suffer — hard to achieve when processing in huge quantities. Eating the jam when it is fresh is also a good way to get the best flavour, but large manufacturers tend to look for long shelf-life.

Look for a jam whose flavour you like! You are more likely to find tasty, fruity versions in your local market or deli, than on the supermarket shelf.

Nuts

I first tasted superb walnuts in a street market in Andalucia, and suddenly understood why anyone would want to include them in baking. They were mild, fresh and sweetly creamy, with none of that nasty bitterness which we expect from shelled walnuts here. Nuts come in quality grades like any other produce, and it's well-nigh impossible to find excellent shelled ones in Ireland — especially walnuts.

Nuts available here are often rancid. Where possible, taste before you buy. Once a pack is open, or if the packaging is not completely airtight, store in the freezer: this prevents the oils in the nuts from going rancid. For flavour, it's always better to use whole nuts and crack them yourself, although it is undeniably tedious. And if your walnuts are bitter — complain!

Look for 'wet' nuts, in season in the autumn, for a moist and fresh flavour. You'll have to crack them yourself, but it's worth it.

Cooking tip

To grind nuts in a food processor: where possible, use some sugar or flour from the recipe and grind with the nuts. This prevents them releasing their oils and going greasy.

Oils

Olive Oil

At its best, olive oil is simply the freshly-pressed juice of the olive. It has mouthfuls of flavour, wonderful aromas and is the crucial fundament of many Mediterranean cuisines.

That's enough to recommend it as far as I'm concerned, but there is also the health angle. The current accepted wisdom is that olive oil, since it contains primarily monounsaturated fats, has the ability to lower your 'bad' cholesterol and raise your 'good' cholesterol levels. See Margarine versus Butter, page 90, for more on this.

The claims being made for olive oil as a result of this are reaching the ridiculous, however. Such is the oil's cachet that a few drops of an industrially refined version, added to any food, appear to confer it with virtue. One company which produces a margarine which contains olive oil has even taken to implying, in its ads, that it is the elixir of eternal life and perpetual sexual function. Meanwhile, the EU is spending millions on advertising campaigns to promote olive oil sales — including sending out crazy recipes telling us to make 'healthy' Colcannon with olive oil rather than butter.

We need to retain a sense of perspective about the Mediterranean Diet. It is definitely a delicious thing, but its health-giving properties are rather more complex. Just a teaspoon of olive oil here and there is not going to ward off heart disease. Eating a great deal of fruit and vegetables is an integral part of it, and having a low-stress lifestyle is considered by some to be an important factor as well.

In addition, no distinction seems to be made between the different grades of oil when dispensing health advice. Yet the lowest-grade 'pure' oil is industrially refined, and has few of the virtues of ultra-natural, extra-virgin.

How to choose?

There's a panoply of wonderful oils out there, but plenty of dross as well. The selection can be befuddling, and the terminology confusing. The most important thing to remember when choosing an olive oil are your own tastebuds: the right oil for you is the one whose flavour you like.

The Categories

Olive oil comes in three categories. First is *olive oil*, formerly known, misleadingly, as pure olive oil. This is the lowest grade, a bland, colourless, flavourless industrially-refined oil which has little to recommend it. It contains an undeclared amount of extra-virgin oil to give it a little character. Refining also strips it of its natural vitamins.

The other two grades are the ones worth bothering about: *virgin* and *extra-virgin*. The difference between these two is technically defined as a 'percentage of oleic acid'. To you and me, lower acid levels in extra-virgin oil mean the olives were in better condition and were treated more carefully during harvesting and pressing. Extra-virgin oil, not surprisingly, is the more pure.

What kind of virgin?

The differences don't end with the various virgins. The flavour of olive oil depends on the variety of olive used, as well as how and when it was harvested. In addition, there are radically different types of extra-virgin, with prices ranging from £5 to £15-plus for a litre of oil.

The region This makes a difference. Oils from northern Italy tend to be very delicate, yellow, often with almondy aromas; their Tuscan counterparts are much greener and often have a peppery kick. French oils are typically sweeter and more rounded, often tasting of black olives. Spanish oils are often quite light but earthy; Greeks are muscley and assertive. So it's worth tasting around until you find one you like.

Where is it really from? You don't know. EU labelling regulations allow for a foodstuff to be called 'product of' if it has been significantly transformed in that country — and blending counts. So olive oil imported from Spain and bottled in Italy can be called 'product of Italy'.

Now that extra-virgin oils are at such a premium, fraud is all too tempting. In 1996, reports emerged in the US that European extra-virgins being sold there contained up to ninety per cent cheaper seed oils.

Extra, extra . . . There are two distinct types of extra-virgin olive oil. One is the commercial variety. These are blended oils from large bottlers in Europe. You haven't any guarantee of where the oil comes from, but the brand is your guarantee of flavour; oils are bought in and blended to match their expected characteristics. These oils cost around £5-£7 a litre and can range from very good indeed to so-so.

The other kind of extra-virgin is the single estate oil. These are the ones which usually carry the £15-plus price tags. What are you paying for? For something very special indeed. These oils will have been harvested by hand, with a comb and great care: there's half an hour's work per bottle of oil in the harvesting alone. Expect to find named varieties of olives, and also numbered and dated bottles. The oil inside has exciting flavours and aromas. The thing to remember is that it's a condiment, it's not for frying the onions. The other important point is that these oils are highly volatile, and they are at their best only for a year. So if you treat yourself to one, use it and enjoy it, don't hoard it for so long that its magic has evaporated.

Which kind of olive oil should I use?

Ideally, you could do with two or three different olive oils. A basic, commercial, reasonably-priced virgin or extra-virgin for frying, since heat destroys the finer, more volatile aromas; perhaps also a full-flavoured commercial extra-virgin for gutsy, mustardy salad dressings. And a single estate extra-virgin for pure, oil-and-vinegar only dressings as well as for finishing cooked foods: just try pouring a few teaspoons on a plate of hot lentils, or perhaps asparagus; that aroma rising in the steam is a dish fit for kings.

You Don't Need to Pay a Fortune

There's no denying that some of the special extra-virgins are pure magic. But one taste test in which I participated rated a £6 bottle of Portuguese Andhorina oil above many of the fancy £15-plus single estates. Use your taste buds. Seek out a shop which allows you to try. This is rarer than it should be — the only one I know of which does it regularly is Cooke's Food Hall. Toby Simmonds' Real Olive Company's olive stands at markets around the country have for the last five years consistently been one of the best sources of reasonable, fantastically-flavoured olive oils. Keep asking to taste! A good olive oil should taste full and it should not be 'greasy'.

Storage

Olive oil deteriorates with light and heat, so keep it in a cool dark place if you don't use it up quickly. Fine extra-virgins should come in dark bottles for that reason. Cold turns the oil lumpy and cloudy, but it runs again once returned to room temperature.

Vegetable, Seed and Nut Oils

Most of these are refined to be as neutral in flavour as possible and differ very little from each other — sunflower, rapeseed, corn, groundnut, etc. Various claims are made for their 'healthy' polyunsaturated natures vis-a-vis each other. My attitude is, they don't taste of anything, and too much fat isn't a good idea, so keep their use to the minimum. The ones to beware of are the unspecified 'vegetable' fats and oils on food labels which often conceal the use of cheap palm oil, the most highly-saturated fat of them all.

Some nut and seed oils are pretty expensive, but they, like single estate extra-virgin olive oils, are used by the spoonful for their intense flavours. Most commonly, these are Hazelnut, Walnut and Sesame.

Hazelnut and Walnut

These are used primarily in salad dressings, often diluted with a neutral oil or olive oil; they lend a fantastic aroma. Like the nuts from which they derive, they go rancid very easily, so store in a dark cool place and use up reasonably quickly. Don't buy them in clear containers: display in these may already have damaged them.

Sesame

This oil comes in two varieties. The French type is quite mild; the Asian variety has been toasted, for a much more intense flavour. Again, these are very prone to rancidity, especially once opened. A few drops of sesame oil is

enough to finish a dish — or to ruin it, if the oil was rancid, so keep a close
eye on your supply. Try adding a few drops of sesame oil and soy to a
vinaigrette as a dressing for an Asian-flavoured salad.

Sunflower Seed Oil
Less common, but absolutely delicious, is fine sunflower seed oil, sometimes
called extra-virgin or unrefined. This has a delicate nutty flavour, wonderful
for salad dressings and also for finishing food with.

Storage
All fine seed and nut oils should be stored in the fridge after opening.

The most recent 'health' angle on oils comes from US author Udo Erasmus.
Vegetable oils, he says, contain valuable essential fatty acids. But in processing,
these are destroyed. Standard refined oils, though often advertised as
'healthy', are 'value-subtracted', since their essential nutrients have been
removed (this includes vegetable, sunflower, groundnut or corn oils.) The oils
are produced by stripping seeds with solvent, then de-gumming them with
water and phosphoric acid, then refining them with caustic soda, then
bleaching with Fuller's earth and deodorising with steam.

Erasmus only recommends extra-virgin olive oil, since it is cold pressed,
not industrially refined.

Olives
'A taste older than meat, older than wine. A taste as old as cold water.' Thus
Laurence Durrell summed up the elemental appeal of this noble fruit of the
Mediterranean. Black olives are the ripe ones; green are (usually) picked
earlier. Green olives should have a fresh, nutty flavour; black ones are softer,
far more complex; savoury and winey.

Unstoned olives have far more flavour than stoned ones. Look for olives
named by variety, rather than by flavouring or filling.

When is a Black Olive Not a Black Olive?
There are olives which look black, but which are strangely tasteless; you'll
usually find them in brine, in supermarket jars or tins. These are actually

green olives blackened by the curing process, and have nothing to recommend them as far as I'm concerned. Avoid them if a recipe calls for black olives — the result will be sadly lacking in oomph.

How was the Olive Cured?

If you've ever plucked an olive from its silvery-leafed tree while on holiday and bitten into it, you'll have discovered that all olives need to be treated in order to become edible. Curing the olive diminishes the naturally-occurring bitter oleuropein in them. How this is done makes for some of the huge differences in olive flavours.

Lye-curing

This method, known to the Romans, works very quickly (so is loved by processors) to remove most bitterness from the olive. It leaves an olive which tastes of very little. It's the kind most often found in jars in supermarkets. Some Spanish and most American olives are treated this way. 'Black' olives (sometimes referred to as 'processed' black olives) have been lye-cured and then oxygenated to cause them to turn black. You can recognise them by their uniform blackness through and through. Real, ripe black olives come in all shades, from mottled mauve to deepest dark, and the flesh is usually lighter than the skin.

Salt-curing

This is done either in a wet brine or in a dry-cure. Either way, it takes longer, and it means that the olives ferment while they cure. The result is an olive which has real, olivey flavours. The brine-cured olives (green or black) will look plump and smooth; the dry-cured ones (black only) are as wrinkled as your fingertips after a long soak in the bath.

After curing, the olives may be further preserved in brine, or in olive oil, with or without flavourings. These also affect the flavour of the olive, but are less crucial than the initial curing method.

Cooking tip

To stone olives quickly, squash with the heel of your hand or roll over them with a rolling pin.

Pasta
Dried Pasta

This is not a poor relation to the fresh; not according to the Italians, anyway, and they ought to know. Good dried pasta has a lively flavour and a firm, bouncy texture when cooked. Bad dried pasta is impossible to cook 'al dente'; it collapses to sticky sludge no matter how carefully you cook it. The best brands are Italian. Two widely-available excellent ones are De Cecco and Barilla.

Cooking tip

Use a full litre/1¾ pints of water for every 100 g/4 oz pasta you cook and it will be much less stodgy than you often encounter it; also use one teaspoon salt for every litre of water. And never drain any pasta until completely dry, or it will be sticky no matter how well it's cooked. It should remain a little slippery.

Fresh Pasta

This can be sublime, when made well: light, tender, slippery. Almost all fresh pasta available in Ireland, even the pricier stuff, is plain nasty: heavy and gummy, poor quality and bad value, considering how expensive it is. Much of the time, you'd be better off with a good dried pasta.

Cooking tip

Fresh pasta is usually cooked in seconds rather than minutes; treat packet instructions with scepticism.

Filled Pastas

Whether fresh, long-life packaged, or dried, filled pasta varies from delicious instant food to dire dumping ground for revolting ingredients. Pick your brand and check ingredients with care; the dried ones are usually worst.

Rice

Long grain rices

Mostly used for savoury cooking, these come in several different varieties:

Straightforward long-grain rice

Perfectly OK, but essentially characterless and bland; its main virtue is cheapness. It needs lots of seasoning or sauce.

Basmati rice

Good-quality Basmati from the Himalayan foothills of India can be exquisite, with a penetrating perfume which is released as it cooks. It has the elegant habit of not swelling plump when cooked, but rather doubling in length instead. It cooks to quite dry, separate grains. Brands matter a good deal here. Tilda is very good, if pricey in tiny supermarket packs. I find Roma disappointing considering the premium price; it seems to me to lack flavour. Likewise, I find that Uncle Ben's Boil-in-the-Bag Basmati does not deliver that distinctive basmati flavour or aroma.

Your best bet? Buy basmati, e.g. Tilda, in large bags from Asian food suppliers, when it will cost the same as ordinary long-grain from the supermarket.

Thai fragrant rice

Less well-known but worth trying is Thai fragrant (Jasmine) rice, another Asian long-grain. Despite its name, its aroma is less pronounced than basmati. It has a light, moist stickiness which I find addictive — less sauce needed to accompany it. Slightly cheaper than basmati, it's my everyday rice.

Short-grain rices

With their stubby, rounded little grains, these rices are used around the world for both sweet and savoury dishes.

Pudding rice

This is right for rice puddings, but not for the famous Italian risottos.

Risotto rice (Arborio, Vialone or Carnaroli)

These are grown in the Po Valley in northern Italy and cook differently: starchier than other rice types, they can retain their shape over a long cooking time, to gradually become infused with all the flavours which are added to the pot — and still stay firm (al dente) in the centre. Whether you think the resulting dish is sumptuous or upmarket porridge depends on your perspective — Madhur Jaffrey once disdainfully compared risottos ('peasant dishes') most unfavourably to the fine, aristocratic pilafs of India and the Middle East!

Calasparra rice

Spanish Calasparra rice, expensive and with its own *Denominacion de Origen*, is for paellas, but I haven't seen it yet in Ireland. Substitute risotto rice rather than long-grain.

In Japan, they also use short-grain rice for savoury food, and love its stickiness. This is essential for sushi, and the rice is often called *sushi rice*.

Brown rice

This rice comes both short- and long-grain. With the outer husk intact, it contains more nutrients and fibre than its polished brethren; it is chewier, has a nutty flavour and takes about twice as long to cook.

Easy-cook rices

You would expect these to be a modern development. Not so. This golden rice has been made for centuries in India. Steamed before it is milled, its B vitamins are driven into the grain so they aren't removed by milling. Thus it is particularly valuable where nutritional considerations are paramount. It also retains separate grains no matter what you do to it. Flavour-wise, it doesn't compare to the finest of rices. It depends on your priorities.

Wild Rice

This is not a rice at all, but rather a water grass. It was once wild, gathered in north America by native Americans, but is now cultivated. Extremely expensive and very chewy, with a nutty, liquorice flavour. It's a bit dense to eat on its own, but works very well mixed in with another long-grain rice after cooking.

Camargue Red Rice

From the wetlands in that part of France, this rice is making the occasional appearance now. It too is chewy and nuttily earthy-flavoured. Beware — it dyes other foods its reddish-brown!

Salt

Most ordinary salt comes from underground sources, and is refined. It usually has anticaking agents added to it, and sometimes iodine. It is perfectly fine for most cooking uses. If you are watching your salt intake, you need to beware of pre-prepared and processed foods, which tend to have very high salt levels. This is particularly important for children, as many of these foods are aimed at them.

Sea Salt

As its name indicates, sea salt comes from various coastal sources. It is very variable in appearance and quality. Some comes as highly refined lumps, as hard as hailstones, which need to be ground in a salt mill. French *fleur de sel* is more or less the equivalent of the 'top of the milk' — the top crystals of shallow coastal salt pans which some claim have the taste of the breeze. It is usually grey, since it is not refined.

Maldon sea salt is a personal favourite for the table — its fine, tender crystals are like snowflakes, can be crushed between the fingers, and are very tasty, with a delicate crunch. Sea salt aficionados claim that it has more flavour and thus you use less of it. I've never found this to be the case. (I know of one food writers' taste test where the resounding winner was . . . Saxa).

Sauces (Bottled)

The quality of these varies from abysmal to reasonably good. They have mushroomed so enormously that I could fill this book checking them out. Check out the label for mysterious ingredients which make no appearance in any home kitchen. Be suspicious of 'cream-based' ones, which tend to be most unsuccessful — floury and sticky. In general, Indian sauces and tomato-based ones have the potential to be the best. See also Chapter 11 Convenience Foods, page 161.

Stock Cubes

These are a mixed blessing. Not many of us have time for home-made stock, not even those of us who believe passionately in the virtues of real stock. However, most stock cubes produce broth which is just nasty. The more delicate the flavouring of the food you're cooking, the more likely the cube taste is to penetrate.

If you look at the ingredients, stock cube flavour is not much of a surprise: most list salt or fat as their first ingredient; many rely on hydrolised vegetable protein, MSG and other flavour enhancers to substitute for real stock flavour. It is rare to see 'concentrated stock' actually listed.

Acceptable stock cubes are few and far between. Look for one which lists ingredients you might want to put into a pot yourself — meat, vegetables and so on. The chicken stock cube which I prefer is Kallo's Just Bouillon.

Sugar

A multitude of varieties of the little sweetener exists. Sugar, once the bugbear of a dieter's existence, has had something of a rehabilitation in recent years: it's now decreed to be bad for your teeth, but not so bad for your health, as long as you don't eat too much of it. It's very easy, if you eat a lot of pre-prepared or processed foods to do just that, though. A lot of sugar goes in, in the name of making the food more palatable for you. Read the label — and watch out for that common manufacturers' habit of listing sugars separately in several different forms, which can disguise a high overall sugar content. This is particularly worrying in the case of some children's foods. See Chapter 16 Labelling, pages 224–5.

Take 'reduced sugar' claims with a pinch of salt. One children's biscuit manufacturer recently produced a 'reduced sugar' version which was higher in sugars than the original! Read the label with care.

When is Brown Sugar Not Really Brown?

When it is white sugar with molasses added. Sugar is refined either from the cane, in tropical countries, or from sugar beet in temperate ones. The sugar beet, however, can only supply white sugar, so if it's a natural product with the best flavour you're after, check the label of brown sugars you buy. (Some like to point out that the natural brown sugars contain various trace elements which are not present in white, but if you're looking to sugar to supply these in your diet, then you're kidding yourself!)

True brown sugars have fantastic flavours running the gamut from mildest toffee all the way through to near-bitter liquorice. Billingtons are particularly good, with an intensity of flavour unmatched by other brands.

In baking, it's important to use the right sugar for good results.

Granulated

Granulated sugar is quite large-grained.

Caster

Caster is the same, only finer-grained, so it's preferable for baking, as the crystals dissolve more readily. (If you run out, whizz granulated in the food processor to reduce crystal size.)

Golden granulated and *caster* sugars are the first extraction of the sugar cane, with a delicate hint of that liquorice flavour which their darker relations have.

Dark Brown (or Rich Brown, or Dark Muscovado)

This sugar has a wonderful, dense, liquorice-like flavour. It comes from the second extraction of the cane. Soft and firm, it doesn't flow freely like granulated and caster sugars.

Soft Brown or Light Muscovado

A lighter, creamier version of the same. These sugars are wonderful for baking spicy cakes, for crumble toppings, and perhaps best of all just with a little cream on the side of a homely fruit tart, or sprinkled on plain yoghurt with fruit.

Demerara

Originally crystallised from sugar syrup, demerara can also be made by adding cane molasses to refined white sugar. Either way, it's a crunchy, big-crystal sugar, good for crunchy toppings for biscuits and fruits.

Vanilla Sugar

One of the cook's most useful companions. Bury used and unused vanilla pods in a large jar of caster sugar, then use this fragrant sugar for baking and for flavouring cream. Delicious.

Things in Tins

There are some things in tins which it is most useful to have to hand. *Chick peas* are the most successful tinned pulse, always good for two-minute hummus, or adding to soups or stews. Just remember to rinse them very well to get rid of that strange tinny odour.

Tinned fruit is not to be sneered at. It's really useful for baked desserts and saves you peeling and poaching fruit. Most successful? *Pears* and *apricots*. *Lychees* are a favourite for dessert, doused in fresh-squeezed lime juice with some of their syrup added.

Anchovies are essential — for Caesar salads, pizzas and pastas. Difficult to track down really good ones in Ireland. The salted ones are usually best. Ortiz fillets in olive oil are a favourite — pink-tinged and much less bristly than most.

Coconut milk for Thai and Indian curries. Some are revoltingly grey. Chaokoh (Asia Market) is pretty good. Or look out for *Coconut powder*, which is much more handy, since you only mix up as much as you need. *Tinned tuna* is not a love of mine, but if it's in good-quality olive oil it can be delicious.

Things Tomatoey

One of the great larder staples, utterly essential for pasta sauces and all kinds of stews and sautés. Don't spurn them for being tinned — the fresh ones we get here are vastly inferior in flavour most of the year.

To mitigate the slightly tinned flavour, add a couple of fresh tomatoes to a pasta sauce.

At any one time, I'm likely to have all of the following: tinned chopped tomatoes (without herbs — they're usually musty dried herbs); passatta (bottled or tetra packed purée, perfect for pizza); Grand'Italia sugo casa (made in Spain despite its name) is a great instant sauce for kids' pasta.

Generally, the best are Italian so check where the tomatoes came.from.

Vanilla

Vanilla is the fruit of a rambling orchid. The tropical vine is native to Central America. Its splayed flowers can only be pollinated by a single species of local bee or hummingbird, so when grown elsewhere it must be pollinated by hand. This makes it expensive already, but even then the work isn't over. When the pods are picked, they're tasteless and yellow. They must be cured in the sun and dried until they ripen and can release their vanillin. It can take a year.

No wonder that a single vanilla pod can cost a pound or more, and that attempts began last century to synthesise vanilla synthetically. Artificial vanillas are made from wood pulp leftovers, or coal tar derivatives, and you can spot them at thirty paces with their acrid knockout pong — precious little relation to the sweet, seductive smell of the real thing. Vanilla nomenclature can be confusing.

Vanilla Essence

Essence means the artificial stuff. Natural or nature-identical essence is still a poor imitation. Always use these by the drop.

Vanilla Extracts

These are distilled from the real pod, and vary from indifferent to superb. Good delis ought to sell them (though surprisingly few do). They cost more, and you need to use more: half to one teaspoon instead of a drop or two. Still, the flavour is incomparably better.

Vanilla Pod

Finally, the pod (Americans call it a bean), also to be found in good delis and some health food shops. Slit it open and infuse in hot liquid, letting the speckles swim out to flavour the food. But don't throw out the used pods — see Vanilla Sugar, opposite, for what to do with them.

Vinegars

Curiously, hardly any attention is paid to different vinegars. Yet they have the ability to make a hit of a dressing or a dish — or reduce you, literally, to tears.

Wine Vinegars

There are very few good vinegars available in Ireland. Smart bottles and bits of herbs predominate, but what matters more is how the vinegar was made.

The best wine vinegars are ones which start with good wines. Then they should be turned into vinegar by the Orleans method: they are put in barrels, where air and natural bacteria can get at them to turn the wine to vinegar; this takes over a month. Then the vinegar should be aged, preferably in wood, for several months. This last step in particular is almost always skipped, and skipping it makes for harsh vinegar, no more than it would for wine.

Price variations are huge, but are not necessarily a guide to flavour or quality. In a recent taste test, there was little difference between various supermarket vinegars despite large price differentials — £1–£2.50 for 500 ml — nor between these and many smart deli versions around £5 for the same amount. So shop sceptically. Best ordinary buy: mellow Champ's French white and red wine vinegars (currently in Terroirs, Donnybrook, Dublin; around £2 for 500 ml).

Champagne vinegars

These vinegars are, in effect, more expensive white wine vinegars. Of course they don't have the bubbles, so you're paying extra for the cachet.

Flavoured wine vinegars (tarragon, raspberry, etc.)

So often, these just mask nasty vinegar and yet command a very high premium for something so easily made: DIY is well worth the trouble here. Just add a sprig of tarragon to a bottle of good vinegar and wait a while.

Sherry vinegars

These vinegars taste distinctly of their origins. Their pronounced flavour can be strident: buy carefully, or mix with plain in your salad dressings.

Cider vinegar
Usually very mild, cider vinegar is a good bet when you don't want to overpower other ingredients.

Rice vinegar
Used in Asian cuisine, rice vinegar is clear, the mildest of all, with very little flavour; substitute cider vinegar if you can't get it.

Malt vinegars
Brown or white, these don't find much favour in my kitchen: very powerful, yet little flavour. Chutneys taste much less harsh and mature more quickly made with wine or cider vinegars. And just try chips sprinkled with wine vinegar . . .

Balsamic Vinegar
This is one of those trendy condiments which varies so much in quality that you can be left wondering what all the fuss was about.

Like extra-virgin olive oil, balsamic vinegar comes in two grades. One is an extraordinary concoction, a much-reduced, incredibly aromatic vinegar, aged for years in successive barrels of different woods which lend their flavour to the resulting syrup; it must by law be at least ten years old and the best may reach a century in age. It's called *aceto balsamico tradizionale*, and can cost from £20 for the tiniest bottle; it can reach into the hundreds of pounds.

The other balsamic vinegar (just plain old *aceto balsamico*) is quite different. It becomes dark not by lengthy ageing but by the addition of caramelised sugar; it's not syrupy, but pours freely. It is not a con, just a different product. It makes for milder, more rounded salad dressings than other wine vinegars. This is the one you will usually buy! Just remember that certain recipes, such as ones which recommend anointing strawberries with balsamic vinegar, are calling for the posh stuff . . .

13

How Was It Produced?

If you've read this far, you'll have realised that there are many questions hanging over the way we produce our food today.

The Roasted Carrot

S ome years ago, I did a series of taste-tests comparing organic carrots and standard, supermarket ones. Flavour differences varied from one grower and one batch to the next, and I found that the organic ones were not necessarily more flavoursome. But one thing remained the same. When roasted, the supermarket carrots deflated. The organic carrots always held their shape. I found this very puzzling.

I was later to learn that artificially-fertilised crops tend to have thinner cell walls and a higher water content than organically-grown ones. It was only a bunch of carrots, but I found it one of the most compelling arguments I've encountered for the superior quality of slow-grown food.

A Radical Experiment in Farming

What we eat nowadays is produced by a new system of farming. The few short decades since the middle of this century have brought revolutions in the way our food is grown. It is a system based not just on mechanisation, but also on new ingredients. Current agriculture is addicted to oil, in the form of artificial fertiliser, and to chemicals, in the form of pesticides and antibiotics.

Artificial fertiliser means extra-high yields can be wrested from the soil. Pesticides mean that weeds and pests can be attacked as never before. Antibiotics mean that animals can be persuaded to grow faster while eating less food.

These farming methods are often described as 'conventional'. Yet in fact they are new methods, a worldwide experiment which is beginning to show one problem after another. Many commentators now feel that these methods are fundamentally unsustainable. They are certainly the cause of many of the problems we face with our food today.

With these wonder ingredients, many farmers have abandoned traditional husbandry practices. Crop rotation, once needed to build the natural fertility of the soil, was deemed unnecessary. Now, fertility comes out of a bag. Traditional practices of caring for the health of animals are often abandoned, and antibiotics used as substitutes.

The Problems with Intensive Farming

Throughout the book, we have seen many of the problems which intensive farming methods bring. Using antibiotics to rear pigs and chickens has given us drug-resistant super bacteria. Using liberal doses of pesticides to grow crops leaves residues in our food, the health consequences of which are gradually becoming apparent.

At the heart of all these problems lies the fact that intensive agriculture is a fundamentally unhealthy system.

The Pesticide Treadmill

Artificially fertilised crops are encouraged to grow extra-quick. As a result, they have thin cell walls and are more prone to pest attacks and disease. In current systems, vast tracts of land are sown season after season with identical crops; this also encourages colonies of pests to arrive for feeding frenzies. Both these factors mean that these intensively-grown monoculture crops require more pesticides. Using more pesticides unfortunately also eliminates 'good' insects which act as predators on crop-damaging insects; once 'good' insects are killed, man inherits their work.

In addition, over 400 species of pest have now evolved resistance to the chemicals which once destroyed them. All this means that more pesticides are needed . . . and so the cycle continues. See Chapter 14 Pesticides, page 205, for more on this.

Unhealthy Animals

Animals kept in intensive, crowded conditions are more prone to disease. This is partly because they are stressed, and partly because they are exposed to so many germs when kept in very close quarters.

Stress is also increased by intensive breeding, which has selected animals for fast growth over all other characteristics. Antibiotics are often used the world over to 'clean up' sick animals and to encourage still further rapid growth in factory-farmed animals. All these factors mean that multi-drug resistant bacteria are emerging worldwide, a most urgent problem, which should be addressed immediately.

There is further concern that even without the use of antibiotics, intensive farming systems where animals are kept in crowded conditions can greatly increase the occurrence of rare genetic exchange of antibiotic resistance between bacteria.

Animal Welfare

I have no desire to be a vegetarian. But I do believe that the animals we grow for food have the right to be treated as living beings and not just viewed as units of production, to be converted as 'efficiently' as possible, irrespective of the effects on their well-being. We should not keep them in conditions where they cannot express natural behaviour, nor breed and rear them for commercial advantage in a way that damages their health. Both these practices are common.

Nutritional Value of High Yields

There is evidence that artificially-fertilised, high-yielding crops are less nutritious than organically-grown equivalents. It appears that plants forced with artificial fertilisers to give higher yields have fewer vitamins and trace elements, and more water. This area is woefully under-researched, something that is difficult to understand as the connection between food and health becomes ever more apparent.

We have such a rich diet in the developed world that this is not a critical issue for most of us. But in the developing world, lower nutritional values can mean the difference between health and dysfunction. It has been reported that high-yielding 'green revolution' crops have led to a generation of children with low IQ and reproductive capabilities, due to zinc and iron deficiencies.

Healthy food is much more than a matter of tinkering with fat and sugar levels. It is a fundamental question of how we look after the soil in which our food crops grow.

Environmental Problems

We haven't the room to go into these here, but intensive farming can have devastating consequences for the environment. It gives the illusion that the food it produces is cheaper, but that's because someone else is paying for the clean-up. Artificial nitrogen fertilisers enter water and food. Pesticides from both land and fish farming enter water.

Current farming practice does not count the cost of environmental capital, which can be degraded without being accounted for on the balance sheet.

Biodiversity

Perhaps the most worrying environmental consequence of intensive farming, and most likely one you've never heard about, is the loss of biodiversity.

It is hard to picture this in the developed world, where we are swamped with food, but crop experts are warning that our food crops face a potentially catastrophic loss of genetic diversity. Modern breeding methods for pure hybrid lines have reduced the variability of genetic material in the crops we grow, as farmers concentrate on just a few high-yielding varieties. And the take-up of these high-yielders the world over is crowding out the variety from which we will need to draw if crops are to be able to resist pests and disease in the future.

Indian farmers, for example, once grew over 30,000 rice varieties. Now it's estimated that just ten varieties cover three quarters of the country's rice-growing acreage. Meanwhile, eighty to ninety-nine per cent of US fruit and vegetable varieties available early this century are now extinct.

'The single greatest threat to our agricultural heritage comes from agriculture itself, from the replacement of traditional seeds and farming practices by modern, inbred crop varieties,' crop experts Cary Fowler and Pat Mooney conclude. And 'with the advent of biotechnology, the threat would seem to be even more severe and more immediate.'

The Irish, of all people, ought to know about the devastating consequences of relying for food on crops which have a very narrow genetic base. We starved as a result of it, 150 years ago.

Is There a Future?

It is difficult to understand why, faced with so many question marks over intensive farming methods, governments are not energetically pursuing research into alternatives. But this is hardly taking place. We pride ourselves on a green image in Ireland, but in fact what we have is a schizophrenic approach. We want to be seen to be green for the purposes of selling Irish food. But we also want to be competing on the world stage with maximum 'efficiency'. In some areas these desires are contradictory.

There are observers who firmly believe that in the early decades of the new millennium, Western governments will have to adopt organic farming strategies as the best methods for dealing with the twin challenges of food safety and agricultural and environmental sustainability. At present, however, there doesn't seem to be any indication of this. If anything, agriculture seems to be turning the other way: towards high-tech solutions such as genetic engineering or irradiation, to solve problems created by intensive farming. BSE should have taught us to apply the precautionary principle when it comes to different ways of growing and producing our food. It seems the world has yet to learn this lesson.

Blinded with Science

Science has a lot to contribute to farming and food, but it is a limited tool. Above all, the way it is used and interpreted needs to be questioned fundamentally. A simple scientific motto is this: absence of evidence is not evidence of absence. The logic of this is that innovations in food production should be rigorously tested. All too often, problems are only identified decades, or even generations, later.

Yet 'absence of evidence' is used time and again to reassure concerned consumers. It was the approach adopted for many years to BSE, and it is the approach adopted for pesticides and genetic engineering.

Those who think that science has clear, simple answers seem to have forgotten that we live in a world whose interconnected ecologies are far more subtle than we have even begun to chart. Good agriculture is not an appointment with the science lab, it is a dance with nature.

World Trade Pressures

You might think that GATT, the World Trade Organisation (WTO) and other such acronyms have little to do with you. Think again. The current trends towards global trade agreements means that it is becoming nearly impossible for countries to impose their own health standards for food. Countries such as Austria and Luxembourg which do not want genetically engineered crops or food are being accused of operating trade barriers.

Sustainable Alternatives
Safer Farming: A Middle Ground?

There are of course farmers who still respect the land and the soil. Farmers who do not reject innovations, but who approach them cautiously and who keep chemical use to an absolute minimum.

Unfortunately, agricultural policies of recent decades have done everything to discourage this approach. The Common Agricultural Policy (CAP) of the EU has always focused on yield, to the detriment of the quality of our food. In Ireland, beef has been an excellent example. The ready availability of intervention meant that it was so tempting for unscrupulous farmers to use growth promoters to boost the weight of cattle. They were just producing an anonymous commodity, not meat for their neighbours. On balance, Ireland benefited greatly from the CAP, but it was a regressive policy. The largest farmers benefited most, intensification was encouraged, and the environment and the quality of our food suffered.

Safer farming could provide an acceptable 'middle road', if quality was rigorously considered and chemical use regulated. It can certainly result in marvellous food; some wonderful producers do exist. But how can you find their food? You'll have to rely on luck, since there's no way in which the system encourages or rewards them.

REPS (Rural Environment Protection Scheme)

This is one of the results of the MacSharry reforms of the CAP. It rewards farmers for more extensive production and for caring for the environment, and is a step in the right direction.

The Swedish Farmers' Association Model

This was adopted by the Swedish government in 1992. The underlying philosophy is that good animal and plant husbandry, set within a less intensive production system, rectifies problems at source rather than attempting to cure symptoms. The policy is voluntary, yet it has already led to drops of fifty per cent in nitrogen use, eighty per cent of cadmium in phosphorus fertilisers and seventy per cent in pesticide use, since 1985. The Swedes have also banned the use of antibiotics as growth promoters, which has led to a thirty-five per cent reduction in antibiotic use.

Reduced Pesticide Use: IPM

Integrated Pest Management is a system which seeks to use natural predators instead of pesticides. It can be very successful in the closed environment of glasshouse cultivation — indeed it is the only alternative in some of these where pests are so resistant to chemicals now. See page 214 for more on this.

Organic Farming

At present the only coherent, sustainable alternative offered to current agricultural practice is organic farming. It is such a pity that this system still carries the baggage of subsistence-farming, 1970s sandal-wearing hippies, in so many people's minds. Good organic farming is a highly sophisticated system which can be profitable for the farmer and produce still-affordable food for the consumer. And it can produce food that is vibrant with flavour and wonderful to eat.

Organic farming uses crop rotation to build soil fertility. This also immediately reduces weeds, pests and diseases. Contrary to many people's image of organic food being bug-ridden, in fact organic farmers report fewer pests and disease, as well as weeds. That's not an accident — the farming system is designed to grow as healthy animals and plants as possible. There are strict rules regarding the medication of animals.

The fundamental principle of organic farming is respect for the soil and for animals. The further we move from that principle with current ways of growing our food, the more urgent is the need to examine alternatives. Unfortunately, organic farming is the Cinderella of Irish agriculture. A curious blindness means that it as almost completely unrecognised, and there is a sad dearth of government and research policy in the area. Organic cultivation is 'negligible' in Ireland, the Department of Agriculture says, 'Less than one per cent of the country's land.' Acreage is increasing, however. IOFGA's acreage has doubled since 1995 and nearly as much again is in conversion. But there is scant interest at policy level.

Elsewhere in Europe, attitudes are different. The Swedish Parliament has set a goal of ten per cent organic land by the year 2000, and there are already over 350 companies producing over 1500 organic food products. In Austria, which is quite similar to Ireland, with plenty of extensive grazing, the government made a concerted decision that the only way to survive as a small country in the EU was to specialise in organic farming. With targeted government support, they have increased their acreage tenfold in three years, reaching ten per cent already. In Germany, the market for organic food is growing by twenty-five per cent a year, and several agricultural professorships are devoted to organic agriculture. In Denmark, fifteen per cent of all fresh milk sold is organic; one agricultural school is devoted entirely to organic farming.

In Ireland, there's no policy, no research, no training. An Organic Consultative Committee does exist, but the Department of Agriculture has been unable to inform me how the Minister plans to act on its advice.

Organic farming may not provide all the answers, but failing to ask the questions is foolish. The madness of all this is that organic farming can be very profitable. Teagasc research has shown that organic beef suckler and sheep production is more profitable than its 'conventional' equivalent. In a feasibility study for The Organic Centre in Leitrim, an average Leitrim farm (income £2500 a year) was compared with a below-average sized and land quality organic farm (income £17,000). That's seven times as profitable. Research by the National Academy of Sciences in the US showed that well-run organic farms were more profitable than 'conventional' equivalents.

From the point of view of food eaters, the small organic sector is particularly frustrating, because it means economies of scale don't apply; prices in

Ireland are often a great deal higher than elsewhere in Europe for organic food. However, the argument that higher prices make organic food an indulgence only for those with money to spare just doesn't hold true. Research by An Bord Glas has shown that the same proportion of people buy organic food, irrespective of social class. Clearly a motive other than extra disposable income is the cause for people to buy organic.

Ultimately, we will have to examine farming systems if we are to have safe food. It is short-sighted for government research bodies to co-operate with tests of genetically engineered herbicide resistant crops, as Teagasc did, and at the same time to neglect research into other farming systems which can offer lower herbicide use.

Ireland is adopting a blinkered attitude, which will endanger our green reputation in Europe. Ireland's failure in early 1998 to support a German proposal for zero pesticides in baby food at the European Commission is a case in point. It is time Irish policy makers and farmers woke up, or one day we may find ourselves left behind in the safe food stakes.

Globalisation

Those of us lucky enough to shop in the supermarkets of the developed world are no longer bothered by thoughts of scarcity. Never have we had such a variety of foods to choose from, with the seasons no longer an issue. Have a look in your shopping basket one week. You could easily fill it entirely with imported foods from around the world. Beans flown in from Kenya are now standard. There might be apples from New Zealand, oranges from South Africa, stawberries from Spain, aubergines from Holland, prawns from South Asia, and ready meals from the UK, perhaps made up with fish from Norway and broccoli from Italy.

'Globalisation' is one of the buzz-words of the end of this millennium, and perhaps nowhere does it affect us as intimately as in the globalisation of the world food supply.

Of course, trade in food is nothing new. It has been part of our lives for millennia; the search for spices, fish and sugar for example was the impetus for much exploration. For centuries, we've enjoyed the tea and coffee, nuts, fruits and spices which trade brought. But we now have trade in food as never before. As someone who loves the foods of other countries, I'd be the first to consider my life enriched by much of this variety — I love to cook a Thai green curry in darkest January. Yet unfettered trade in food comes with a whole host of implications which we are hardly considering.

Trade in food means more 'food miles'

In late spring and early summer there will be Spanish asparagus in the shops, when Irish asparagus should be in season, strawberries from Spain sitting shoulder-to-shoulder with punnets from Wexford. Of course I bemoan the lack of freshness and flavour in the food which results from this insanity. But it's also a concern because the use of fossil fuels is already excessive in most aspects of our lives in the developed world, not least the fertilisers used in intensive agriculture. Adding more and more miles to each mouthful we eat means those fuels are being burned up even more quickly.

Trade in food means trade in bugs

Bacteria which are resistant to multiple antibiotics are emerging worldwide, much of this the result of factory farming of animals and the use of antibiotics to do so. Food poisoning is on the rise worldwide, and this is one of the reasons.

Trade in food means trade in standards

This often means settling for the lowest common denominator in our food. Is that good enough? Take the question of pesticides. Once EU Maximum Residue Levels are set, countries can't demand more stringent standards. Germany fell foul of this when it refused Spanish baby food which contained pesticide levels higher than German regulations permitted.

Food from developing countries, meanwhile, may contain suspect pesticides. We may have banned these in the developed world, but we still manufacture and export them. The fact that they may arrive back on our plates is called the 'circle of poison'. See Chapter 14 Pesticides, page 205, for more on this.

'Free trade'

This is often invoked now by bullying governments and multinationals to force the reluctant to accept their produce. You might think that the WTO has little to do with Tuesday morning's breakfast. You might be wrong. It may yet, for example, foist milk produced with a genetically-engineered hormone,

BST, on unwilling EU consumers. The EU has a ban in place on BST until the year 2000. It encourages cows to even higher milk yields; it is linked to higher levels of mastitis, and some research has also linked it to higher somatic cell counts (pus) in milk. EU scientists have said that BST doesn't affect consumers, but the ban remained because EU consumer opinion was so strongly against it. In early 1998, the WTO declared the EU ban unscientific, and is pressurising the EU to rescind it.

Increasingly, food is being viewed as a neutral, industrial commodity, rather than part of the fabric of our communities and, indeed, the sustainer of life. We're going to see more and more food grown wherever it is cheapest to do so, rather than close to its markets. Next time you reach for a food which has flown thousands of miles to be with you, you might pause for thought. What do you know about the food and how it was produced? Should we really be encouraging this?

14

Pesticides

W ould you hesitate to buy an orange labelled 'Produced with P-326, P-265, P-987, and P-321, P-214 and P-387 used post-harvest, skin not suitable for eating'? Or hold back on an apple labelled 'May contain residues of P-986, P-645, P-376, P-329, P-295'?

About half of the food we eat is contaminated with detectable pesticide residues and much of it is contaminated with residues of more than one pesticide. The Department of Agriculture's Pesticide Control Service (PCS) reports that, 'The fact that the majority of residues detected were well below the established MRLs is reassuring.'

Indeed it appears to be reassuring to hear that just two to four per cent of residues detected were above the Maximum Residue Limit (MRL).

Yet many experts don't think so, the US National Academy of Sciences (NAS) among them. They argue that MRLs create a false illusion of safety. That our regulatory agencies the world over are ignorant of many of the potential damaging effects we may suffer from the cocktail of pesticides we are exposed to daily. That no-one is keeping track of them. And that, according to Professor John Wargo of Yale University (a member of that NAS research team) 'Current legal and scientific approaches . . . give little hope that we are even aware of the magnitude and distribution of significant threats.'

More and More Pesticides

Five to six billion lbs of pesticides are added to the world's environment every year. You'd have thought that we would have had the pest problem licked under that onslaught. Yet pests quickly evolve resistance to each chemical designed to kill them. Worse, pesticides kill beneficial predators of the pests, so leaving more of a job for pesticides to do. It is often called the pesticide treadmill. Insecticide use has increased tenfold in the US since the war. But crop losses haven't decreased — they have doubled. The situation is reaching crisis proportions according to those in the industry, and companies are developing more toxic compounds to cope.

Maximum Residue Limits

Maximum Residue Limits, set by governments, have a reassuring ring of safety. Yet in a 1993 report from the US National Academy of Sciences, this approach to pesticide residues was likened to setting the speed limit at 500 mph and then declaring the roads to be safe, since everyone was only travelling at 200 mph.

How Do Pesticides Work?

Pesticides are designed to be damaging to living things. Their early benefits in the 1950s, such as in the control of malaria epidemics, were undeniably enormous. Yet as time has gone on, we have discovered more about their potential effects on our bodies and on the environment. And what we are learning is most disquieting.

Initially, pesticides were presumed safe because they disappeared into the environment. Then, in 1962, Rachel Carson published *Silent Spring*, in which she marshalled an impressive body of evidence to show that pesticides like DDT accumulated in food chains and were finally found, sometimes in very high concentrations, in human fat. She was subjected to scathing attacks by the industry, but ultimately supported by the Science Advisory Committee which President Kennedy set up to investigate her claims.

DDT and related organochlorine pesticides were subsequently banned in the developed world, although they continue to be used in developing countries. However, the compounds which have replaced them are also causing concern. Organophosphates degrade more quickly, but they are damaging to our nervous systems.

The Burden of Proof

The burden of proof is the wrong way round: chemicals we release into the environment are presumed to be reasonably safe unless proved otherwise. Yet it can take decades for new health threats to emerge. Very little is known about the long-term effects of low dosage exposure to pesticides, which we all undergo. Few, if any, comprehensive safety data exist for many chemicals.

When older pesticides are tested with up-to-the-minute systems, new hazards are discovered. About a third are suspected of causing cancer in laboratory animals; another third may disrupt the nervous system; others are suspected of interfering with our hormones and reproductive systems.

Cancer . . . Or Something Else?

Since the 1960s, research into the health risks to humans of pesticides has focused specially on carcinogenic effects. Experts are now warning that this focus has been too narrow. We may be at risk, not just of cancers, but also of damage to our neurological, immune and reproductive systems.

Most recently the spotlight has fallen on the potential which organochlorine compounds, some pesticides as well as industrial chemicals, have to disrupt our hormones. 'The impacts on wildlife and laboratory animals as a result of exposure to these contaminants are of such a profound and insidious nature that a major research initiative on humans must be undertaken,' a group of US scientists from many disciplines concluded in a statement at Wingspread, Racine in 1991. They warned of possible 'large-scale dysfunction' in humans. The most dramatic warning sign is the plummeting of male sperm counts in the last fifty years. The damage is thought to have taken place, and to continue to be taking place, as foetuses develop in the womb.

Children Are Most Vulnerable

A landmark study was published by the US National Research Council (NRC) in 1993. They discovered that regulatory authorities are operating in the dark when it comes to assessing the risks children face, and came to the unambiguous conclusion that children face higher risks from pesticides than experts had anticipated.

Children Are Doubly Susceptible

Firstly, their bodies are different from those of adults. They are extra sensitive during periods of rapid growth (in the womb, during infancy and during puberty).

Babies triple in weight during the first year — and of course grow even faster in the womb. Children's kidneys and liver are less efficient at eliminating toxins; their gastro-intestinal tracts and nervous systems are thought to be more permeable. From conception to age five, they may be especially vulnerable to carcinogens, because their cells are reproducing so rapidly. In addition, their central and peripheral nervous systems are thought to be particularly vulnerable to the neurotoxic agents in many pesticides.

Yet most toxicity studies are performed on mature animals. This is a poor basis for estimating the effects on the foetus, infants, children, and young adults. As the NRC report put it:

> The data strongly suggest that exposure to neurotoxic compounds at levels believed to be safe for adults could result in permanent loss of brain function if it occurred during the prenatal or early childhood period of brain development . . . policies that established safe levels of exposure to neurotoxic pesticides for adults could not be assumed to adequately protect a child less than four years of age.

Secondly, young children eat differently. Anyone with small children knows that they eat much more of much fewer foods than adults do, particularly taking a lot of fruits, fruit juices, some vegetables and milk. A four-month-old may be weaned almost exclusively on banana, cereals and milk, for example. This means that the average adult consumption patterns with which risks are calculated also underestimate the potential risk to children.

Authorities calculating risk have always worked on averages — they have not calculated for the high food intake, low bodyweight and extra sensitivity of the most vulnerable. In failing to do this, they have consistently ignored the threat children may face from pesticides.

Cumulative Effects

Most recently, concerns have been raised about the cumulative effects of the consumption of several pesticides which act in a similar way. The Environment Working Group (EWG) in the US released a report, *Overexposed*, in early 1998. It concluded that one in twenty children under six is affected, and that most risks are posed by apples and apple products, including apple juices, grapes, peaches and nectarines. (The report was based on US eating patterns, and the key foods in Ireland may be different — we just don't know, because such studies have not been done here.) For infants aged six to twelve months, commercial baby food was cited as the major source of unsafe levels of organophosphate (OP) insecticides — although the report stresses that baby food is in fact safer than other foods infants may be fed.

OPs may cause long-term damage to the brain and nervous system, which are rapidly growing and extremely vulnerable during foetal development, infancy and early childhood. They are close relatives of nerve gases developed during World War II. Many OPs have the common effect of disturbing the normal transfer of nerve signals. When residues of several OPs are combined, an unsafe dose can result, even though each single residue may fall below standard safety limits.

The EWG concludes that 'It is probable that these high OP exposures early in life are causing long-term functional and learning deficits.'

The report calls not for a drop in fruit and vegetable consumption, but for fruits and vegetables to be rid of the most toxic pesticides. It wants the five highest-risk OPs (methyl parathion, dimethoate, chlorpyrifos, pirimophos methyl and azinphos methyl) to be banned immediately for all agricultural use, and for all OPs to be banned in commercial baby food. This latter demand echoes an amendment passed by the European Parliament in December 1997 for all baby foods to be pesticide-free (see Baby Food, page 167).

New US food safety legislation requires the government to consider the total risk faced by consumers where groups of pesticides act in a similar way and have similar toxic effects. No such protective legislation exists in the EU. Pesticides are assessed one at a time, and regulations do not take account of combinations of pesticides with similar effects.

David Buffin, of the London-based charity The Pesticides Trust, commented, 'Although this is a US report, the sorts of figures involved have a similar application in Europe, where pesticide usage is similar. A very stringent reduction in the use of these chemicals is the only solution, since there are so many uncertainties.'

What Can You Do?

1. Give your babies and children organic foods and drinks wherever possible. This is the only safe advice currently available.
2. If fruit and vegetables are not organic, the best strategy is to peel them.
3. Pregnant women should also follow this advice.

If you find it hard to source organic foods, tell your retailer you want them, and why. The most pressing gap in the Irish market at present is organic milk and fruit juices. I know how difficult this can be. You have to retain a sense of perspective. Young childrens' eating habits can be curious, and they can break you with their determination, no matter how creative or sly your food solutions for them attempt to be. (My young son existed almost exclusively on a diet of processed potato waffles and ketchup, supplemented by non-organic plums and clementines, for quite some time.)

In addition, organic foods and drinks are not very widely available.

Inadequate Testing

The Department of Agriculture's Pesticide Control Service is underfunded. It only tests for residues of fewer than a quarter of pesticides in common current use. In addition, the number of samples it takes is tiny. In 1996, just 103 samples of cereals, 409 of meat, milk and dairy products and 505 of fruits and vegetables were tested.

Such paucity of testing is not peculiar to Ireland. Testing is expensive, and governments worldwide don't do very much of it. For example, in a two-year period, the US FDA tested seventy-two banana samples for benomyl, a suspected carcinogen; during the same period, nearly twenty-five billion bananas were imported. In Ireland in 1997, just one courgette, one nectarine, one pepper, one baby milk powder, two cucumbers and three parsnip samples were analysed for pesticide residues.

The Cocktail Effect

Pesticides are studied one by one, usually by the companies which produce them. The complex mix of the pesticides we are exposed to is not allowed for in toxicity studies. No individual manufacturer has any incentive to fund complex mixture studies, which would normally involve products produced by other firms. Understanding the effects for a single pesticide may cost millions of pounds. Understanding the effects for thousands of separate licensed products along with their combinations is a virtual impossibility. And yet that is what we are eating.

Asked how many pesticides were permitted to remain as residues on apples and in milk, a Department of Agriculture spokesman could only reply that it would be 'a major task' to sort this out. It is not confidence-inspiring to learn of such ignorance in our regulatory authorities. Ireland should be pressing at EU level for fundamental changes in the current system of testing.

Russian Roulette at the Fruit and Vegetable Counter

Which nectarines have twenty-nine times the residue level of the rest in the punnet? New research by the UK Department of Agriculture's Working Party on Pesticide Residues demonstrates that residue levels vary enormously between one vegetable or piece of fruit and another. This calls current testing methods and safety margins into question.

In 1995, the UK government issued a health warning about carrots. They should be topped, tailed and peeled generously, since very high residues of organophosphate insecticides in single carrots had been discovered. Research released in 1997 has discovered that this variability is the *norm* in fruit and vegetables, not an exception. Apples, pears, tomatoes, bananas, nectarines, peaches and oranges were tested. Highest residue levels were up to twenty-nine times the average level. Normal residue testing can't show this up, since it reveals only average levels.

The 'variation of residues is no longer within the control of pesticide regulators or users', the UK's Pesticide Trust commented. It pointed out that these variations occur with legal use of the chemicals. 'The only viable strategy is one of overall reduction of the use of and reliance upon pesticides in agriculture.'

The Circle of Poison

This is the ominous name given to the situation created by the explosion of international trade in pesticides and food. Not in My Back Yard was the developed world's response, when it was discovered how dangerous some pesticides could be. We have banned DDT and other organochlorine compounds, but we are still exporting them to developing countries. (The US exported a tonne of DDT a day in 1996.) Tropical countries tend to use more pesticides, because their climates give them more severe pest control problems. They are also under pressure to expand lucrative export agriculture, and their environmental health regulations are generally weak. A 1996 study by the University of Hanover of Thai farmers concluded that they were overdosing with pesticides by a factor of eight because of pest resistance.

The developed world may export pesticides, but it can get them back in its food. We are importing more and more food from developing countries. Just think of all the orange juice our children drink.

What Happens to a Pesticide?

When foods are processed into juices, oils, dried foods or are cooked, pesticides are altered. This is the least understood area of pesticide chemistry, but one of the most relevant for understanding pesticide exposure. Some may be reduced; others magnified. We just don't know.

Picture-Perfect Food

Our expectations of utterly unblemished fruit and vegetables (and EU grading regulations which demand the same) are encouraging the use of still more pesticides. One estimate concluded that sixty to eighty per cent of the pesticide use on oranges was to enhance the cosmetic appearance of the skin.

Ironically, some processed foods, which we may think of as inferior in quality to fresh, may contain fewer pesticides, as a result of this fixation with appearance. This was the case for tomato-based products tested by the UK's Working Party on Pesticide Residues 1996; only one residue of the fifty-four sought was detected. 'This profile was likely to be the result of the lower aesthetic requirements for tomatoes used in processing,' it commented.

Getting Rid of Pesticides
Can they be washed off?

Pesticides are formulated to resist easily being washed off by rain. After washing, 70–93.5 per cent of surface residues remain on fruit and vegetables.

Peeling

Consumer tests have reported that peeling removes seventy-five to ninety per cent of post-harvest pesticides. However, they can also travel into the flesh of fruit and vegetables. These figures do not take account of systemic pesticides, which enter the interior of the food. Of course, peeling also removes up to a fifth of the fruit or vegetable, taking with it fibre and nutrients. And clearly in some cases it's just not practical, or even possible: would you peel a grape?

It's Not Just Fruit and Vegetables

We have an image of pesticide residues primarily in fruit and vegetables, but they are also to be found in many other foods. It is thought that adults receive many residues from bread and cereals, because we eat a lot of these. With these foods, we don't even have the option of peeling residues off.

Post-Harvest Pesticides: Storage Aids

These cause most concern. In the growing, pesticides are at least supposed to wear off. Applied after harvesting, for example as fungicides, there's nowhere for the pesticide to go. Nearly all lemons and oranges, and many apples, potatoes and wheats are treated.

This leads to another irony. Brown bread is usually thought of as healthier than white. Yet pesticide residue testing in the UK reveals higher residues in wholemeal breads than white breads — this is because the outer bran is likely to contain most of the residue.

There was a proposal in the EC's Residues Directive that post-harvest treatments of food crops be labelled. This laudable suggestion was unfortunately put off for consideration, and has fallen by the wayside.

Reduced Pesticide Use is Feasible

Sweden has cut its levels by fifty per cent, and achieved similar yields; UK trials have cut use by fifty to seventy-five per cent and achieved normal or slightly reduced yields. However, encouraging reports of reduced volumes of pesticide use may mask the fact that chemicals are tending to become more potent.

Some crops are produced using systems which encourage natural pest predators and reduced pesticides. These are often referred to as IPM — Integrated Pest Management. IPM is most often employed in glasshouse production, where pest problems are most acute. You may come across references to them on labels of imported tomatoes, for example. It is also used in Ireland, though the produce is unlikely to be labelled.

IPM sounds encouraging, but it pays to ask searching questions. Just because a predatory mite is used to tackle whitefly doesn't mean that the food is free of other chemicals.

Meaningful Warnings

If governments license the use of toxins which may persist in our food to affect our health and that of our children, they have a duty to warn us 'in a way that has some relation to everyday choices', Prof Wargo of Yale concludes.

These should include P-numbers on foods which should be simple to understand and international. Your oranges could say 'produced with P-127, P-232 and P-376. P-456 and P-976 on skin. Peel not safe to eat.'

These should be introduced as a matter of urgency, where post-harvest chemicals have been used, and not just for raw foods but also for products such as bread.

15

Genetic Engineering

When the Tomato Met the Flounder Fish . . .

Genetic engineering promises so much for our food. According to its proponents, it will improve food quality. It will mean higher crop yields, and reduced chemical use. It will lower the cost of raw materials. It will reduce the environmental impact of intensive agriculture. This all at a time when the world's population is expected to double by 2030.

Sounds promising. Yet there are ominous question marks hanging over the technology, questions which have yet to be answered.

Scientific Impartiality

Most worrying of all is the question of the loss of scientific impartiality. One senior food industry source, who didn't wish to be named, said this:

> Now that genes may be patented, scientists are no longer impartial, they often stand to gain financially from the research they are doing . . . It worries me a great deal, but we in Ireland must take part, or we won't be taken seriously by the rest of Europe.

Genetically modified foods are being rushed to market by companies anxious

215

for the speediest return possible on their high-investment crops. It may emerge that some are perfectly safe. But until long-term studies have been done, it makes no sense at all to be eating these foods — in effect participating in a large-scale uncontrolled trial of their effects on human beings. Yet this is precisely what we are doing. Since 1997, genetically modified soy from the US has been mixed with the standard crop. Soy is a major international commodity and is estimated to be found in about 7000 foods, as flour, oils, lecithin and vegetable proteins. So you just don't know if you have been eating it. In 1997 and 1998, the EU made weak attempts at devising a labelling system. But unless crops are segregated, any labelling will be utterly meaningless.

The Claims and Concerns

Here are some of the claims being made for genetic engineering — and some of the concerns.

Genetic Modification will bring Better Food Quality

The 'quality' we hear about is mostly for the convenience of manufacturers. Longer shelf-life. Higher solids contents for cheaper processing. Increased protein or oil quantity. There are also suggestions that high-vitamin foods will be produced. Why? What suggestion is there that the vitamins in current varieties of tomato, or of a spinach leaf, are not enough?

There are also more worrying ideas being tested. Give a tomato a gene from the North Atlantic flounder fish, in the hope that it will be frost resistant. Add genes from intestinal bacteria to potatoes so they will absorb less oil on frying. Insert growth hormones genes into salmon so that in fourteen months they can weigh up to thirty-seven times more than an ordinary fish. These are not morbid fantasies, they are happening.

Better food quality would come from raising crops and animals with more respect for them, their natural attributes and the soil.

All Commercial Fruits, Vegetables and other Foods have been Genetically Modified

Please don't insult our intelligence. Of course it is true. But until now, they have been modified by natural breeding methods. A tomato does not naturally breed with a fish.

Biotechnology Will, with Higher Crop Yields, Feed the World

This is most unlikely. This claim was made a generation ago for new, high-yielding food crops. They would, it was promised, create a 'green revolution' in the developing world. The result has been quite different. Rich farmers, who could afford the high-investment farming that these varieties require (with high fertiliser and pesticide uses), have got richer, while the poor have got poorer. Most hunger in the world is caused not by low-yielding crops, but by inequitable distribution of food.

High-yielding crops cause problems, and are more prone to disease. The Ethiopian famine had many causes, but one of them was pressure exerted by experts on Ethiopians to abandon their drought-tolerant crops for 'green revolution' varieties. Indeed, there are cogent warnings that biotechnology-based agriculture will speed the loss of vital genetic diversity in the world's food crops. See Biodiversity, page 197, for more about this.

Genetically Modified Crops Mean Fewer Herbicides

Planting genetically modified crops which won't be affected by herbicides may mean that chemical use is lower at first. But what of the consequences? Being able to douse a crop with a chemical (which would once have killed it) means there will probably be higher residues of the chemical in the food. And when surrounding weeds mutate or cross-breed with the resistant crop and acquire its resistance, as they surely will, then new, stronger herbicides will need to be invented to deal with the superweeds.

Genetically Modified Crops Won't Cross With Others

Despite this claim, in November 1997, French scientists showed that genetically modified herbicide-resistant oilseed rape crossed with unrelated wild radish weeds. Within four generations, the weed had acquired the resistance.

Genetically Modified Crops Have Been Well-Tested

Bill Meredith, a geneticist and research manager with the US Department of Agriculture in Mississippi, was quoted in 1997 in the *New York Times*. He had wanted a pound of seed to test the new herbicide-resistant cotton which Monsanto had developed. Monsanto said they couldn't spare it. 'These new . . . technologies are going out with less evaluation than . . . traditional varieties,' Meredith remarked.

Many unexpected side-effects are found with genetically modified crops. This is not surprising. In fact, it is to be expected. 'Genetic engineers will always be limited by an incomplete understanding of the infinite interactions between plants and the environment,' commented international crop experts Cary Fowler and Pat Mooney.

These crops have been shown to shorten the life span of bees and ladybirds. The 1997 genetically modified cotton crop in Mississippi failed dramatically, and farmers sued Monsanto. An experiment with a red colour gene in white petunias resulted in quite unassociated effects: more leaves and shoots and lowered fertility. Geneticists believe that altering genes affects a plant's system in ways which we don't fully understand yet. The complexity of ecology should not be underestimated, and it should lead us to proceed with great caution.

There are also concerns about antibiotic-resistant 'marker' genes. These are used while the genetic engineering takes place, and help technologists to know whether the inserted genes have been taken up. It is not sure whether these could pass on antibiotic resistance to bacteria. This concern alone has led Norway to ban the importation of several genetically modified products.

Science Chasing Technology: Where is the Burden of Proof?

The science of assessing genetically modified crops has not caught up with the technology of creating them. While this remains the case, the burden of proof should remain with the manufacturers to show that the foods and crops are safe. Long-term studies should be required. As the history of pesticide use has shown, the crucial question usually turns out to be the one we never thought to ask. The effects on humans are often ones which scientists never thought to look for.

Unfortunately the regulatory authorities aren't operating according to these principles. The US Food and Drug Administration has come up with the term 'substantial equivalence'. If a genetically engineered food is found to be substantially equivalent to its normal relations, it doesn't require extra testing. This ignores questions now being raised about how genes can behave differently depending on where they are sited.

The pressure of world trade regulations mean that it is very difficult for Europe, once something has been declared safe in the US, to close its doors to it.

It is possible that the proponents of genetic engineering may be right. But what if they are wrong?

What Can You Do?

Generally, global issues like this seem to be overwhelming. But here, it's quite simple. If you refuse to buy these foods, there is no market for them. If you are concerned about this, tell your retailer that you will not buy genetically modified foods, or foods produced using such products. And tell them why.

16

Labelling

'**H**oney roast ham' which has no honey. Spanish olive oil, 'produce of France'. 'Smoked' fish which has never seen a smokehouse.

Food labelling is a tussle between advertising and honesty, and it is largely unregulated. The Consumers' Association regularly calls for claims on foods to be dealt with, and to be given some legal definition, but so far little has happened. There are only two broad rules governing food labelling. One says that if a claim (e.g. 'low fat') is made, then nutritional labelling must be included. The other says that food labelling claims should not 'mislead the consumer to a material degree'. Plenty of products sail pretty close to the wind on this one.

Names and Images

Sometimes you get the feeling that you need to proceed around the supermarket with a magnifying glass and calculator in hand. A generous pinch of scepticism is no harm too. Many food products create an image with their advertising and brand names which is rather at odds with the nutritional information on the small print. To pluck but a few at random from the shelves . . .

Take Kellogg's Special K, aimed at those who'd love to be svelte — yet it contains exactly the same number of calories as their cornflakes, and twice the sugar.

Or Ballyclough Light Butter, which proclaims 'all the natural taste of Irish creamery butter', but check the label and you discover added 'flavouring', plus a host of other ingredients.

Try Tesco's Olive Spread, presumably appealing to those who are interested in the health benefits of olive oil — but it contains more vegetable oils and hydrogenated vegetable oils than it does olive oil.

Or Ballyfree's Country Kitchen 'butter basted' Chicken, which has more vegetable oil than butter, plus a few ingredients you'd be hard pressed to find in a country kitchen: sodium polyphosphates, emulsifier, mono and di-glycerides of fatty acids, carrageenan . . .

Or Irish Cereals Crunchy Oat Bran which says it 'can help reduce cholesterol': 'As part of a cholesterol-lowering eating plan', it adds helpfully on the side of the pack. Well, of course! A Mars Bar could no doubt help reduce cholesterol, if it formed part of a cholesterol-lowering eating plan . . .

Product Names

Another dubious area is the naming of products. 'Farmhouse', 'home-made', 'selected', 'natural' . . . all these are words which try to create a cachet for the food they're selling, yet are almost always utterly meaningless. More questionable are misleading product names, such as 'Cheese, Spinach and Potato Bake', which might sound as if it's packed with protein and calcium — but cheese is the eleventh ingredient listed.

Certainly, consumers are adults who are entitled to make choices about the food they eat. But it's also clear that a lot of consumers are confused about many claims made for foods nowadays. In one British study, over half the people questioned thought that a 'low-fat' sausage would have less fat than an ordinary yoghurt. (The reverse is true.) Many people also believe, perhaps because 'low-fat' milk is so widely available, that full-fat milk is high in fat. Yet it only contains three to four per cent fat.

This kind of ignorance puts the concept of what may be 'misleading to a material degree' in a very different light.

Do You Read the Label?

One European survey revealed that only three per cent of consumers read the label. Another British study revealed that only half of shoppers ever scrutinise the contents label on a pack of food. Does this matter? If you don't read the label, you are at the mercy of the manufacturer. You won't know if their implied claims are correct. And you won't know what kind of additives you are eating.

It has been estimated that essential preservatives account for fewer than one per cent of chemicals used in food processing. Eighty-eight per cent of additives are for cosmetic reasons — colourings, flavourings, flavour enhancers, sweeteners and so on. The final eleven per cent goes on processing aids — things needed not for the food, but to make large-scale production possible. The more processed foods you eat, the more additives you will be getting. The effect of many of these on our health is questionable and most are under-researched.

How to Read a Label

Ingredients are listed in descending order of weight, so the heaviest is mentioned first. This gives you a modicum of information, but not enough. If water is first in the list of ingredients, does that mean forty-one per cent water, or eighty-one per cent? You have no way of knowing. Ingredients listings which include the percentages of ingredients used are common in other countries. They should be introduced here as soon as possible.

This is highly unlikely to happen, however. For nearly ten years, the EU has been grinding its way through the issue of food labelling, and it still hasn't come to a decision. You can't help but arrive at the conclusion that manufacturers are reluctant to let us know what they are putting into the food we eat.

Look for ingredients you recognise

A list of ingredients that sounds more like the contents of a Junior Chemistry Set than a kitchen cupboard is a sure sign that the food is over-processed and full of under-tested, often suspect, chemical ingredients.

E-numbers

These are on the way out. Not of our food, unfortunately. But manufacturers have cottoned on to the fact that we don't much like to see a string of E-numbers listed. So instead they are citing the ingredients by name.

Words and Claims
Free From . . .

'Free from artificial colouring'; 'free from artificial flavouring'; 'free from artificial preservatives'. Sounds good, doesn't it? However, always check the small print; it's surprising how often a no-artificial-flavours food contains artificial colouring and/or preservatives, and vice versa. Chemically synthesised 'nature-identical' flavourings are permitted to be described as 'natural'.

Light/Lite/Extra light

Most people take these to mean 'lower in calories'. Yet 'light' olive oil, for example, is light in colour and taste, not lower in calories; 'light' bread is light in texture!

Low Fat

- a low-fat spread is about forty per cent fat
- a low-fat yoghurt is about one per cent fat
- low-fat milk is about 1.5 per cent fat
- low-fat sausages are around ten to fifteen per cent fat
- low-fat cream cheese has more fat than full-fat cottage cheese.

You'd need to be a nutritionist to negotiate your way around this minefield. Many people automatically reach for the 'low-fat' option, thinking it must be healthier. Sometimes lower-fat foods may be a sensible option, but usually you're just getting a more processed product, often more additives, and almost certainly less flavour.

Low in Cholesterol/Cholesterol-Free

This is less important than it appears. First of all, eating cholesterol-free fats doesn't necessarily mean your body will have less cholesterol in it. (If you need to worry about your cholesterol levels, you need to worry about your total fat intake, not just your cholesterol intake, since our bodies make cholesterol themselves.)

In addition, a food can be cholesterol-free and still high in fat. Only animal fats contain cholesterol. All vegetable fats are cholesterol-free. But two kinds of cholesterol-free vegetable fats cause problems: 1. those vegetable fats which are highly saturated (palm and coconut oils); and 2. those vegetable fats which have been hydrogenated and thus contain trans-fats. These trans-fats are now thought to pose even more of a risk for heart disease than saturated fats. (See Margarine versus Butter, page 90, for more on this.)

Vegetable Fat

This term is used indiscriminately in processed foods like confectionery and ready meals and on margarine spreads. Many people are under the erroneous assumption that vegetable fats are a 'Good Thing': that they contain fewer calories, and are better for you. No, on both counts. The calories are broadly the same. Are they 'better' for you? Not necessarily. They may even be worse than good old butter! (See Low in Cholesterol, above, and Margarines and Spreads, page 89.) I'd rather enjoy the taste of butter in my biscuit.

Reduced Fat/Reduced Sugar

Cast a cold eye on these. Sometimes fat and sugar are 'reduced' by the simple expedient of reducing pack size! Often, fat or sugar may be lowered, but calories remain nearly the same. 'Reduced sugar' often means 'added artificial sweeteners'.

Sugar-free/No Sugar Added

Sweetness may be achieved, however, by fruit syrups, honey or other sugar-containing ingredients. 'Sugar free' also often means 'with artificial sweeteners and extra preservatives'.

Sucrose-Free

Yet the product may contain plenty of other sugars like glucose, glucose syrup, dextrose, corn syrup, maltose, fructose, lactose . . .

High In . . .

Inappropriate or irrelevant nutrients are often highlighted. One spread, for example, announces that it is 'high in protein'. It does have more than other spreads, but it still only has a miniscule 7 g protein per 100 g. You wouldn't want to be relying on it for your protein intake!

Farm Fresh, Country

These are usually meaningless terms. Often applied to eggs, many people confuse them with free-range eggs. In fact, if you see such terms you are almost guaranteed that the eggs come from a battery system.

However, 'farm fresh' chicken is a common term (see Chapter 4, Chicken and Other Poultry, page 49).

Home Cooked and Home Made

This is most often seen in relation to ham, cakes, marmalade and jam. The meaning is often very dubious; potentially misleading. Be sceptical, especially if the words are in inverted commas!

Healthy

One of the biggest cons of all. Used to create an image, but quite meaningless. 'Healthy' is often applied to prepared foods which are intended to appeal to slimmers. Many of these meals, though, if examined for nutritional content, are not good; often they contain too few vegetables, carbohydrate or fibre, and are high in salt. Remember: there's no such thing as a healthy food, just balanced and unbalanced diets.

Natural

This vies with 'healthy' for the biggest con. It's often used where the food is anything but natural. Examine with care! For example, Dairygold spread declares 'All natural ingredients'. Although it doesn't contain the additives, emulsifiers and preservatives so common in other spreads, it contains hydrogenated soya oil. There's nothing natural about this industrially-hardened oil.

Fortified With . . .

Extra vitamins and minerals make a food seem healthier. But most of us get enough nutrients from our natural diets, and don't need extra boosting. These foods may be helpful in the case of children who are poor eaters. It's worrying, however, to see a new development: fortifying inappropriate foods such as confectionery and fizzy drinks, particularly those aimed at children, in order to give them a false veneer of 'goodness'.

A Europe-wide study of fortified foods, published in *Consumer Choice* in February 1998, discovered that only thirty-two per cent of foods analysed contained the levels of vitamins and minerals stated on the packet. Most were in fact higher, but ten per cent were significantly lower.

With . . .

One to set the alarm bells ringing. 'With . . .' nearly always means there's an ingredient the manufacturer would like to tell you all about — and also a lot more they'd prefer you didn't notice. One example is Dolmio Pesto. 'With basil, cheese and pine-nuts' it declares, and also 'with extra-virgin olive oil'. Sounds like the real thing. It doesn't choose to say: 'with canola oil, onion, garlic, lemon juice, vegetable shortening, glucose, chicken bouillon, salt, spices, cheese extract, thickener (modified cornstarch), vegetable gum (sodium alginate) and water'. Apart from the garlic, these extras are all ingredients foreign to a true pesto . . .

'Honey Roast', 'Smoked'

Hard to understand this, but you can call foods these things even if they're not. Honey flavouring will do. Liquid 'smoke' is fine.

Flavouring

There are thousands of flavourings. They do not have to be listed in ingredients, and they do not have E numbers. If it says 'flavouring', you don't know what you're eating.

Product Of . . .

You can import something, alter it, then call it your product. So olive oil from Spain blended and bottled in France is 'product of France'.

Organic

There are three organic certification bodies in Ireland. Look for one of their symbols to be assured that the food you are buying is honestly organic. They are: IOFGA (Irish Organic Farmers and Growers Association), Organic Trust, and Demeter (the Bio-Dynamic Agricultural Association, which farms to rules even more stringent than organic). Retailers must also be registered in order to prevent fraud.

Q-Mark
Some foods carry the Quality Mark (awarded by Excellence Ireland). All this means is that the production system has been certified; it's a mark of quality for the system, not the product. So battery eggs with a Q-mark may well be good battery eggs, but that doesn't make them good quality eggs. (See Eggs, page 109.)

Fairtrade
Production of food in developing countries often involves exploitation of workers who are vulnerable to fluctuating world commodity prices, and who often use large quantities of pesticides to the detriment of their own health. This foundation was set up by Oxfam and other development agencies to ensure that producers in developing countries are given a better deal; the mark is issued to some teas, coffees and chocolates and other products.

Fairtrade products mean that more of the product's price goes back to the local communities, and in some cases also means reduced pesticide use. However, it is not a guarantee of eating quality. Some of the products are very good, and some are not.

Quality Assurance
There are several meat quality assurance schemes in various stages of development. In most cases, 'Quality' means traceability, to assure you that the meat doesn't contain illegal substances. (See Beef, page 15, and Pork, page 32.) It doesn't mean exceptional eating quality.

Adding Water to Food
You can buy water in so many colours and flavours, and so many different price ranges nowadays. It's one of the miracles of modern food processing: they sell water to you at £4 a lb — and persuade you that you're saving money.

Of course, there are plenty of perfectly reasonable places to find water in food. We add it all the time when we're cooking, and meat and fish are naturally mostly water. But added water has become one of the most common ways to make food cheaper. Unfortunately, the only thing that's genuinely cheapened is the quality of the food. You get less nutrition for your money — and a good deal less flavour too.

You do, however, often get more of *something* for your money: more additives in the food, to hold all that water in place. And more salt, sugar, flavourings and flavour enhancers in order to make up the taste.

Manufacturers are not required to tell you how much water is in food. Some do include it in the list of ingredients. But since they usually don't give the percentage of water, it's very difficult to compare products on the shelf. These are some to watch out for.

Rashers

Water oozes out in the pan, and your rashers end up swimming rather than frying. Water is injected as a brine solution and held in place by polyphosphates. It's possible to add fifteen, even twenty, per cent water to bacon. Even Quality Assured bacon may contain ten per cent added water.

Ham

As for rashers, only more so. Lots of added water makes for a rubbery slice, and it also means the ham can be sliced extra thin. Picnic hams may be one-third added water. In 1996, an EU Directive on additives actually increased the range of water-holding additives permitted to the manufacturers.

Bread

'Water standing up' is what they call a lot of the sliced pans available now. Add more water, and you can squeeze an extra penny or two off the price of the loaf. Modern mechanical agitation and extra-fine flour milling mean flour can be induced to hold more water.

Margarines and Dairy Spreads

This is an interesting one. Work a lot of water into artificially-hardened vegetable oil, plus extra stabilisers and emulsifiers to hold it in place, and call it an extra-healthy food. Perhaps it is. The water is certainly better for you than the rest of the contents of the tub.

Breaded Chicken

The crumb conceals a lot. What's inside may be a piece of natural chicken. Or it may be a slush of minced chicken bits, with up to twenty per cent added water, and a dash of polyphosphates to hold it all in place.

Breaded Fish Products

The same goes for fish. The fish content of most breaded fish was lowest in Ireland, when analysed Europe-wide by the Consumers' Association.

Shellfish Glazes

They don't defrost, they melt away. Just watch those prawns and scallops end up in a sad little puddle on the plate. It's all the more galling when shellfish is so expensive. A fine coating of water is needed to protect shellfish from being burned by the cold of the freezer, but this is all too tempting to overdo. Don't buy frozen shellfish except from an exceptionally good shop, unless it states the percentage of glaze on the packet. Even then you're limited in your protection, since processors may soak the shellfish in water first to increase its weight.

Baby Foods

Some water is needed to make most fruit and vegetable purées. But how much are they using? They never say. And why should a baby yoghurt contain more water than yoghurt?

Cheese

Processed cheese is lowest-grade cheese melted with added emulsifiers, flavourings, and added water.

Other Foods

There are some other foods where water is not actually poured in by the jugful, but where production methods mean we get more water, and less texture, flavour and nutrition in our food.

Modern-grown vegetables and fruit are encouraged, by chemical fertilisation, to take up more water. It makes them grow bigger. But tests have shown them to be less nutritious. Modern hard cheeses are ripened in plastic. They miss out on traditional maturing, where they exhale their moisture and increase in flavour; instead of being deliciously flaky or firm, they are squidgy and pasty.

Finally, there's the mystery of the modern chicken, to which I haven't found a definitive answer. It sheds so much water in the cooking, and no-one can say why. The current theory at the moment is that the speed-reared, extra young flesh is low in what the scientists call WHC — water holding capacity. Slightly more matured free-range birds don't do this. Perhaps this is one case where we want a food to hold on to its water!

17

Food Poisoning

ood poisoning is a thorny issue. It is on the rise worldwide. It makes headlines and it scares us. There are new bugs about, some potentially very dangerous, and some are now resistant to many antibiotics.

You can't be too careful. Or can you? It's worth remembering that there is no such thing as one hundred per cent guaranteed safe food. It's a question of balancing risks.

Time for a bit of psychology: it's about the illusion of control. We are prepared to take extraordinary risks driving cars, because we feel safe and in control behind the steering wheel. With food, we once had a measure of control too. We had relationships with the people who produced our food. Our networks were small, and we soon heard about bad practices. Now, it's different. What do we know about the Spanish farmer who's growing the lettuce on our shelves in February? Or about the pig producer at the other end of the country with a few thousand pigs in his sheds?

Have We Gone Too Far?

So now, we want 'safe food'. Fair enough. We have a right to expect people to produce food for us that will be clean and wholesome, and that's what much of this book is about. But it's important to keep it in perspective: it may be possible to push food safety too far. It is ironic that in recent decades, some 'food safety' concerns have actually led to an impoverishment in the quality and variety of food available to us. They have closed down small local producers, often the guardians of the best foods we could buy. Excellent butter, superb cheese, wonderful breads, exceptional chickens — there are many examples. Often over-zealous environmental health officers have failed to appreciate that you don't need acres of tiling and stainless steel to produce good healthy food.

EU regulations and policies have played a part in this. Small local abattoirs have been closed down; abattoirs are getting larger. Grants are often given for large-scale food processing developments, but not to encourage smaller local producers. Increasingly we are heading towards larger-scale food production, and food safety agendas can speed up that trend. Yet it may mean that we get more sterile, less flavoursome food as a result. Is that really what we want?

Fortunately there seem to be some glimmerings of light. The Department of Health, for example, formed guidelines for small-scale producers of food in the home in 1996, although it is most frustrating that these have still not been implemented as this book goes to press. Sources suggest they have met with resistance from some Environmental Health Officers. The Department of Health hopes that the guidelines will finally be introduced at the end of 1998. Many a local shop has felt the lack of delicious local baked foods for some time now. Meanwhile, in 1997, the Department of Agriculture rowed back on an attempt to impose even more exacting standards on producers of raw milk cheese.

It's certainly true, though, that vigilance is called for at a time when food poisoning is rising. Ireland is the only EU state without a National Reference Laboratory, without which adequate studies are impossible. The new Food Safety Authority of Ireland (FSAI) has targeted this area as a priority. It remains to be seen how long it will take before we see some information which is pertinent to Ireland.

Food Poisoning on the Rise

Why is food poisoning on the up? The way we shop, the way we eat, and the way we produce food has changed. We shop less often than we used to, and we expect food to last much longer. We want our food to be cheap, and intensive farming has been the response to this. Unfortunately, it brings with it problems: less healthy animals in particular. We eat more processed food, yet we want it with fewer preservatives. And our food now travels from all over the world, exposing us to a wider variety of bugs.

Food is Not Sterile

A farm is not a factory, and food is not sterile. Raw foods, by their very nature, can have some pathogens (disease-causing bacteria) on them. So it's a good idea to know the basics of safe food preparation in the home.

Unfortunately, some food safety advice goes over the top: 'Think of every food scrap, crumb or spot as a potential reservoir of germs,' one guide recommends. This is a recipe for a nation of food phobics. A bread crumb is not a problem. On the other hand, a spot of raw meat which might be picked up by a crawling child certainly could be.

Or take the contentious issue of eggs. Standard advice tells us never to touch another food made with raw or undercooked egg. The FSAI's advice is to use liquid pasteurised egg. Is this necessary? No. You just need to know that you should buy eggs from salmonella-controlled flocks.

Understanding the Risks

One problem is that the widespread ignorance of the basics of food hygiene includes many people who prepare food for us. People producing and handling food, down to the sandwich maker at the local deli, should have simple, basic hygiene training to alert them to the vital danger points. This is a matter which the FSAI should address immediately. Basic food knowledge should also be incorporated into our children's education.

The FSAI's Food Safety Information Centre opened this year to provide information on food hygiene, safety and nutrition (see Further Information, page 253). You can phone them or call in.

The Most Important Safety Rules

Most of us know the basics of how to keep our kitchens clean and our food safe to eat. Don't we? 'I'm constantly amazed at the questions I'm asked,' says Dr Mary Upton, microbiologist at UCD. 'People just aren't aware of the hazards.'

To Minimise Bugs in your Food

1. *Wash hands thoroughly, and wash utensils well.*
    Hot soapy water is effective at removing most bacteria from hands and surfaces.
2. *Wash raw vegetables, fruits, herbs etc. carefully.*
3. *Be careful with raw meat. This applies both to poultry and other meats.*
    - Poultry have a high chance of carrying salmonella or campylobacter.
    - E coli O157 may be on the outside surface of meat, and so it may be distributed all the way through mince or sausages.
      Fortunately all these bugs are easily killed by cooking and are removed by routine kitchen hygiene.
    - *Don't* let raw meat touch or drip onto ready-to-eat food in the fridge or while shopping.
    - *Don't* handle raw meat in the kitchen without immediately cleaning up: hands, surfaces, boards, knives.
    - *Is rare or pink meat safe?*
      Standard advice now is that poultry, burgers, mince, sausages and rolled roasts must be cooked until well done (there should be no more blood in the juices). Your rare steak or pink lamb is perfectly safe, though, once the outside is cooked.
4. *Be careful with cooked meats.*
    If you buy loose *cooked* meat from a butcher, be *sure* he or she has washed their hands after handling raw meat. If they don't wash their hands — don't buy the cooked meat, and tell them why!
5. *The buzz word is 'cross-contamination'.*
    This means that raw food which may contain disease-causing bacteria should not touch food which is ready to eat. So fill the fridge sensibly: raw meats at the bottom, where they can't drip onto the cheese, the cooked ham or the baby food. And wash up immediately after preparing raw meat. You may wish to keep one board for raw and another for cooked food.
6. *Don't give bugs an opportunity to multiply.* They do this best given time and the right warm temperature. So it means:

- Keep food very cool or piping hot.
- Check that your fridge is kept at or below 5°C. (Get a fridge thermometer; many fridges are closer to 10°C.)
- Don't fill the fridge too full, or it won't be able to stay cold.
- Cool food down quickly if you're going to keep it; if reheating, make sure it's very hot all the way through.
- Keep eggs in the fridge.
- Don't leave the week's shop hanging around in the boot of the car, especially on a warm day. (And if the weather is warm, consider a cool box for a picnic.)
- Observe best-before dates on food — don't keep them too long.
- Thaw frozen food in the fridge, and cook soon after thawing.

7. *Be especially vigilant if preparing food for 'at risk' groups whose immune systems are low*: babies, the elderly, pregnant women and those with compromised immune systems.

Antibacterial soaps, detergents and chopping boards?

Some companies are marketing these products to cash in on increased concern about food safety. Treat their claims with scepticism. One project at the Young Scientists Awards in 1997 showed that most detergents were ineffective at killing bacteria or controlling bacterial growth; one prominent brand failed to kill any bacteria at all! Basic washing with hot soapy water is enough.

Chopping boards: wood or plastic?

Some years ago, wooden chopping boards got the chop when it was deemed that plastic was more hygienic. Since then, research at the University of Wisconsin has demonstrated that bacteria multiply on plastic but actually diminish on wood. The added bonus is that wooden boards are better for our knives.

Storing Food in the Fridge

Surveys often find that most fridges are kept at a higher temperature than recommended. It should be at or below 5°C. Get a fridge thermometer — these cost only a few pounds — especially if you shop just once a week and regularly keep ready meals for several days. Keep the thermometer on the middle of the top shelf, which is usually the warmest.

The Main Bugs

These are the food poisoning bugs causing most concern at present. Firstly, it's worth noting that while we have no figures yet for food poisoning levels in Ireland, food safety experts are saying at the moment that they believe Irish food is comparatively safe. 'We never tracked anything back to Ireland,' says Chief Executive of the FSAI Dr Patrick Wall, of his time spent in charge of investigating foodborne disease at the UK's national Communicable Disease Surveillance Centre until 1997. So he is optimistic: 'I think that augurs well.' However, until a national reference laboratory is established, we can have no idea.

Always remember that particular care must be exercised if you're serving food to vulnerable people: babies and infants, the elderly, pregnant women, and those who are ill or have weak immune systems.

E coli O157

This most unpleasant and dangerous bug has been described on page 9. It can cause kidney failure and even death, especially in young and elderly sufferers. It has become part of the normal intestinal flora of cattle, so a healthy animal is no guard against it. Meats other than beef have been discovered to carry it too. E coli O157 may transfer to the surface of meat in the abattoir, so butchers must be aware of hygiene. It can therefore be on any surface of meat. For this reason, *minced meat* (including *burgers* and *sausages*) and *rolled roasts* must be cooked all the way through until juices run clear and no pink remains.

E coli O157 may also get into *milk*, so the FSAI has warned against farm consumption of unpasteurised milk. *Water* may also be contaminated. It has implications for the spreading of slurry on land since the organism may live for up to one hundred and thirty days in soil. *Vegetables* fertilised with manure may also carry E coli O157, so vegetarians are not immune! Always wash vegetables and salads well.

International research into E coli O157 is being co-ordinated in Dublin. We can only hope that measures to control it are found soon, since its infectious dose is very small, and research at the National Food Centre has shown that even visually clean cattle can carry E coli O157 into the abattoir.

See also Milk, page 81, and Cheese, page 95.

Salmonella

There are many different varieties of this bacterium. Salmonella enteritidis is found only in poultry — *eggs* or *poultry meat*. (See Eggs, page 111, and Chicken, page 45, for more on this subject.) It is perfectly possible to produce poultry and eggs free of salmonella. Sweden does so, and Ireland should focus on doing the same. You should buy eggs only from salmonella-controlled flocks, and cook chicken through until the juices run clear.

Other salmonella strains may be found in other meats. At present, food safety sources tell me that over fifty per cent of pig herds in the Republic carry some strain of salmonella. Salmonella typhimurium DT 104, meanwhile, which doesn't have a predeliction for one species and is found in *cattle, sheep and pigs*, is now resistant to most major antibiotics. This highlights the foolishness of using antibiotics in intensive farming: as a result, we have grown several bacteria which are resistant to major antibiotics.

Campylobacter

This is thought to be the commonest cause of bacterial food poisoning, although because it causes sporadic cases rather than outbreaks it is harder to quantify. *Chicken* and *pork* seem to be most implicated in its spread. See Chicken, page 45, for more. Cooking meat until the juices run clear kills the bacterium.

Listeria

Listeria monocytogenes was in the news a decade ago but seems to have slipped off the agenda now. It is a very widely spread organism and is found in soil, animals, vegetation and water. Today we still don't understand why most people do *not* become ill, while occasionally it *can* cause serious illness. Pregnant women in particular should be careful since it can cause miscarriage. Vulnerable groups should avoid *soft ripened cheeses* (both pasteurised and unpasteurised), *pâtés, ready meals* which won't be reheated thoroughly, and *salads and vegetables* which may have been inadequately washed.

SRSV

These are small, round-structured viruses. They are found where human sewage may be present and have been associated with eating raw and lightly-cooked *shellfish* from areas where raw sewage goes into the water. The viruses cause vomiting but are destroyed by cooking. You should be very careful about your source of shellfish if you eat it raw: accept it only from beds classified as 'A' (see Shellfish, page 70).

Bacillius cereus

These can multiply in cooked cereals, especially rice, at room temperature, and can produce a toxin; so cool cooked rice right away if you plan to keep it.

Staphylococcus aureus

These are found on our skin and in our noses and can contaminate food, producing a toxin; so hygiene while cooking is important.

The FSAI produces leaflets on *Food Safety When Shopping*, *At School and Work*, *In the Home*, *Outdoors*, *When Eating Out*, and *Microwaves*, as well as other information leaflets. See Further Information, page 253, to contact them.

Irradiation

Opinions are sharply divided on this technology, with some seeing it as part of the future of food safety, while others view it as a potential danger itself. This subject is likely to come more to the fore as food safety becomes more of a consumer concern, and large companies seek quick solutions to making food 'safe'.

What is Food Irradiation?

Food is irradiated by exposing it to a radioactive source. The rays destroy bacteria, and have long been used as a process to sterilise medical equipment. The scientific evidence available to date does not suggest that the practice is unsafe. Irradiation does not just kill bacteria; it can also delay fruit ripening and vegetables sprouting, and kill pests which may attack foods in storage. So it can also increase the shelf-life of fresh foods.

There are limitations on the use of irradiation, since it alters the flavour of foods which contain fat.

The Concerns about Irradiation

There is no way of knowing
There is currently no test method available which can detect whether a variety of foods has been irradiated.

Vitamin loss
Some studies have demonstrated high vitamin losses in irradiated foods.

Cleaning up dirty food
Irradiation may be used to clean up food which has unacceptably high bacteria counts. Not only is this undesirable — food should be produced in a wholesome manner in the first place — but it is also potentially dangerous. Some bacteria leave behind toxins which cause illness, even if the bacteria themselves have been removed. Irradiation does not eliminate viruses. Nor does it necessarily kill all bacteria, especially if the food was badly contaminated in the first place.

A false sense of security
Using irradiation may lead to more shoddy food production, if it is perceived as being available to clean up food. Irradiation should not be necessary if food is produced cleanly.

Making food more susceptible
If beneficial bacteria present in food are eliminated, it is easier for it to be contaminated subsequently by harmful bacteria. Irradiated food would require even more careful handling than un-irradiated food.

More centralised food production
Relying on technologies like irradiation, which require vast investment in the machinery necessary, means food must be produced on an ever-larger scale, and makes it much harder for small, quality producers to enter the market. As we have seen throughout this book, the pressures of high-volume, centralised food production tend to make for lower-quality food.

18

Where to Buy

G ood eating begins with shopping. You can be as good a cook as you like, but unless the ingredients you buy are carefully produced, the food will never be the best.

Here are some tips about where to find the best.

Supermarkets?

Glittering with choice, aisle after aisle bombarding us with options. And yet the vast variety offered by supermarkets often turns out to be an illusion. Thirty-seven varieties of chicken product, but not one single well-reared chicken with flavour. A wide array of never-tasted tropical fruits, but never a spear of Irish asparagus picked fresh this morning. An entire counter full of the world's cheeses, and not one of them ripe.

Supermarkets' size gives them their muscle, but it's often their downfall when it comes to food quality. They buy in bulk, so can't (or won't) offer you great food from smaller producers. Their many staff serve you quickly, but most are utterly ignorant about what they're selling.

Supermarkets' systems also militate against the best food. Buyers often move from one area to the next; the average age of a supermarket buyer in the UK is twenty-six! The consequent lack of experience means they are not in a position to develop mature expertise and understand the factors which make for the best food.

Supermarkets can do some things well. For starters, they offer a dry place to shop. That's a big plus in this climate. They also offer a trolley to corral the kids into, perhaps a well-run creche if you're lucky. Anyone who has to factor small people into their shopping list knows the immense value of that. They're also great at dried goods and washing-up liquid.

Ask For It!

One of the problems with large-scale shops is that communication between customers and shop owners is made more intimidating and difficult. As a result, people become easily defeated when an item is not on the shelf. Shop owners, in turn, think that since no-one's asking for it, no-one wants it. Remember — if you ask for it, you will create a demand. If more of you ask for it, it will be stocked!

When it comes to some fresh food quality, the bonuses are not so great. As we saw, the meat *can* be reasonably good if it comes from a rigorously-monitored assurance system that encompasses eating quality as well as safety. Some sell organic meat which can be good. Some are now a good source of store cupboard items for cooking from all over the world. But if you want the very best fish, or great cheese, or exciting vegetables, or chicken that tastes of chicken, you'll have to get to an independent retailer, or to a market.

Superquinn have led the way with meat quality, though their beef and lamb are substantially better than their pork; far and away the best supermarket butchery staff too. Fish is often better than other outlets, but suffers as they all do from central buying and filleting. Their baking breads scent store entrances temptingly, but most taste like the same squidgy dough moulded into a dozen different shapes. They usually have the best range of store cupboard exotica, very valuable if you can't get to a specialist shop. Most of their deli counter ready-meals are utterly uninspiring and rather sludgy.

Super Valu are most definitely not to be underestimated. Easy to do if you expect supermarkets to be wide of aisle and smooth of trolley. But the Super Valu system can lead to great supermarkets. They are privately-owned, but take advantage of central buying power for the group. This means that, if the owner so chooses, the store can sell a good array of foods from small, local producers. And some of them do. It gives them character and gives you better food. Two excellent Super Valus are: Fields of Skibbereen; Kieran's of Mount Merrion, Co. Dublin.

Quinnsworth/Tesco With one fell swoop, a UK multiple became the largest owner of grocery stores in Ireland and there are still many concerns about the potential this has to affect Irish suppliers. The stores have become somewhat schizophrenic since the take-over, with Tesco ready-foods in particular flooding the freezer and chill cabinets — all produced in the UK. This was never more apparent than when Tesco advertised proudly in Britain that they only bought British beef, much to the chagrin of the Irish management. In early 1998, the Irish stores then carried advertisements saying they only carried Irish beef.

These shops vary a great deal, depending on location. Some pluses in some stores: good organic vegetable ranges; Ballybrado organic lamb and beef; Cooke's and other good breads; Rudds dry-cured rashers.

Dunnes Stores and **Roches Stores** are something of a mixed bag. Where price is the only factor, their stores offer little but anonymous food and glum staff. In some flagship stores standards are much better. Dunnes in Cornelscourt in Co. Dublin, for example, took the radical step of siting its organic vegetables section at the entrance to the store. Roches may offer good treats such as Rudds rashers and often buy from local suppliers.

The Specialists

The best of the small shops sell you a quality of food that gets your tastebuds begging for more. They also offer something else invaluable: knowledge, and a relationship with you. As you get to know each other, this becomes one of the most important factors in coming home with the best food. If something wasn't good enough, you can say so, and be sure it is making an impact, rather than disappearing into the vacuous expression of a pasty-faced youth. And you can benefit from the experience of someone who really cares about the food they're selling, and who knows where it has come from.

However . . . Just because a butcher, greengrocer, fishmonger or deli-owner is local and small doesn't mean that the food is guaranteed to be better. There are plenty of retailers who just buy in an anonymous commodity about which they know nothing, and sell it on to you in cheerful indifference. If that's your option, you're better off in the supermarket. At least they have standards which you can find out about.

Markets

The energy and fun to be found in the good food at a market is something we associate with other countries, with shopping on holiday. Some say we lack the climate for it. Having shopped for olives in the market in Freiburg with the snow crunching underfoot, I find this unconvincing. But the great news is that the market is finally inching its way into the Irish food scene. Here you will find the best of seasonal vegetables, carefully-grown, and excellent foods from small artisan producers who don't have the kind of volume which a supermarket considers worthwhile. And you can meet the people who make the food.

Galway Saturday morning, the longest-established. Excellent local organic growers, good cheese (great Dutch cheeses), rather worthy wholefood breads. 'Galway is wonderful, the people who buy are so appreciative,' one producer said. 'They really come to buy food here.'

Limerick Saturday morning — very limited, but some good cheese, olives and preserves.

Dublin-Temple Bar, Meeting House Square Finally, the capital got its market in 1997. Not to be missed. Look out for: Denis Healy's vegetables; Sheridan's cheesemongers stall; Jenny McNally's vegetables and yoghurt; Hederman's fish; and more. Everywhere you go, there is the unmissable whiff of Toby Simmonds' marinating olives, bringing garlicky olive oil to the four corners of Ireland.

Irish Country Markets are an independent organisation. The place for the old-fashioned flavour of home-baked sponge sandwiched with real lemon curd, or piles of blackcurrants for a summer pudding.

They vary a great deal from place to place, depending on who's cooking and growing for them. Some of the best are: Kilternan, Co. Dublin; Kilcoole, Co. Wicklow; Carrigaline, Co. Cork. For information about one in your area, Tel.: 01 668 4784.

How to Buy

A little-appreciated skill. I've talked elsewhere in the book about that enduring cook-book cliché, having a relationship with your butcher. That relationship should be one of mutual respect. Let staff know that you want the best, and be exacting in your standards. It helps to get to know staff and to ask questions. With time, shopping will become so much more fruitful. And remember — the customer deserves to get what she wants. But the customer is not always right, and should enjoy learning too.

Some Great Small Shops and Delis

This list is by no means exhaustive. In particular it only contains a very few special butchers to whom I have spoken at length. For more information on exceptional butchers, try IQ butchers (see page 16).

Dublin

Asia Market, 18 Drury St, Dublin 2. Tel.: 01 677 9764.
Essential regular stop-off. Many Asian specialities much cheaper than the supermarkets, and better local brands too. Fine Basmati and Jasmine rices in large bags, and spices. Regular supply of fresh Chinese vegetables such as pak choi and choi sum, plus generous bunches of fresh coriander year-round. Divine, ripe, meltingly soft Alphonso mangoes in season. Also many specialities from other cuisines such as the Middle East.

Big Cheese Company, Andrews Lane, Dublin 2. Tel.: 01 671 1399.
The widest range of cheeses from Ireland and around the world. Choose carefully and you can find good things. Also interesting range of deli items with a strong bias towards American essentials.

Caviston's, Glasthule, Dun Laoghaire, Co. Dublin. Tel.: 01 280 9120.
One of the great food shops in the country. Poulterers and fishmongers, they are supremely skilled at these tasks, especially the fish, and at Christmas poultry. Also a very good deli range of meats, salads and so on, plus great dried goods. Cheeses can be erratic, but often serve up a gem. Time a visit to

eat lunch in the tiny and exceptional seafood restaurant.

Cooke's Food Hall, 15 Castle Market, Dublin 2. Tel.: 01 679 9923.
Ultra smart food shop opposite the restaurant can seem pretty intimidating, and some food is horrendously pricey. But excellent Italian and French specialities are to be found, much from the Carluccio's range. Best plus: they let you sample those expensive olive oils.

Downey's Butchers, 97 Terenure Rd East, Dublin. Tel.: 01 490 9239.
Butcher and poulterer, selling some extremely good produce, with a bias toward the wild, free-range and organic.

Roy Fox, 49a Main St, Donnybrook, Dublin 4. Tel.: 01 269 2892.
An essential Dubliner's shop for big bags of herbs year-round. Also a first stop if ever looking for a slightly unusual deli item. Good De Cecco pastas, everything imaginable in tins, plus fish sauce, candied peel, real essence . . .

Hicks, Woodpark, Sallynoggin, Co. Dublin. Tel.: 01 285 4430. Also 18 Castle St, Dalkey, Co. Dublin. Tel.: 01 285 9568.
Best pork butchers in the country. Donal (Dalkey) and Ed (Sallynoggin) follow faithfully and creatively in the footsteps of father Jack, to produce exceptionally well-handled and consistently delicious pork. Famous for sausages, smoked black pudding, and range of German and other European cured meats, sausages and cooked meats. Best Kasseler (smoked cured pork loin) in the country.

Little Italy, 139 North King St, Dublin 7. Tel.: 01 872 5208.
Good spot for certain Italian staples.

Magills, 14 Clarendon St, Dublin 2. Tel.: 01 671 3830.
One of the originals and still very good; a wide range of deli essentials. A few good cheeses and often the best place to happen upon that rare thing, a well-ripened dote of Milleens. As we go to press, daughter Kim Condon is due to take over the business, so the family commitment to good food in Dublin city centre looks set to remain.

C. Morton & Sons, 15 Dunville Ave, Dublin 6. Tel.: 01 497 1254.
Lovely privately-owned supermarket with carefully-chosen ranges of food. Some excellent ready meals from their kitchen on the premises.

K. and C. Norton, 37 Dunville Ave, Dublin 6. Tel.: 01 497 3411.
Italian specialities in this tiny, unexpected shop, many a great deal cheaper than smart shops elsewhere.

O'Tooles Butchers, 138 Terenure Rd North (at the Terenure crossroads), Dublin. Tel.: 01 490 5457. Also 1 Glasthule Rd, Dun Laoghaire. Tel.: 01 284 1125.
Danny O'Toole was the first organic butcher, and is still going strong.

Ow Valley Farm Shop, Powerscourt Townhouse Centre, Dublin 2. Tel.: 01 679 4079.
This shop has some excellent vegetables and other unusual treats, such as Turkish delight, smoked garlic and great nuts.

Sheridans Cheesemongers, 11 South Anne St, Dublin 2. Tel.: 01 679 3143. Also Kirwan's Lane, Galway.
Seamus and Kevin Sheridan are staunch supporters and lovers not just of the Irish farm cheeses but also of a few gems from England and Holland. These young men are ones to watch; eager to learn, they are working hard at cheese maturing. Very good selection, often in good condition. Also to be found in Galway and Temple Bar Saturday markets.

Terroirs, 103 Morehampton Road, Donnybrook, Dublin 4. Tel.: 01 667 1311.
Another ultra-smart shop, but don't be put off by the exclusive atmosphere, since the food is chosen with great care; there are some fair-priced essentials, like the country's best value in inexpensive Champ's wine vinegar. Also the place for special treats such as Cluizel chocolates (stunning), tasty foie gras and other things you never knew you wanted.

Around the Country

Cosgrove's, Market Street, Sligo. Tel. 071 42809.
Most surprising — a true old-fashioned, one-room grocers, complete with baked ham, and yet many of the best foods are to be found there as well.

Country Choice, Kenyon Street, Nenagh, Co. Tipperary. Tel.: 067 32596.
A most surprising place to find wonderfully-matured cheese. Peter Ward's little deli and coffee shop is evidence, if any were needed, that superb farm cheese is not just an indulgence for a gastronomic elite. Also excellent local produce — free-range eggs, fruit and vegetables, great deli essentials like olive oils and best chocolate. And good baked hams.

Jim's Country Kitchen, Church Street, Portlaoise, Co. Laois. Tel.: 0502 62061.
'Everything we have is here because someone asked for it', I was told as I browsed; so clearly the townspeople of Portlaoise are having a great time with delicious foods — nice cheeses, Macroom flour and oatmeal, oils, rices, spices and herbs, Seventy-two per cent Callebaut chocolate . . . and more.

Kate's Kitchen, Market Street, Sligo. Tel.: 071 43022.
Good deli range.

Nolan's Butchers, Kilcullen, Co. Kildare. Tel.: 045 481229.
Exceptional local butcher; superb beef and lamb.

John David Power, 57 Main Street, Dungarvan, Co. Waterford. Tel.: 058 42339.
For that rare thing, dry cure bacon.

Shortis Wong, 74 John Street, Kilkenny. Tel.: 056 61305.
Useful for some Asian needs, as well as other things, such as salt-packed capers, good anchovies.

Tir na nOg, Grattan Street, Sligo. Tel.: 071 62752.
Many health food shops labour wearily under the worthy banner, but not Tir

na Nog: Mary McDonnell presides over delicious foods, too. Many interesting imported foods, which you'd be hard pushed to find in the smartest Dublin deli. Plus, best of all, Rod Alston's utterly magnificent organic salads, vegetables and herbs. I'm not kidding when I say it's worth a trip to Sligo for these alone. If you haven't eaten them, you haven't eaten salad.

Tormey's Mullingar. Tel.: 044 42246. Also Galway. Tel.: 091 564067; and Tullamore. Tel.: 0506 21426.
These superb butchers have recently expanded into all kinds of cooked foods too. Superlative beef from father Robin's family farm, and a son in each of the above towns.

Cork

In the English Market
Mr Bell's. Tel.: 021 885333.
Asian supplies — all sorts of essentials.

Iago. Tel.: 021 277047.
Sean Calder-Pott's stall is a delight, with fine Irish cheeses, some in exceptional condition, good two-year-old Parmesan, fresh pasta, excellent pesto, good Spanish cheese, buffalo mozzarella, superb Ortiz anchovies and more.

Katherine's Wholefoods. Tel.: 021 271322.
For wholefoods and Asian supplies as well.

Machanaclai. Tel.: 021 272368.
Have organic vegetables and leaves in season, as well as stunning dried fruits, excellent beans and delicious French sea salt.

O'Connells. Tel.: 021 276380.
Great fish and good advice: rivals Cavistons for best fishmonger in the country, and certainly one of the finest ranges and displays. They will vac-pac your fish fillets for you, a great bonus.

On the Pigs Back. Tel.: 021 270232.
Has some fine pâtés, as well as good French saucisson and cheeses; also breads from the Arbutus Lodge hotel, and that rare commodity Fieldwise free-range pork.

The Real Olive Co. Tel.: 021 270842.
The only fixed abode for Toby Simmonds' peripatetic olive stall, which puts in appearances at just about every market in the country. Excellent marinated olives, fine olive oils and much more.

■ ■ ■

Field's, Skibbereen. Tel.: 028 21400.
A marvel of a shop, a Super Valu with a most magnificent range of foods.

Manning's, Ballylickey. Tel.: 027 50456 and **The Courtyard, Schull. Tel.: 028 28390.**
Two local delis showing what great food in West Cork is all about.

O'Flynns, 36 Marlborough Street, Cork. Tel.: 021 275685.
One of the country's great butchers. Their special home-cured bacon is dry cured: my favourite. Also good for sausages, spiced beef, Kasseler, venison and guinea fowl, smoked chicken and some hard-to-find treats such as lamb sweetbreads.

Galway

Sean Loughnane, Foster Court, Galway. Tel.: 091 564437.
Something of a phenomenon, this Galway town butcher has now expanded to a seven-day mini supermarket and cooked food operation. Much of the cooked food and supermarket range is to my mind plain enough, but the meat has always been exceptional. Loughnane has Connemara lamb in season, one of the few butchers outside the immediate mountain lamb areas to make a feature of it.

McCambridges, Shop Street, Galway. Tel.: 091 62259.
A treasure-trove of a deli.

McGeoughs, Lake Road, Oughterard. Tel.: 091 82351.
Eamonn and son James have Connemara lamb, as do other butchers in the area. A treasure: careful and conscientious, of the old school. Don't miss the 'Connemara' pork and herb pâté.

Kerry

Continental Sausages, Fossa, Kerry. Tel.: 064 33069.
Arnim Weise does wonderful things to meat, and sells other good foods too.

Select Sources

Books and Reports

Colburn, Theo et al., *Our Stolen Future*, London: Abacus 1997.

Beaumont, Peter, *Pesticides, Policies and People, A Guide to the Issues*, London: The Pesticides Trust 1993.

Blythman, Joanna, *The Food We Eat*, London: Michael Joseph 1996.

Cowan, Cathal and Sexton, Regina, *Ireland's Traditional Foods*, Dublin: Teagasc 1997.

David, Elizabeth, *English Bread and Yeast Cookery*, London: Penguin 1977.

Fowler, Cary and Mooney, Pat, *The Threatened Gene: Food Politics and the Loss of Genetic Diversity*, Cambridge: Lutterworth 1990.

Herbst, Sharon Tyler, *The New Food Lover's Companion*, New York: Barron's 1995.

Kurlansky, Mark, *Cod, A Biography of the Fish that Changed the World*, London: Jonathan Cape 1998.

Lymbery, Philip, *Beyond the Battery — A Welfare Charter for Laying Hens*, Hants, England: Compassion in World Farming 1997.

McGee, Harold, *On Food and Cooking*, New York: Collier Books Macmillan 1984.

McKenna, John and Sally, *The Bridgestone Irish Food Guide 1996*, Durrus, Co. Cork: Estragon Press 1996.

National Consumer Council, *Farm Policies and our Food: the Need for Change*, London: National Consumer Council 1998.

National Food Centre, *Teagasc Research Report*, Dublin: Teagasc 1996.

National Research Council, *Pesticides in the Diets of Infants and Children*, Washington DC: National Academy Press 1993.

O'Brien, Tim, *Factory Farming and Human Health*, Hants, England: Compassion in World Farming Trust 1997.

Overexposed, Organophosphate Insecticides in Children's Food, Washington DC: Environmental Working Group 1998.

The Pennington Group, *Report on the Circumstances leading to the 1996 Outbreak of Infection with E coli O157 in Central Scotland*, Edinburgh: The Stationery Office 1997

Pesticide Control Service, *Pesticide Residues in Food, 1994, 1995 and 1996,* and *Pesticide Residues in Food*, 1997, Dublin: Department of Agriculture, Food and Forestry 1997 and 1998 respectively.

Ross, Alison, *Leaping in the Dark*, Perth, Scotland: Scottish Wildlife and Countryside Link 1997.

Sexton, Regina, *A Little History of Irish Food*, Dublin: Gill & Macmillan 1998.

Stevenson, Peter, *The Welfare of Broiler Chickens*, Hants, England: Compassion in World Farming Trust 1995.

Visser, Margaret, *Much Depends on Dinner*, London: Penguin 1989.

Wargo, John, *Our Children's Toxic Legacy*, US: Yale University Press 1996.

'The Welfare of Intensively Kept Pigs', in *Report of the Scientific Veterinary Committee*, Brussels: 30 September 1997.

'The Welfare of Laying Hens', in *Report of the Scientific Veterinary Committee*, Brussels: 30 October 1996.

World Health Report, *Fighting Disease, Fostering Development*, Geneva: World Health Organisation 1996.

Magazines

Compassion in World Farming
Consumer Choice (the magazine of the Consumers' Association of Ireland)
Food Safety Advisory Committee
The Food Magazine
Nature
New Scientist

Nutrition and Health News (National Dairy Council)
Pesticides News

Further Information

An Bord Bia
Clanwilliam Court, Lower Mount Street, Dublin 2. Tel.: 01 668 5155.
Bord Iascaigh Mhara (BIM)
Crofton Road, Dun Laoghaire, Co. Dublin. Tel.: 01 284 1544.
Compassion in World Farming
Salmon Weir, Hanover Street, Cork. Tel: 021 272 441.
Consumers' Association of Ireland
45 Upper Mount Street, Dublin 2. Tel.: 01 668 6836.
The Food Commission
94 White Lion Street, London N1 9PF, England. Tel.: 00 44 171 837 2250.
Food Safety Authority of Ireland (FSAI)
Drop-in Information Centre, Abbey Court, Lower Abbey Street (Irish Life Mall), Dublin 1. Helpline: 1800 33 66 77. E-mail: info@fsai.ie. Website: http://www.fsai.ie
Genetic Concern
Room 13, 24-26 Dame Street, Dublin 2. Tel.: 01 670 5606.
Monsanto
Website: www.monsanto.co.uk This particularly informative website also gives contacts and websites for organisations opposed to genetic engineering.
National Dairy Council
Information Centre on Nutrition and Health, Grattan House, Lower Mount Street, Dublin 2. Tel.: 01 661 9599.
The Pesticides Trust
Eurolink Centre, 49 Effra Road, London SW2 1BZ, England. Tel.: 00 44 171 837 2250.

Information about organic growers, box schemes and more:

IOFGA

Irish Organic Farmers and Growers Association, 56 Blessington Street, Dublin 7. Tel.: 01 830 7996.

Organic Trust

Vernon House, 2 Vernon Avenue, Clontarf, Dublin 3. Tel.: 01 853 0271.

Bio-Dynamic Agricultural Association

The Water Garden, Thomastown, Co. Kilkenny. Tel.: 056 54214.